THE COUNTERFEIT GOSPEL OF MORMONISM

FRANCIS J. BECKWITH ✦ NORMAN GEISLER

RON RHODES ✦ PHIL ROBERTS

JERALD AND SANDRA TANNER

HARVEST HOUSE PUBLISHERS
Eugene, Oregon 97402

Cover design by Left Coast Design, Portland, Oregon

THE COUNTERFEIT GOSPEL OF MORMONISM

Copyright © 1998 by Francis Beckwith, Norman L. Geisler, Ron Rhodes, Phil Roberts, and Jerald and Sandra Tanner
Published by Harvest House Publishers
Eugene, Oregon 97402

Library of Congress Cataloging-in-Publication Data

Geisler, Norman L., general editor
    The counterfeit gospel of Mormonism / Norman Geisler.
        p.   cm.
    Includes bibliographical references and indexes.
    ISBN 1-56507-845-4
    1. Church of Jesus Christ of Latter-Day Saints—Doctrines.
2. Mormon Church—Doctrines. 3. Church of Jesus Christ of Latter
-Day Saints—Controversial literature. 4. Mormon Church-
-Controversial literature.   I. Title.
BX8645.G45   1998
230' .9332—dc21   97-44722
                                                              CIP

Printed in the United States of America.

98 99 00 01 02 /BC/ 10 9 8 7 6 5 4 3 2 1

Contents

Foreword

In recent days, much attention and time is directed at the Church of Jesus Christ of Latter-day Saints. Key and vital questions about this group are discussed everywhere. Are they Christians? Do they uphold the Bible? Do they believe in Jesus Christ and the God of Christian Scripture? Can they expect to reach heaven? When they use Christian or biblical words or terms, do they bear the same meaning that evangelicals would understand them to mean?

All of these issues are addressed in this book. And they are addressed in detail. Each chapter treats the biblical/Christian answer to the major doctrinal issues of Scripture, God, Christ, and Salvation. That section is then followed by an exposé of the Mormon position on each major doctrine. The chapter on Terminology Differences stands on its own. Mormons use Bible words but employ their own dictionary to define them. It may be best for a new student of Mormonism to read this chapter first. It will unlock the door of "Mormonese" and help the beginner to understand the "great divide" between Mormons and biblically based Christians.

Each of the writers for *The Counterfeit Gospel of Mormonism* is uniquely qualified for his or her assignment. Norman Geisler, President of Southern Evangelical Seminary, Charlotte, North Carolina, wrote the chapter on the Bible. Dr. Geisler is a renowned authority on the inspiration of Holy Scripture, being coauthor of major works on the topic, including *General Introduction to the Bible,* and served as cofounder of the Council on Biblical Inerrancy. Francis Beckwith, Professor at Trinity International University, is author of an incisive academic monograph titled *The Mormon Concept of God: A Philosophical Analysis,* among other books. Ron Rhodes is one of the foremost countercult authors. He has written extensively on Mormonism, including *Reasoning from the Scriptures with the Mormons* (Harvest House, 1995).

Jerald and Sandra Tanner of Utah Lighthouse Ministry, Salt Lake City, have researched Mormonism for over 35 years. They are recognized as among the foremost experts on the Church of Jesus Christ of Latter-day Saints. Phil Roberts, director of the Interfaith Witness Division of the North American Mission Board, SBC, has wide experience on Mormonism. He is the producer of the excellent video on Mormonism titled "The Mormon Puzzle."

Mormon authorities and standard works on every topic are examined carefully. Part of the misunderstanding and confusion related to Mormonism is due to Mormonism's failure, especially in its proselytizing work, to be less than candid about its doctrines. Mormons argue that unbelievers cannot digest rich doctrinal "steak." They must have "milk" instead (taken from a misuse of 1 Corinthians 3:2). So, they believe, it is difficult for non-Mormons to understand and grasp the teachings of the Church of Jesus Christ of Latter-day Saints.

In their attempt to make Mormonism appear to be Christian, Mormons are not completely candid in their doctrinal teaching; in fact their treatment of it often is disingenuous. Therefore we have sought to explain what Mormons really believe. How can a judgment be made about the truthfulness of any truth claim unless the claim or doctrine is clearly exposed? Jesus' words are appropriate: "If anyone wants to do His will, he shall know concerning the doctrine, whether it is from God or whether I speak on My own authority" (John 7:17 NKJV).

To tell the full story is our goal and desire. We are absolutely unanimous and enthusiastic in our recommendation to readers to trust and follow the Jesus of the Bible for their salvation.

While this book is partly a response to *How Wide the Divide?* (Blomberg and Robinson, IVP, 1997), its purpose is much broader than that. With Mormonism claiming more fervently than ever that it alone represents the fullness of true Christianity, it is more urgent than ever before for biblical Christians to speak up for truth—truth unmixed and unalloyed. While directness marks our style, it is a directness born of the desire to speak the truth in love (Ephesians 4:15).

Hence this book is written out of love—love for the truth, love for the body of Christ, and love for Mormons, whom we as contributing authors are persuaded need to read this book and heed its message.

Abbreviations of Mormon Works Used in this Book

AF—*Articles of Faith*

BM—*Book of Mormon*

CHC—*Comprehensive History of the Church*

D&C—*Doctrine and Covenants*

DG—*Doctrines of the Gospel*

DS—*Doctrines of Salvation*

EM—*Encyclopedia of Mormonism*

GP—*Gospel Principles*

HC—*History of the Church*

JD—*Journal of Discourses*

JST—*Joseph Smith Translation* ("Inspired Version")

LDS—*Latter Day Saints*

MD—*Mormon Doctrine*

PGP—*Pearl of Great Price*

TPJS—*Teachings of the Prophet Joseph Smith*

1

Scripture

Norman L. Geisler

There is a great gulf fixed between the evangelical and Mormon views of Scripture. For starters, evangelicals believe in *sola Scriptura* (the Bible alone) and Mormons believe there are four inspired books: the Bible, the Book of Mormon (BM), *Doctrine and Covenants* (D&C), and *The Pearl of Great Price* (PGP). In addition, evangelicals believe that the canon of Scripture is closed, and Mormons do not. This is to say nothing of the fact that, unlike Mormons, evangelicals hold that there are no living prophets receiving new normative revelation, while Mormons affirm that the President of the Mormon church is a living prophet.[1]

The Evangelical View of Scripture

There are many dimensions of the evangelical view of Scripture. These include the origin, reliability, completeness, and confirmation of Scripture as God's special revelation.

First a definition of "evangelical" is in order. In agreement with other orthodox traditions, evangelicals accept the doctrinal proclamations of the creeds, councils, and confessions of the first five centuries of the Christian church. Essential evangelical doctrines include the virgin birth of Christ, His deity, the triune nature of God, the completely sufficient substitutionary atonement, the physical resurrection, the sole infallibility of the Bible, the literal

---

Scripture quotations in this chapter are from the New King James Version except as otherwise noted. See Copyright page.

second coming of Christ, and the final and eternal bliss of the saved and the eternal conscious punishment of the lost.

The Origin of Scripture

Evangelicals believe that the Scriptures came from God through men of God who recorded it in the Word of God (the Bible). That is, the Bible has a divine origin, even though it was produced through human instrumentality.

The divine origin of Scripture. The Bible claims to have come from God. Speaking of the whole Old Testament, Paul wrote: "All Scripture is given by inspiration of God and is profitable for doctrine..." (2 Timothy 3:16). Even the New Testament is called "Scripture." Paul cited the Gospel (cf. Luke 10:7) as "Scripture" (in 1 Timothy 5:18). And Peter referred to Paul's epistles as "Scripture" in 2 Peter 3:15,16. So both the entire Old and New Testament, both Gospels and epistles, are said to be writings that are "breathed out" by God. Jesus used a similar expression when He referred to the Word of God coming out of the "mouth of God," saying to the tempter: "Man shall not live by bread alone, but by every word that proceeds from the mouth of God" (Matthew 4:4).

Not only is the Bible a God-breathed writing, but it comes from Spirit-moved writers. Peter referred to the Old Testament prophets as men who were "moved" (carried along) by the Holy Spirit. For "prophecy never came by the will of man, but holy men of God spoke as they were moved by the Holy Spirit" (2 Peter 1:21). David added: "The Spirit of the LORD spoke by me, and His word was on my tongue" (2 Samuel 23:2).

The role of a prophet. The role of the biblical prophets was unique. They were the mouthpieces of God, commissioned to speak His words—nothing more and nothing less. God told Balaam, "Only the word that I speak to you, that you shall speak" (Numbers 22:35). Balaam responded, "Have I any power at all to say anything? The word that God puts in my mouth, that I must speak" (verse 38). As Amos put it, "The LORD God has spoken! Who can but prophesy?" (Amos 3:8).

Of course, the human authors of Scripture were not

mere secretaries or automatons. Evangelicals do not believe in verbal dictation but only verbal inspiration. That is, God used the individual personalities, vocabularies, literary styles, and conscious desires of the biblical authors to produce His Word. Thus, while being completely from God, the words of Scripture are also human words in particular human languages (Hebrew and Greek) expressed in distinctive human literary forms that include narrative (Samuel), poetry (Psalms), and parables (Gospels), as well as some metaphor (John 15:1ff.), some allegory (Galatians 4), and even some hyperbole (Colossians 1:23). Nonetheless, the final product is exactly as God ordained and providentially superintended it to be—the divinely authoritative, infallible, and inerrant Word of God. For Scripture "cannot be broken" (John 10:35) or pass away (Matthew 5:18). It is the truth (John. 17:17) that comes from a God who cannot lie (Hebrews 6:18). In short, it is without error in whatever it affirms, not only on spiritual matters but also on those of science (cf. Matthew 19; John 3:12) and history (cf. Matthew. 12:40-42; 24:37).

Further, what the Bible claims about its own origin in general is also claimed for sections and books of the Bible in particular. Jesus referred to the "Law" (the first five books of the Old Testament) and the "Prophets" (the rest of the Old Testament) as God's indestructible Word, saying, "Do not think that I came to destroy the Law or the Prophets. I did not come to destroy but to fulfill" (Matthew 5:17). Elsewhere He called them "all the Scriptures" (Luke 24:27). Peter referred to "all his [Paul's] epistles" as Scripture (2 Peter 3:16). Indeed, even individual books of the Bible are cited as the Word of God, including Isaiah (John 12:37-41), Daniel (Matthew 24:15), Psalms (Matthew 22:43,44), and the vast majority of all Old Testament books.[2]

No occult means. Unlike some cult and occult literature, biblical revelation was not given in a word-for-word dictation or by means of occult objects. Indeed, God's servants were forbidden to use physical objects to "divine" things. Moses wrote "There shall not be found among you anyone who makes his son or his daughter pass through the fire, or one who practices witchcraft, or a soothsayer, or one who interprets omens, or a sorcerer, or one who conjures spells, or a medium, or a spiritist, or one who calls up the dead. For all who do these things are an abomination to the LORD" (Deuteronomy 18:10-12).[3]

The Urim and Thummim were used by the high priest alone (Exodus 28:30), and the lot was cast to determine weighty matters (Proverbs 16:33). But these were not occult objects like seer stones, crystal balls, or the like. The difference is clear. First, the Urim and Thummim were given only for the use of the Aaronic high priests (Exodus 28:30). And the Aaronic priesthood was dissolved by the work of Christ (Hebrews 7,8). The writer of Hebrews says explicitly that "*the priesthood being changed,* of necessity there is also a change of the law" (Hebrews 7:12, emphasis added). Second, they never produced false results, since God speaks only truth (Romans 3:4; John 17:17). Third, the Urim and Thummim were used only for getting "Yes" or "No" answers from God to particular questions. They were not used to receive content revelations from God or to translate books with alleged revelations in them. Fourth, the lot was cast to determine whether this or that was God's will, but not to spell out discourses from God (Proverbs 16:33). Finally, all use of physical objects to get messages or revelations came under the repeated condemnation of witchcraft in the Old Testament (see Exodus 22:18; Deuteronomy 18:9-14; Leviticus 19:26, 31; 20:6; Isaiah 8:19). There is no case of any author of Scripture using physical objects (such as seer stones) to divine a message from God.

No tampering with the text. Biblical prophets were forbidden to tamper with the text of sacred Scripture. God dealt severely with anyone who attempted to change His words. When King Jehoiakim cut out a section from the Word of God, Jeremiah was told: "Take yet another scroll, and write on it all the former words that were in the first scroll" (Jeremiah 36:28). No one was to add to or take away from what God had said. Agur wrote, "Every word of God is pure....Do not add to His words, lest He reprove you" (Proverbs 30:5,6). Indeed, John was told of his prophecy: "If anyone adds to these things, God will add to him the plagues that are written in this book; and if anyone takes away from the words of the book of this prophecy, God shall take away his part from the Book of Life..." (Revelation 22:18,19). This did not mean they could not receive new revelations. It meant they could not tamper with old ones.

The Reliability of the Biblical Text

Evangelicals affirm the reliability of the biblical text from God to us. This includes the inerrancy of the original text and the accuracy of good English translations based on the copies of them.

The reliability of the witnesses. The dependability of the biblical text begins with the inspiration of God and the reliability of the witnesses. The writers of Scripture were by and large contemporaries of the events. Moses was a witness of the events in Exodus through Deuteronomy (Exodus 24:4; Deuteronomy 31:24). Joshua was a witness of the happenings reported in his book (Joshua 24:26), as was Samuel (1 Samuel 10:25), Isaiah, Jeremiah, Daniel, Ezra, and Nehemiah after them. The same is true in the New Testament. Matthew was a disciple of Jesus. Mark was a contemporary and associate of the apostle Peter (1 Peter 5:13). Luke was a contemporary who knew the eyewitnesses (Luke 1:1-4). John was a disciple of Jesus and an eyewitness of the events. In the case of the New Testament writers, all eight (or nine) of them were either apostles or associated with the apostles as eyewitnesses and/or contemporaries. These were all men who held the highest standard of ethics and who were willing to die for their beliefs, as most of them did.

As their tendency to disbelief in Christ's resurrection (Matthew 28:17; Mark 16:3; Luke 24:11; John 20:24-29) indicated, they were not suggestible. Luke's account, which is basically the same as that of the other Gospels (especially Matthew and Mark) is confirmed by the historical reliability of his writings in general. Noted Roman historian Colin

Hemer has demonstrated that Luke's book of Acts is one of the most reliable documents regarding the first century in existence.[4] Earlier, Sir William Ramsey's work demonstrated the same thing.[5] The New Testament witnesses have been scrutinized by some of the greatest legal minds in our history. A former Harvard professor of law and author of a leading book on legal evidence, Simon Greenleaf, was led to accept the authenticity of the New Testament based on his application of the rules of legal evidence to the Gospel accounts.[6]

The reliability of the copies. The biblical scribes were meticulous in how they copied Scripture. The overall reliability has been measured in several ways. First, with regard to any major doctrine in the Bible there has been no loss whatsoever. Every important truth of Scripture from the original text has been preserved intact in the Old Testament Hebrew and the New Testament Greek manuscripts.

Second, the differences that exist in the copies are in minor matters, such as numbers which affect no major or minor doctrinal matter in the Bible (cf. 2 Kings 8:26; 2 Chronicles 22:2). In fact, in most of these different readings we know either from common sense, the context, or other passages which readings are correct.

Third, not only is 100 percent of all the major and the vast majority of minor truths of Scripture preserved in the manuscripts we have (and in the translations based on them), but more than 99 percent of the original text can be reconstructed from the manuscripts we have. The reason for this is twofold: 1) We have thousands of manuscripts, and 2) we have early manuscripts. So the proximity to the original autograph and the multiplicity of the manuscripts enable textual scholars to accurately reconstruct the original text with more than 99 percent accuracy. The great Greek scholar Sir Frederic Kenyon affirmed that "...all manuscripts agree on the essential correctness of 99 percent of the verses in the New Testament," as even a Mormon New Testament scholar acknowledged.[7] Noted Greek scholar A. T. Robertson said the real concerns of textual criticism are on "a thousandth part of the entire text." This would make the New Testament 99.9 percent pure.[8]

The Completeness of Scripture

Not only is the original text of the Bible faithfully and accurately reproduced in the standard English translations, but there are no books missing from the original Bible either. This is true of both Old and New Testaments.

Evangelicals believe that the canon (normative collection) of Scripture is closed. That is, in the 66 books of the Bible, we possess all the books that God intended to be there from both Old Testament and New Testament times. Further, God never intended for there to be any more books added to the Bible since that time. The Bible was finished by the end of the first century, and we have in the 66 books of our Protestant English Bibles all the inspired books that God intended to be in the Bible.

The completeness of the Old Testament canon is confirmed by several facts. These include the testimony of Judaism, the testimony of Christ, and the testimony of the Christian church.

The testimony of Judaism. The Old Testament is the Jewish canon. It was written by Jews and for Jews, and Jewish scholars have unanimously acknowledged that there are 39 books, which they combine as 24 (or 22 if Ruth is combined with Judges and Lamentations with Jeremiah), no more and no less. That these books comprise the complete Old Testament canon is based on several considerations.

First of all, the very fact that the books are combined in certain ways to make either 24 (or 22) reveals that they were considered to be complete, since this is the number of letters in the complete Hebrew alphabet (there being two double letters making the alternate of 22 or 24). In order to make the 39 books come out to 24 (the number in today's Jewish Bible) they classed all 12 Minor Prophets as one book and combined all the first and second books (1 and 2 Samuel, 1 and 2 Kings, 1 and 2 Chronicles, and Ezra-Nehemiah) as one book for each pair. Some Jewish sources (such as Josephus) renumber them to 22 (the exact number of the root Hebrew alphabet). This numbering of books indicates their belief that their canon was complete.

Furthermore, there are Jewish statements in Judaism affirming the closure of the canon. Josephus stated that "from Artaxerxes [Malachi's day, c. 400 B.C.] until our time everything has been recorded, but has not been deemed worthy of like credit with what preceded, because the exact successions of the prophets ceased" (Against Apion 1:8). The Jewish Talmud adds, "After the latter prophets Haggai, Zechariah...and Malachi, the Holy Spirit departed from Israel."[9]

Finally, Jewish scholars, such as Philo, Josephus, those of Jamnia, and the Talmud all agree on the number of books in their canon. No branch of Judaism has ever accepted any other books nor rejected any of the 39 (24) books of the Protestant Old Testament. The Jewish canon is considered closed, and it has exactly the same books as the evangelical Old Testament canon.

The Roman Catholic additions of 11 Apocryphal books by the alleged infallible proclamation of the Council of Trent (A.D. 1546) are rejected by Evangelicals because:[10] 1) these books do not claim to be inspired; 2) they were not written by prophets; 3) they were not confirmed by miracles; 4) they contain no new supernatural prophecies; 5) they contain false teachings and errors; 6) they were never accepted by Judaism as inspired; 7) they are never quoted as Scripture in the New Testament; 8) Jesus accepted and confirmed the Jewish canon, which was called "the Law [and] the Prophets" (Matthew 5:17,18; cf. Luke 24:27); 9) the Apocrypha were rejected by most major Fathers in the early church, and 10) the grounds on which Roman Catholics accepted them was faulty—claiming Christian usage rather than their being written by a prophet or apostle as the reason (cf. Hebrew 1:1; 2:3,4; Ephesians 2:20; John 14:26; 16:13).[11]

The testimony of Christ. Christ confirmed the closure of the Old Testament canon in several ways. For one thing, in His numerous uses of the Old Testament Scriptures He never cited any book other than one of the 24 (39) canonical books of the Jewish Old Testament. What is more, He cited from every major section of the Old Testament, both Law and Prophets, as well as the later division of the Prophets known as the "Writings." But He never quoted any books in the Apocrypha. Further, Jesus defined the limits of the Old Testament canon as ending in 2 Chronicles (the book listed last in the Jewish Old Testament) by the phrase "from the blood of the righteous Abel [Genesis 4] to the blood of Zechariah [2 Chronicles 24]" (Matthew 23:35). The phrase was a Jewish equivalent of the Christian phrase "from Genesis to Revelation," each indicating a complete Jewish canon of Scripture. Furthermore, the phrases "the Law [and] the Prophets" (Matthew 5:17) or "Moses and all the Prophets" (Luke 24:27) are used by Jesus to indicate the complete canon of Jewish Scripture. Indeed, Jesus used the phrase in parallel with the phrase "all the Scriptures" (Luke 24:27). Being a faithful Jew, Jesus, who came "not to destroy the Law or the Prophets," accepted the same closed Jewish canon as did Judaism, which has always consisted of the exact same books as those in the 39 books of the Protestant Old Testament.

The testimony of early Christians. Early Christians manifested their acceptance of the Jewish canon in several ways. First, they quoted from these books as Scripture. With the exception of the heretical teacher Origin, the consensus of the Fathers of the first four centuries supported the same books as were in the Jewish Old Testament, and no more. When the Apocryphal books were cited, they were not given the divine authority accorded the 39 canonical books. Rather, they were used in a manner similar to that of Paul's use of noninspired Greek thinkers (Acts 17:28; 1 Corinthians 15:33; Titus 1:12) or the Pseudepigrapha (false writings) (Jude 9, 14)—namely, they were cited for some truth in them but not as inspired. Even St. Augustine, whose influence led many after him to accept the Old Testament Apocrypha, recognized that these books were not in the Jewish canon. Indeed, most of the alleged citations of the

Apocrypha by other early writers do not really support the inspiration of these extracanonical books.[12] As noted canonical scholar Roger Beckwith points out, "When one examines the passages in the early Fathers which are supposed to establish the canonicity of the Apocrypha, one finds that some of them are taken from the alternative Greek text of Ezra (1 Esdras) or from additions of appendices to Daniel, Jeremiah or some other canonical book, which...are really not relevant; that others of them are not quotations from the Apocrypha at all; and that, of those which are, many do not give any indication that the book is regarded as Scripture."[13]

The New Testment was written between about A.D. 50 and A.D. 90. There are several lines of evidence that support the evangelical belief that the New Testament canon is closed.

First of all, Jesus promised a closed canon by limiting the teaching authority to the apostles, who all died before the end of the first century. There are clear indications in the New Testament that Jesus' revelation to the apostles would complete the biblical revelation. First, Jesus was the full and complete revelation of the Old Testament. He said of the whole Old Testament in the Sermon on the Mount: "Do not think that I came to destroy the Law or the Prophets. I did not come to destroy [the Law and the Prophets] but to fulfill" (Matthew 5:17). Indeed, Hebrews teaches that Jesus is the full and final revelation of God in "the last days." We read: "God, who at various times and in different ways spoke in time past to the fathers by the prophets, has in these last days spoken to us by His Son...who being the brightness of His glory and the express image of His person..." (Hebrews 1:1,2). Further, the book of Hebrews refers to Christ as better than the angels (1:4), better than the law (7:19), and better than the Old Testament law and priesthood (9:23). Indeed, His revelation and redemption is said to be eternal (5:9; 9:12,15) and once-for-all (9:26; 10:12-14). So Jesus was the full and final revelation of God to mankind. He alone could say, "He who has seen Me has seen the Father" (John 14:9). And of Him alone could it be said that "in Him dwells all the fullness of the Godhead bodily" (Colossians 2:9).

Second, Jesus chose, commissioned, and credentialed the apostles (cf. Hebrews 2:3,4) to teach this full and final revelation that He gave them (Matthew 10:1ff.). And before Jesus left this world He promised these apostles to guide them into all truth, saying: "The Holy Spirit...will teach you all things, and bring to your remembrance all things that I said to you" (John 14:26), and, "When He, the Spirit of truth, has come, He will guide you into all truth" (John 16:13). This is why the church is said to be "built on the foundation of the apostles and prophets" (Ephesians 2:20) and the earliest church "continued steadfastly in the apostles' doctrine" (Acts 2:42). If the apostles of Jesus did not teach this completed revelation of God, then Jesus was wrong. But as the Son of God He could not be wrong in what He taught. Therefore, the full and final revelation of God in Christ was given by the apostles.

Third, the apostles of Christ lived and died in the first century. So the record of this full and final revelation of Christ to the apostles was completed in the first century. Indeed, one of the qualifications of an apostle was that he was an eyewitness of the resurrection of Christ, which occurred in the first century (Acts 1:22). Anyone who lived after that time was a "false apostle" (2 Corinthians 11:13). When Paul's credentials as an apostle were challenged, he replied: "Am I not an apostle?...Have I not seen Jesus Christ our Lord?" (1 Corinthians 9:1). Indeed, he is listed with the other apostles as the "last" to have "seen" the resurrected Christ (1 Corinthians 15:6-8).

Fourth, so that there would be no doubt as to who was authorized to teach this full and final revelation of God in Christ, God gave special supernatural powers to the apostles (who in turn gave them to their associates—Acts 6:6; 8:14-18; 2 Timothy 1:6). That these powers were unique to the apostles is clear from the fact that they were called "the signs of an apostle" (2 Corinthians 12:12) and that certain things could occur only through the "laying on of the apostles' hands" (Acts 8:18; cf. Acts 19:6). Further, this "power" was promised to the apostles (Acts 1:1,8). After Jesus ascended (cf. John 14:12) they exercised or gave special apostolic functions and powers, including striking people dead who lied to the Holy Spirit (Acts 5:1-10) and performing special signs and wonders (Acts 5:12; Hebrews 2:3,4; 2 Corinthians 12:12), which included even raising the dead on command (Matthew 10:8; Acts 20:7-12).

Finally, there is only one authentic record of apostolic teaching in existence, and that is the 27 books of the New Testament. All other books that claim inspiration come from the second century or later. They are known as the New Testament Apocrypha and are clearly not written by apostles, since all the apostles died before the end of the first century. Since we know that these 27 books have been copied accurately from the very beginning (see p.14), the only remaining question is whether *all* of the apostolic writings from the first century have been preserved. If they have, then these 27 books complete the canon of Scripture. And anything written after them cannot be a revelation of God to the church.

The Preservation of the Apostles' Writings

There are two lines of evidence showing that all the inspired writings of the apostles and their associates were preserved and are found in the 27 books of the New Testament. The first reason is based on the character of God and the second on the care of the church.

The providence of God. Since the God of the Bible is all-knowing (Psalm 139:1-6; 147:5), all-good (Matthew 5:48; 1 John 4:16), and all-powerful (Genesis 1:1; Matthew 19:26), it follows that He would not inspire books for the faith and practice of believers down through the centuries which He did not preserve. Lost inspired books would be a lapse in God's providence. The God who cares for the sparrows will certainly care for His Scriptures. And the God who has preserved His general revelation in nature (Romans 1:19,20) will certainly not fail to preserve his special revelation in Scripture (Romans 3:2). In short, if God inspired these truths (2 Timothy 3:16), then God will preserve them (verse 17).

The preservation by the church. Not only does the providence of God promise the preservation of all inspired books, but the preservation of these books by the church confirms it. This preservation is manifest in several ways.

First, a collection of these books was made from the earliest times. Even within the New Testament itself this preservation process was put into action. Luke refers to other written records of the life of Christ (Luke 1:1-4), possibly Matthew and Mark. In Paul's epistle of 1 Timothy (5:18) the Gospel of Luke (10:7) is quoted. Peter refers to a collection of Paul's epistles (2 Peter 3:15,16). Paul charged that his epistle of 1 Thessalonians "be read to all the holy brethren" (5:27). And he commanded the church at Colosse: "Now when this epistle is read among you, see that it is read also in the church of the Laodiceans..." (Colossians 4:16). Jude (6,7,17) apparently had access to 2 Peter (2:4-6). And John's book of Revelation was circulated to the churches of Asia Minor (Revelation 1:4). So the apostolic church itself was involved by divine imperative in the preservation of the apostolic writings.

Second, the contemporaries of the apostles showed a concerned awareness of their mentors' writings, quoting from them prolifically. Following them, the Fathers of the second to fourth centuries made some 36,289 citations from the New Testament, including every verse except 11! This includes 19,368 citations from the Gospels, 1,352 from Acts, 14,035 from Paul's epistles, 870 from the General Epistles, and 664 from Revelation.[14] The Fathers of the second century alone cited from every major book of the New Testament and all but one minor one (3 John), which they simply may have had no occasion to cite. This reveals not only their great respect for the writings of the apostles but their ardent desire to preserve their written words.

Third, when challenged by heretical teaching, such as that by Marcion the Gnostic, who rejected all but part of Luke and ten of Paul's epistles (all but the Pastorals), the church responded by officially defining the extent of the canon. Lists of apostolic books and collections of their writings were made from early times, beginning with the second century. These include the Muratorian (A.D. 170), Apostolic (c. A.D. 300), Cheltenham (c. A.D. 360), and Athanasian (A.D. 367) lists, as well as the Old Latin translation (c. A.D. 200). This process culminated in the late fourth and early fifth centuries at the Councils of Hippo (A.D. 393) and Carthage (A.D. 410), which listed the 27 books of the New Testament as the complete canon.[15] Every major branch of Christendom, Catholics of all kinds, Protestants, and Anglicans have accepted this as the permanent verdict of the church. Evangelical Protestants agree that the canon is closed.

Finally, it is important to note that the material of textual criticism does not contradict this conclusion. The many variant readings of verses do not deal with lost books or even sections of books. They simply provide extra material within existing books, and not lost books.

The completeness of the collection. There is no evidence that any inspired book has been lost. This is confirmed by: 1) the providence of God, 2) the immediate and careful preservation of the church, and 3) the absence of any evidence of any other prophetic or apostolic book. Alleged contrary examples are easily explained as either a) uninspired works to which the biblical author made reference, or b) inspired works contained in the 66 inspired books but with another name. The following list illustrates the point.

Uninspired books mentioned in the Bible. Sometimes a biblical author cited uninspired books even as the apostle Paul cited some truths from pagan poets (Acts 17:28; 1 Corinthians 15:32,33; Titus 1:12) or as Jude may have referred to some Pseudepigraphal (false writings) books (Jude 9,14), which are rejected by both Judaism and all sections of Christianity. These include the book of Jasher (Joshua 10:13), the Wars of the Lord (Numbers 21:14), and the Acts of Solomon (1 Kings 11:41). These were simply sources to which the biblical author had occasion to refer for some truth contained in them. Books in this category could even have been written by a prophet or apostle who made no pretense on that occasion to be offering a revelation from God for the people of God. After all, even authors of inspired books had occasion for normal correspondence relating to business or family. "The records of Shemiah the prophet" (2 Chronicles 12:15) seem to fit in this category.

Inspired books mentioned by another name. Some inspired books are referred to by different names but are contained in the 66 inspired books known as the Bible. These include: 1) the "letter...from Elijah," which is contained in 2 Chronicles 21:12-15; 2) the contents of the chronicles of "Samuel... Nathan the prophet...Gad the Seer" (1 Chronicles 29:29), which parallel that of 1 and 2 Samuel; 3) the "vision of Isaiah the prophet" (2 Chronicles 32:32), which are probably the same as the book of Isaiah; 4) the other accounts (Luke 1:1) of the life of Christ, which may refer to Matthew and Mark; 5) the "epistle from Laodicea" (Colossians 4:16), which is probably Ephesians, for it was written at the same time and had not yet reached there; and 6) the letter to the Corinthians (1 Corinthians 5:9), which may refer to 1 Corinthians itself by a device known as an "epistolary aorist," which stressed the urgency of the message, a device Paul used elsewhere in the same letter (1 Corinthians 9:15). There is simply no evidence that any inspired apostolic work is missing from the New Testament.

The Confirmation of Scripture

Unlike other holy books, including the Qur'an[16] or the Book of Mormon, the Bible alone has been supernaturally confirmed to be the Word of God. For only the Scriptures were written by prophets who were supernaturally confirmed by signs and wonders. When Moses questioned how his message would be accepted, God performed miracles through him "that they may believe that the LORD God of Abraham, the God of Isaac, and the God of Jacob, has appeared to you" (Exodus 4:5). Later, when Korah rose up to challenge Moses, God again miraculously intervened to vindicate His prophet (Numbers 16). Likewise, Elijah was confirmed to be a prophet of God by supernatural intervention on Mount Carmel (1 Kings 18). In the Gospels, even the Jewish teacher Nicodemus said to Jesus, "Rabbi, we know that You are a teacher come from God; for no one can do these signs that You do unless God is with him" (John 3:2; cf. Luke 7:22). Luke spoke of "Jesus of Nazareth, a Man attested by God to you by miracles, wonders, and signs which God did through Him..." (Acts 2:22). Hebrews affirms that "God [was] also bearing witness [through the apostles] both with signs and wonders, with various miracles, and gifts of the Holy Spirit, according to His own will" (Hebrews 2:4). And the apostle Paul proved his apostleship by affirming, "Truly the signs of an apostle were accomplished among you with all perseverance, in signs and wonders and mighty deeds" (2 Corinthians 12:12).

No other book in the world has authors who were confirmed in this miraculous manner. Of all the world religious leaders, neither Confucius, Buddha, Muhammad, nor Joseph Smith was confirmed by miracles that were verified by contemporary and credible witnesses. The Bible alone proves to be the Word of God written by prophets and apostles of God (cf. Ephesians 2:20) who were confirmed by special acts of God (miracles).[17]

The Mormon View of Scriptures

The Mormon view of inspired writings stands in stark contrast to the evangelical view on virtually all major points. This includes the writings' origin, means, reliability, prophecies, completeness, and confirmation. While there are many similarities in form and overlap in content between the evangelical and Mormon views of divine revelation, the differences are both multiple and crucial. Judging the two to be essentially the same because of superficial similarities while overlooking crucial differences is a fatal mistake. It is like insisting that a counterfeit 20-dollar bill is genuine because it has many similarities to a genuine one, while overlooking the crucial differences that make it a counterfeit. In the final analysis it is the differences that really make the difference between authentic Christianity and counterfeit forms of it.

Mormons affirm things about the Bible that sound identical to what evangelicals believe, but they are not. One Mormon New Testament scholar even claimed to believe that the Bible is the inerrant Word of God in the originals, accepting the widely acknowledged 1978 ICBI Statement on Inerrancy.[18] As a drafter of the statement and author of the official commentary on it, I can say with authority that there is a great gulf between what evangelicals affirmed in this statement and what the Mormon Church teaches on this matter. In contrast to evangelicals, Latter-day Saints (LDS) teaching has consistently affirmed that our present translations of the Bible are neither accurate nor complete. In fact Mormon leaders have proclaimed the Bible we possess to be completely corrupted in essential elements of the Gospel, which they believe was restored only in the Book of Mormon and other revelations of Joseph Smith. They believe it to be "another Testament of Jesus Christ" containing a record of Jews who allegedly lived in North America between 600 B.C. and A.D. 400, after they had fled Israel in 587 B.C. Jesus allegedly appeared to them after His resurrection. The tablets of this book were supposedly hidden and later discovered by Joseph Smith.

Mormon Claims About
Substantial Changes in the Biblical Text

While in theory Mormons accept the inspiration of the original manuscripts of the Bible, in actual practice they believe the copies are riddled with errors. The *Missionary Pal: Reference Guide for [Mormon] Missionaries & Teachers*[19] lists a section on "Bible Errors" and gives examples of what they believe are errors in the Bible, such as the two accounts of Judas' death (Matthew 27:5; Acts 1:18) and two reports of Paul's vision (Acts 9:7; 26:13,14). In fact, Joseph Smith made his own "inspired" translation of the Bible which has thousands of changes from the King James Version.

The official statement of Mormonism about the Bible is "We believe the Bible to be the word of God as far as it is translated correctly; we also believe the Book of Mormon to be the word of God" (AF no. 8). But in actual practice

Mormon leaders from Joseph Smith onward have said that *the Bible has not been translated accurately*. So Mormons leave the wrong impression when they say they believe the Bible is the Word of God. If it is, then why did God command Joseph Smith to make an "inspired translation" of the Bible which contains thousands of changes from the Bible, even omitting a whole book of the Bible?

Mormon Apostle Orson Pratt declared, "The Hebrew and Greek manuscripts of the Bible from which translations have been made are evidently very much corrupted....This uncertainty, combined with the imperfections of uninspired translators, renders the Bibles of all languages, at the present day, emphatically the words of men, instead of the pure word of God." But even Joseph Smith's successor, Brigham Young, agreed (JD 3:116) that Apostle Pratt went too far in rejecting the Bible. For the Book of Mormon itself quotes hundreds of verses from the Bible which almost always carry the same meaning they have in the Bible. Thus the Bible cannot be discredited without also discrediting the Book of Mormon.

While some current Mormon scholars would like to discard the official Mormon position, even the Book of Mormon charges that "...through the hands of the great and abominable church...there are many plain and precious things taken away from the book [the Bible]..." (1 Nephi 13:28). In 1832 the Mormon publication *The Evening and the Morning Star* said the changes in the Bible were made "by the Mother of Harlots while it was confined in that Church,—say, from the year A.D. 460 to 1400" (vol. 1, no. 1, p. 3).

However, since we possess manuscripts of almost the whole New Testament that date well before that time, from A.D. 250 to 350 (Chester Beatty Papyri, Vaticanus, and Sinaiticus), that are substantially the same in all major and most minor points, this position is untenable.[20] Further, the Isaiah A scroll from the Dead Sea Scrolls (c. 100 B.C.) reveals that the Christian church, even beginning in the time of the apostles, did not take away any precious truths, since they reveal no substantial changes in the book of Isaiah or in other Old Testament books in the King James Bible.

One recent Mormon scholar, Stephen E. Robinson, attempts to avoid this problem by predating the time of the corruption to between A.D. 55 and 200.[21] However, this is refuted by the facts that: 1) there was no corrupt "Mother of Harlots" church at that time; 2) the Bodmer Papyri contain whole books of the New Testament from A.D. 200 that are substantially the same as the Bible today; 3) the John Ryland manuscript (A.D. 117-138) contains whole verses from the Gospel of John that are the same as later manuscripts; 4) the closer the manuscripts are to the original, the less likely there would be corruption, not the more likely; 5) there is no motive for the early church to corrupt the truth it was dying for under the great Roman persecutions; 6) the hypothesis is practically unverifiable, since we have no complete Greek manuscripts from before A.D. 200; 7) it is contrary to almost universal Mormon teaching that the corruption was due to the Roman Catholic Church, which did not really begin to develop until the fourth century and later; and 8) indeed, it is contrary to the Book of Mormon itself, which implies that the corruption was during the Middle Ages (BM, 1 Nephi 13:28); 9) it does not explain the lack of corruption in the Old Testament as verified by the Dead Sea Scrolls, many of which date from 200-100 B.C., which is long before A.D. 50-200.

Even a Brigham Young University (BYU) New Testament scholar, Dr. Richard L. Anderson, acknowledged that "there is more reason today, then, to agree with him [Sir Frederic Kenyon] that we possess the New Testament, 'in substantial purity' and to underline that 'the variations of the text are so entirely questions of detail, not of essential substance.'" But if this is so, then both the Book of Mormon and the Mormon Apostles must have been wrong in their statements about the corruption of the Bible during the Middle Ages.

The Need for New Revelation

Since Mormons believe that the Bible as we have it is an unreliable guide, they claim this reveals the need for new revelation, such as the Book of Mormon. In a pamphlet

titled "The Bible Alone An Insufficient Guide," Apostle
Orson Pratt wrote: "We all know that but a few of the
inspired writings have descended to our times, which few
quote the names of some twenty other books which are
lost..." and "What have come down to our day have been
mutilated, changed, and corrupted in such a shameful manner that no two manuscripts agree." For "verses and even
whole chapters have been added by unknown persons; and
even we do not know the authors of some whole books; and
we are not certain that all those which we do know, were
wrote [sic] by inspiration, and who, in his right mind, could,
for one moment, suppose the Bible in its present form to be
a perfect guide?" In fact, "Who knows that even one verse of
the whole Bible has escaped pollution, so as to convey the
same sense now that it did in the original?" In view of this,
"no reflecting man can deny the necessity of such a new revelation [as the Book of Mormon]."[22] In point of fact, Joseph
Smith claimed that the Book of Mormon was given to
restore the fullness of the Gospel that had been lost.

Further, the alleged corruption of the Bible is evident
from what LDS Apostle Bruce R. McConkie affirmed:
"...[A]t the command of the Lord and while acting under
the spirit of revelation, the Prophet [Joseph Smith] corrected, revised, altered, added to, and deleted from the
King James Version of the Bible to form what is now commonly referred to as the Inspired Version of the Bible."
Thus the "...marvelous flood of light and knowledge
revealed through the Inspired Version of the Bible is one of
the great evidences of the divine mission of Joseph Smith
(MD, 1958, pp.351-52).

Joseph Smith's Inspired Version of the Bible

Actually, this so-called "Inspired Version" of the Bible has
been an embarrassment to the Mormon Church. It was never
published during Smith's lifetime, nor has the Mormon
Church ever made an official publication of it. It was given in
1886 by Smith's wife Emma to the Reorganized Church,
which denies Smith's later revelations and Brigham Young's

leadership. Their edition of 1887 is even sold in the Mormon Deseret Book Store and is cited by Mormon scholars.

The origin of the "Inspired Version." Apostle John A. Widtsoe declared that "Joseph Smith accepted the Bible as far as it was translated correctly but felt that many errors which should be corrected had crept into the work of the copyist and translators....He endeavored through inspiration from on high to correct those many departures from the original text....It is a remarkable evidence of the prophetic power of Joseph Smith. Hundreds of changes made clear a disputed text."[23]

According to Mormon scholar Reed C. Durham, Jr., "There are eighteen sections in the Doctrine and Covenants wherein the Lord gives commands and specific instructions relating to the Revision."[24] In a revelation given to Joseph Smith on January 10, 1832, he was commanded by God: "Now, verily I say unto you my servants, Joseph Smith, Jun., and Sidney Rigdon, saith the Lord...it is expedient to continue the work of translation until it be finished" (D&C 73:3,4). It is clear from this that God expected him to finish the work. If it was a revelation from God, the fact that Smith did not finish it would indicate either that he was a disobedient prophet or that God was wrong!

The Mormon dilemma. The leaders of the Mormon Church are faced with a dilemma. On the one hand, they cannot deny that Joseph Smith was commanded by God and actually made the hundreds of changes in the Bible found in his "Inspired Version," since it exists in both handwritten and printed copies. On the other hand, they acknowledge that "there are many parts of the Bible in which the Prophet did not change the meaning where it is incorrect," yet insist that "he revised as far as the Lord permitted him at the time, and it was his intention to do more, but because of persecutions this was not accomplished" (DS 3:191).

However, this claim is insufficient for several reasons. First of all, Mormon scholars admit that there are errors in the "Inspired Version," even in sections that Smith revised under God's direction. But an all-knowing God certainly would have known they were in need of correction when He "inspired" Joseph to make the changes. Second, surely God would have known in advance about Joseph's busy schedule. If He knew Joseph would not be able to complete it, then why did He command him "to continue the work of translation until it be finished" (D&C 73:4)?

Furthermore, early Mormons considered it a completed version. In the *History of the Church* we find this statement by Joseph Smith under the date of February 2, 1833: "I completed the translation and review of the New Testament, on the 2nd of February, 1833, and sealed it up, no more to be opened until it arrived in Zion" (HC 1:324). And in the *Church Chronology* by Andrew Jenson the entry of the same day (February 2, 1833) we read: "Joseph Smith, jun. Completed the translation of the Bible." And in a letter of July 2, 1833, signed by Joseph Smith, Sidney Rigdon, and F. G. Williams, this statement is found: "We this day finished the translation of the Scriptures, for which we returned gratitude to our Heavenly Father..." (HC 1:368).

Finally, Mormon writer Arch S. Reynolds asserted that "the scriptures at that time were considered finished. This is proved by revelation from the Lord commanding the printing and publishing the same...the Lord felt that the Bible contained his word and also was given in fulness."[25] Even the *Doctrine and Covenants* supports this, saying, "...I have commanded you to organize yourselves, even to shinelah [print] my words, the fulness of my scriptures..." (D&C 104:58). Even though the Mormons were unsettled and persecuted, they were able to publish many other works. Why then do they not publish their prophet's Inspired Version of the Bible?

An evaluation of the Inspired Version. There are many problems with Smith's alleged inspired Bible. In each case, the consistency and/or credibility of the LDS claims are at stake.

For one thing, if it was an inspired revision of the King James Version, then why did Smith overlook some verses contrary to Mormon teaching? First John 5:7,8a is a classic case in point. Most orthodox Christians admit this is an interpolation. Why an inspired Mormon Prophet who rejected the doctrine of the trinity would miss correcting this verse is not easy to explain. Even LDS scholars reject this verse. Why then did their Prophet not delete it from his Inspired Version of the Bible?

Further, Smith's renditions of verses that are clearly authentic is without justification. John 1:1 reads, "In the beginning was the Word, and the Word was with God, and the Word was God" (KJV). Yet Smith rendered it, "In the beginning was the gospel preached through the Son. And the gospel was the word, and the word was with the Son, and the Son was with God, and the Son was of God." But no such rendering is found in any of the thousands of manuscripts of the Gospels. Indeed, many of these manuscripts come from a time long before the Roman Catholic Church could possibly have changed or distorted it—namely, from between A.D. 200 and 350 (e. g., Bodmer Papyri, Chester Beatty Papyri, and Vaticanus manuscripts).

What is more, Smith missed a great opportunity to restore some of the so-called "lost books" to the Bible while he was "restoring" what was allegedly lost. But instead of restoring them, he actually took one book out of the Bible— the Song of Solomon—claiming that "the Songs of Solomon are not inspired writings."[26]

Furthermore, there are strange interpolations in Smith's Inspired Version, such as an 800-word addition to Genesis 50:24 which includes a prophecy about Joseph Smith by name. Even his bias against Blacks came out in some "inspired" changes—a bias that the Mormon church hoped to overcome in a later revelation (1978) which finally allowed Blacks into the priesthood. In addition, Joseph's Inspired Version contains a strange anachronism in which Adam was baptized and received the Holy Ghost like the early believers in Acts 2!

In addition, the very nature of the revision process indicates that it was entirely human and not divine in origin. As a follower of Joseph Smith (from the Reorganized Church) put it, "Many tests reveal that the process was not some kind of automatic verbal or visual revelatory experience on the part of Joseph Smith. He often caused a text to be written in one form and later reworded his initial revision. The manuscripts in some cases show a considerable time lapse between such reconsiderations." In fact, "when one turns to nearly any page of OT #3 containing substantial initial revisions of the King James Version, different colors of ink appear, showing later revisions, written between the lines or on separate scraps of paper and pinned to the manuscript pages."[27]

Finally, the Inspired Version corrects verses in the Bible which are cited by the inspired Book of Mormon as true. It would follow logically that at least one, if not both, of these books is not inspired.

Incompleteness of LDS Scriptures

Unlike evangelicals and other Christians, Mormons believe that the Bible is not the complete canon of Scripture. They have four books they believe to be inspired: the Bible [insofar as it is correctly translated], the Book of Mormon, *Doctrine and Covenants*, and *The Pearl of Great Price*. What is more, Mormons believe that the sitting President of the LDS Church is a living prophet. In the 1988 edition of *Gospel Principles* we read: "In addition to these four books of scripture, the *inspired words of our living prophet become scripture to us*. Their words come to us through conferences, Church publications, and instructions to local priesthood leaders" (GP 49-51, emphasis added).

Aside from the words of the living prophet, even the LDS Scriptures are not complete for a number of reasons. First of all, as noted above, Joseph Smith omitted the Song of Solomon from his Inspired Version. Yet it is in the King James Version which the LDS Church accepts. Second, as will be shown below, there were many errors in Joseph Smith's canon that both he and later Mormon editors had to correct. Third, the LDS Scriptures contain false prophecies (see below) which, therefore, should be omitted from the inspired writings, since God cannot err (Hebrews 6:18; Titus 1:2). Fourth, Smith failed to restore the so-called lost

Apocryphal books to the Bible, even though he borrows ideas from them. Fifth, since the Mormon Church claims to have a living prophet who can receive new revelation from God, the canon of Scripture will always be open. This idea of an open canon is emphatically rejected by evangelical Christians, as well as all other major branches of Christianity. As quoted above, the LDS handbook *Gospel Principles* declares: "In addition to these four books of scripture, the inspired words of our living prophets become scripture to us. Their words come to us through conferences, Church publications, and instructions to local priesthood leaders."[28] Indeed, Brigham Young affirmed, "I have never yet preached a sermon and sent it out to the children of men that they may not call Scripture" (JD 13:95).

Not only is the Mormon canon incomplete, but it is unconfirmed. There are no accompanying miracles to confirm the new revelations such as there were for biblical prophets and apostles (Exodus 4:1ff.; 1 Kings 18; Acts 2:22; Hebrew 2:3,4).

Confirmation of LDS Scriptures

Unlike the Gospels, the witnesses to the claims of the Book of Mormon were not supported by supernatural events, as were Jesus and the apostles. That is, neither Joseph Smith nor his witnesses were confirmed by a multitude of miracles including healing the blind, lame, and deaf, and even raising the dead (cf. Matthew 10:8; Luke 7:22).

Mormons offer the 11 witnesses to the Book of Mormon as proof of its divine origin. Their testimony is recorded in two separate statements in the forepart of the Book of Mormon. In the first statement Oliver Cowdery, David Whitmer, and Martin Harris claimed that an angel of God showed them the golden plates from which Joseph Smith later translated the Book of Mormon. The second statement claimed to see the plates, though no mention is made of an angel showing the plates to them. It is signed by Christian Whitmer, Jacob Whitmer, Peter Whitmer, Jun., John Whitmer, Hiram Page, Joseph Smith, Sen. Hyrum Smith, and Samuel H. Smith.

The LDS Church claims that the witnesses never denied their testimony. However, there are numerous reasons to deny that they confirm the truth of Mormonism.

First, even if the alleged witnesses did see some kind of plates, it does not mean that what was written on them was true. And even if some of them believed they saw angel-like beings, it does not mean they were not hallucinating. Further, even if they actually saw some angels, it does not mean that they were good angels. The Bible warns that the devil himself is transformed into an angel of light (2 Corinthians 11:14) and that we should reject a false gospel even if it were proclaimed by an angel from heaven (Galatians 1:8). Indeed, Mormons themselves admit that the devil gives false revelations (see below).

Second, the 11 witnesses could not read what was on the plates. Only Joseph Smith was able to translate them, and that some time later. So they could not even vouch for the content of the message on the plates. Indeed, the plates were said to be taken by the angel back to heaven. So there is no way for anyone to verify what was on them.

Third, in another case where Joseph claimed to be able to translate the Book of Abraham the manuscript was later discovered, translated by competent scholars from Egypt, and proved to be a total fraud having nothing to do with Abraham.[29] Rather, it was the Egyptian "Book of Breathings."[30] Why then should the Book of Mormon be considered anything but fraudulent?

Fourth, there is a serious question about the credibility of the witnesses even seeing what they claimed to have seen, which even if seen proves nothing about the truth of the content of the Book of Mormon.

Oliver Cowdery. According to Joseph Smith himself, Oliver Cowdery was later led astray by Hiram Page's "peep stone"—something forbidden in the Bible as an occult means of divination (Deuteronomy 18:9-12). Cowdery was even excommunicated from the Mormon Church and joined the Methodist Church at Tiffin, Ohio. In 1841 the Mormons published a poem which stated that the Book of Mormon was "denied" by Oliver. Mormons claimed he joined "a gang of counterfeiters, thieves, liars, and blacklegs." Although there is evidence that Cowdery may have returned to Mormonism before he died, even David Whitmer claimed Joseph Smith was a fallen prophet and that his revelations in the *Doctrine and Covenants* must be rejected. Why then accept his alleged revelation of the Book of Mormon, especially when he had no idea of the content of what he originally said and later "denied" he saw in those plates?

David Whitmer. Whitmer eventually left the Mormon Church and never returned to it. Joseph Smith himself said of Whitmer that he was of those who were "too mean to mention" and called him a "dumb ass."[31] Whitmer changed his allegiance several times, first supporting Joseph Smith, then James J. Strang, and eventually the McLellin group. When discontent with the Mormons he claimed: "God spake to me again by His own voice from the heavens, and told me 'to separate myself from among the Latter Day Saints, for as they sought to do unto me, so should it be done unto them'"[32]—obviously not from the same God who revealed the Golden Rule (Matthew 7:12). In short, David Whitmer was not a man of strong character or credibility. Rather, he was gullible, being influenced by Hiram Page's "peep-stone" and possibly by a woman with a "black stone in Kirtland, Ohio." Whitmer eventually joined a small sect that accepted the Book of Mormon. But the question remains as to why Mormons accept the testimony of a man who defected from Mormonism and received what they believe to be a false revelation, and whom they claim to be a liar, counterfeiter, and thief.

Martin Harris. There is evidence that Harris was religiously, if not psychologically, unstable. G. W. Stodard, a resident of Palmyra, New York, made the following statement in an affidavit dated November 28, 1833: "I have been acquainted wth Martin Harris, about thirty years....Although he possessed wealth, his moral and religious characer [sic] was such as not to entitle him to respect among his neighbors....He was first an ortha dox [sic] Quaker, then a Universalist, next a

Restorationer, then a Baptist, next a Presbyterian, and then a Mormon." Even Mormons admitted that Harris "became partially deranged...flying from one thing to another (*Millennial Star* 8:124). One Mormon writer, Richard L. Anderson, acknowledged that Harris "changed his religious position eight times when he was in Kirtland, Ohio." Joseph Smith referred to Harris as a "wicked man," and the Mormon *Millennial Star* said he had "a lying and deceptive spirit."[33]

Other Considerations About the Witnesses

First of all, as one former Mormon put it, "It would appear that some of the witnesses to the Book of Mormon would follow almost anyone who had a peep stone or claimed to have been visited by an angel."[34] For example, they believed James J. Strang, who claimed to translate ancient plates with Urim and Thummim. Martin Harris even served as a missionary for the Stranites. The Mormons admit that Harris even joined the Shakers, who did not accept the Book of Mormon and who had their own book called *A Holy, Sacred and Divine Roll and Book; From the Lord God of Heaven, to the Inhabitants of Earth.*

Second, there is conflicting testimony as to whether the witnesses actually saw the tablets. Mormon writer Marvin S. Hill said that "...there is a possibility that the witnesses saw the plates in vision only....There is testimony from several independent interviewers, all non-Mormon, that Martin Harris and David Whitmer said they saw the plates with their 'spiritual eyes' only...." Indeed, "Stephen Burnett quotes Martin Harris that 'the eight witnesses never saw the plates when they were not covered....'"[35]

Third, the Shakers had eight witnesses who signed a statement claiming to have seen an angel holding their book. Yet Mormons reject this signed testimony. Why then should others accept the testimony of only three Mormons who claimed to have had a similar experience? Indeed, one Mormon source claimed that Harris believed the testimony for the Shaker book to be "greater than it was for the Book of Mormon."[36]

Fourth, there is evidence of hallucination among the witnesses. In his *History of the Church*, Joseph Smith admits that Martin Harris was not with the other two when they saw the angel. Smith had them pray continually in an effort of obtaining a vision for Harris. After failing twice, Harris volunteered to leave. This proved to be the charm, and the two witnesses saw the angel again and invited Harris to rejoin them. Harris wrote, "We accordingly joined in prayer, and ultimately obtained our desires, for before we had yet finished, the same vision was opened to our view..." (HC 1:54,55). These are almost classic conditions for a hallucination.

Highly imaginative and even hallucinatory experiences were not uncommon among early Mormons. John Pulsipher recorded in his journal that he saw "a steamboat past [sic] over Kirtland in the air!...Old Elser Beamon, who had died a few months before, was seen in the bow of the Boat."[37] Even the Mormon historian of Smith's time, John Whitmer, admits the false visions that some Mormons had. He wrote, "For a perpetual memory to the shame and confusion of the Devil, permit me to say a few things respecting the proceedings of some...who have come under the error and enthusiasm they had fallen. Some had visions and could not tell what they saw." And "some would fancy themselves that they had the sword of Laban, and would wield it as expert as a light dragon; some would cut like an Indian in the act of scalping...." Whitmer concludes, "Thus the Devil blinded the eyes of some good and honest disciples."[38]

Fifth, there is nothing really supernatural about the contents of the Book of Mormon. Its contents can be readily explained from known sources. Just to mention a few: 1) It reflects the religious controversies of the ninteenth century, attempting in vain to solve them (see Alexander Campbell, *Millennial Harbinger*, p.93); 2) it shows resemblance to the *Westminster Confession and Catechism*, with which Smith's Presbyterian family was undoubtedly familiar; 3) it reflects an awareness of Josiah Priest's *The Wonders of Nature and Providence Displayed*, published in 1825; 3) the King James Version of the Bible is widely used, even though it anachronistically had people speaking in 1611 English more than

2000 years before the KJV was written (in A.D. 1611); 4) the Apocryphal books found in many King James Bibles use the name "Nephi," which is also used in the Book of Mormon (cf. 2 Maccabees 1:36). Mark Twain said that the Book of Mormon "seems to be merely a prosy detail of imaginary history, with the Old Testament for a model, followed by a tedious plagiarism of the New Testament."[39]

The Problem of Plagiarism

There is another thorny problem for Mormons with regard to the authenticity of the Book of Mormon: It has some 27,000 words taken directly from the King James Version of the Bible.[40] There are many complete verses lifted out of the King James text that was written in A.D. 1611. But the Book of Mormon is alleged to have been written between 600 B.C. and A.D. 421. So it is using the King James Version 1200 to 2000 years before there was a King James Version! The Book of Mormon even uses the *italicized* words from the King James, which its translators admit were not in the original but were inserted for clarification!

Alleged Prophecies

The thing that could have supernaturally confirmed Joseph Smith's writings—his sometimes predictive prophecies—turns out to be one of his worst enemies, since there are many false prophecies. A few examples will illustrate the point.

The Canadian revelation. One of the three witnesses to the Book of Mormon, David Whitmer, relates one of Smith's false prophecies. Once when they needed money to finish their project, "Joseph looked into the hat in which he placed the [seer] stone, and received a revelation that some of the brethren should go to Toronto, Canada, and that they would sell the copy-right of the Book of Mormon." When the mission failed and Joseph was asked why the revelation went wrong, God revealed to Joseph, "'Some revelations are of God; some revelations are of man; and some revelations are of the devil.' So we see that the revelation to go to

Toronto and sell the copy-right was not of God, but was of the devil or the heart of man."[41]

Mormon historian B. H. Roberts admits this was a false revelation, excusing it on Joseph being "overwrought in his deep anxiety for the progress of the work" (Roberts, CHC 1:165). However, Mormon apologists do not seem to appreciate how this tends to undermine Smith's other revelations, especially in view of the fact that David Whitmer admits that there were "other false revelations that came through Brother Joseph as a mouthpiece."[42] The Bible teaches clearly that false prophecies demonstrate a false prophet (Deuteronomy 18:22).

Prophecies about the coming of Christ. In 1835 Joseph Smith prophesied that Christ would return in 56 years. In *History of the Church* (HC 2:182) we read that "President Smith then stated...it was the will of God that those who went to Zion...should be ordained to the ministry, and go forth to prune the vineyard for the last time, or the coming of the Lord, which was nigh—even fifty-six years should wind up the scene." It has now been well over 156 years, and Christ has still not come.

On another occasion Smith wrote, "I prophesy in the name of the Lord God—& let it be written: that the Son of Man will not come in the heavens till I am 85 years old 48 years hence or about 1890..." (ibid). Indeed, on the basis of this statement there was a widespread belief among Mormons of the time that Christ would return in 1890. But Christ did not come as predicted, the Saints were disappointed, and Joseph Smith was again proven to be a false prophet.

Predictions about building a Mormon temple in Zion. On September 22 and 23, 1832, Smith predicted: "Yea, the word of the Lord concerning his church, established in the last days for the restoration of his people...for the gathering of his saints to stand upon Mount Zion, which shall be the city of New Jerusalem. Which city shall be built, beginning at the temple lot, which is appointed by the finger of the Lord, in the western boundaries of the State of Missouri, and dedicated by the hand of Joseph Smith, Jun., and others." He added, "...which temple shall be reared in this generation. For verily this generation shall not all pass away until an house shall be built unto the Lord..." (D&C 84:2-5,31). However, no such temple was built. Since that whole generation died before the prophecy came to pass, it is clear that God did not speak it. Again, Smith was a false prophet.

Prophecy about the Civil War. On December 25, 1832, Joseph Smith made a prediction about the Civil War (D&C 87:1-5). It reads in part as follows: "1. Verily, thus saith the Lord concerning the wars that will shortly come to pass, beginning at the rebellion of south Carolina, which will eventually terminate in the death and misery of many souls. 2. And the time will come that the war will be poured out upon all nations beginning at this place. 3. For behold the Southern States shall be divided against the Northern States, and the Southern States will call on other nations, even the nation of Great Britain....4. And it shall come to pass, after many days, slaves shall rise up against their masters, who shall be marshalled and disciplined for war."

While this prediction is now offered by Mormons as an example of the supernatural gift of prophecy Joseph Smith possessed, there is evidence that even they were embarrassed by it. First of all, it was never published during Joseph Smith's lifetime. It first appeared in 1851, seven years after his death. Second, over 300 words were deleted in the first two editions of the *History of the Church.* Third, there is nothing really supernatural about the things that did come to pass, since they were not an uncommon view of the times. It simply represented the trend of the times. Fourth, and most significantly, verse 2 never came to pass, since the war was not poured out on all nations. Here again Smith proved to be no more than a purely human prognosticator and no less than a false prophet.

Changes in Revelation

Another embarrassing contrast between the Mormon and Christian Scriptures is seen in the many substantial changes that have been made in the Mormon revelations. As already noted, the biblical prophets were forbidden to make changes in their revelations (Proverbs 30:5,6; Revelation 22:18,19). By contrast, Joseph Smith made thousands of changes.

Noted Mormon researchers Jerald and Sandra Tanner have published *3,913 Changes in the Book of Mormon* (1965). While most of these are grammatical in nature, even these are significant in the light of early Mormon claims that Joseph received these word-for-word revelations directly from God. Indeed, Joseph himself claimed it was "the most correct of any book on earth." Olive B. Huntington recorded in his journal that Joseph F. Smith, who became the sixth President of the Mormon Church, claimed: "Joseph did not render the writing on the gold plates into the English language in his own style of language as many people believe, but every word and every letter was given to him by the gift and power of God...." For "the Lord caused each word to appear on the stones in short sentences or words and...when the scribe had written it properly, that sentence would disappear and another appear." In fact, "if there was a word wrongly written or even a letter incorrect the writing on the stone would remain there...and when corrected the sentence would disappear as usual."[43] If this is so, then God made at least 3913 mistakes in his word-for-word dictation to Joseph Smith!

Mormon scholars today find it easier to resort to the view that God only gave Joseph Smith the *ideas*, which he then put in his own plainly errant words. But this explanation will not suffice, for many of the errors are not merely grammatical; there are errors in content and even in important doctrines. Several examples will illustrate that there have been changes in content in the Book of Mormon, as well as changes in doctrine through the years.

Plurality of Gods. The Book of Mormon teaches that there is only one God. The later *Book of Abraham* affirms that there are many gods. A comparison of the two books reveals the former saying over and over "I, God" or "I, the Lord God" while the latter affirms "the Gods" or "they [the Gods]" (cf.

Moses 2:1,10,25; 3:8 with Abraham 4:3,10,25; 5:8). By 1844 Smith came to believe that "God himself, who sits in yonder heavens, is a man like unto one of yourselves, that is the great secret....I am going to tell you how God came to be God...God himself; the Father of us all dwelt on an earth the same as Jesus Christ himself did....You have got to learn how to be Gods yourselves. No man can learn [sic] you more that what I have told you."[44]

Apostle Orson Pratt declared that "there are more Gods than there are particles of matter in those worlds" (JD 2:345). And President Brigham Young claimed that God "was once a man in mortal flesh as we are, and now an exalted being... God has once been a finite being..." (JD 5:19). Apostle LeGrand Richards summarized it well: "As man is, God once was; as God is, man may become."[45]

Not only have Mormon leaders taught that there are many Gods, but they also affirm that there are many goddesses. Although Mormons do not worship God's wife, they teach that she is our "Eternal Mother." Apostle Bruce McConkie asserted, "Implicit in the Christian verity that all men are the spirit children of an Eternal Father is the usually unspoken truth that they are also the offspring of an Eternal Mother...the begetting of children makes a man a father and a woman a mother whether we are dealing with man in his mortal or immortal state." McConkie appealed to the First Presidency to justify his conclusion, noting that they referred to man as "begotten and born of heavenly parents [plural]" (MD 516). Milton Hunter, who served in the First Council of the Seventy, affirmed that "the stupendous truth of the existence of a Heavenly Mother, as well as a Heavenly Father, became established facts in Mormon theology."[46]

No virgin birth. It follows logically from the foregoing that Jesus, like the rest of us, was begotten of two human parents, which directly contradicts the Bible and the Book of Mormon (Alma 7:10). Indeed, Brigham Young said, "Now remember from this time forth, and for ever, that Jesus

Christ was not begotten by the Holy Ghost" (JD 1:51). He added, "The birth of the Saviour was as natural as are the births of our children; it was the result of a natural action" (JD 8:115). Apostle Bruce McConkie added, "Christ was begotten by an Immortal Father in the same way that mortal men are begotten by mortal fathers" (MD 1966, pp. 546-47). But this is a change from what the Book of Mormon teaches. For Alma 7:10 reads: "And behold, he shall be born of Mary...she being a virgin, a precious chosen vessel, who shall be overshadowed and conceived by the power of the Holy Ghost, and bring forth a son, yea, even the Son of God." In view of this it is difficult to understand Joseph Fielding Smith's denial of the virgin birth: "They tell us the Book of Mormon states that Jesus was begotten of the Holy Ghost. I challenge that statement. The Book of Mormon teaches no such thing! Neither does the Bible!" (DS 1:19). This is, of course, exactly opposite of what the Bible teaches (cf. Isaiah 7:14; Matthew 1:18-25; Luke 1:26-38).

The changeableness of God. If Gods are begotten like we are, then it follows logically that they change as we do. Apostle Orson Pratt said, "Remember that God, our heavenly Father, was perhaps once a child, and mortal like we ourselves, and rose step by step in the scale of progress..." (JD 1:123). Wilford Woodruff, who became the fourth President of the Mormon Church, said, "God himself is increasing and progressing in knowledge, power, and dominion, and will do so, worlds without end" (JD 6:120). Brigham Young declared, "We are now, or may be, as perfect in our sphere as God and Angels are in theirs, but the greatest intelligence in existence can continually ascend to greater heights of perfection" (JD 1:93).

But this is a change in revelation from the Book of Mormon, which affirms: "For I know that God is not a partial God, neither a changeable being; but he is unchangeable from all eternity to eternity" (BM 517:18). What is more, it stands in contrast to orthodox Christians, who affirm what the Bible teaches. Malachi wrote: "For I am the Lord, I change not..." (Malachi 3:6; cf. Hebrews 1:12; James 1:17).

God is the same "from everlasting to everlasting" (Psalm 90:1), and there was no God before Him. Further, God said through Isaiah: "...I am He. Before Me there was no God formed, nor shall there be after Me" (Isaiah 43:10).

Plural marriages. The Book of Mormon never approved anything but monogamy, one wife for one man (BM; cf. Jacob 2:26-29; 3:3-11). Even the first (1835) edition of *Doctrine and Covenants* emphatically denounced polygamy: "Inasmuch as this church of Christ has been reproached with the crime of fornication, and polygamy; we declare that we believe, that one man should have one wife: and one woman but one husband, except in the case of death, when either is at liberty to marry again" (D&C 101:4, 1835 edition). This section was deleted from *Doctrine and Covenants* in 1876. Smith had earlier received his revelation about many wives on July 12, 1843. This change in revelation is printed as part of LDS Scripture in *Doctrine and Covenants* (D&C 132:1-62).

King Benjamin. Another change in revelation from the first Book of Mormon (1830) to that of the later edition relates to king Benjamin. The earlier version reads: "...king *Benjamin* had a gift from God, whereby he could interpret such engravings...." Later versions read: "...king *Mosiah* had a gift from God, whereby he could interpret such engravings..." (1964 edition). Based on the chronology of the Book of Mormon (Mosiah 6:3-7; cf. 7:1), king Benjamin should have been dead by this time, and church leaders thought it best to change the wording.

Another change involving king Benjamin once read (in 1830) "...for this cause did king *Benjamin* keep them..." (page 546). Today it reads "for this cause did king *Mosiah* keep them..." (page 485).

Other content changes. Even the signed statement by the eight eyewitnesses has been altered. In the 1830 edition it read, "...Joseph Smith, Jr. The *Author and Proprietor* of this work, has shown unto us the plates...." In more recent editions it reads, "...Joseph Smith, Jun., the *translator* of this work, has shown unto us the plates...."

The first edition reads, "...the mean man boweth down...." (page 87). In later editions the meaning is reversed to "...the mean man boweth *not* down..." (page 74).

The first edition reads, "My soul was *wrecked* with eternal torment..." (page 214). This was altered to read, "My soul was *racked* with eternal torment..." (page 188).

The 1833 *Book of Commandments* (44:26) reads, "And behold, thou shalt consecrate *all* thy properties, that thou hast unto me, with a covenant and a deed which can not be broken; and they shall be laid before the bishop of my church...."

However, this covenant that could "not be broken" was broken only two years later (1835) in *Doctrine and Covenants* (13:8), which reads, "And behold thou wilt remember the poor, and consecrate *of* thy properties for their support that thou hast to impart unto them, with a covenant and a deed which cannot be broken...and they shall be laid before the bishop of my church...."

The *Book of Commandments* (Chapter 4) speaks of an "only gift," and *Doctrine and Covenants* (Section 5) changes this to "first gift."

Conclusion. Not only were there substantial changes in Mormon revelation, revealing that they were not from God, but some changes even resulted in opposite meanings. And many changes were in major doctrines. Indeed, the "Introduction" to the Book of Mormon claimed to contain "the fulness of the everlasting gospel." Yet one searches in vain to find many of the essentials of this Mormon "gospel," including deification (polytheism), the priesthood, baptism for the dead, and celestial marriage. All of these changes came in later revelations. Hence, the Book of Mormon made a false claim from the beginning, and there is no reason to accept any of its so-called "revelations" as from God, for false revelations and false predictions come from a false prophet (Deuteronomy 18:22). But no follower of Christ should be surprised, for Jesus warned that "false prophets will arise and show great signs and wonders, so as to deceive, if possible, even the elect" (Matthew 24:24).

Occult Means of Revelation

As mentioned above, all use of physical objects to get messages or revelations came under the repeated condemnation of witchcraft in the Old Testament (see Exodus 22:18; Deuteronomy 18:9-14; Leviticus 19:26,31; 20:6; Isaiah 8:19). There is no case of any author of Scripture using physical objects (such as seer stones) to divine a message from God. The Urim and Thummim was given for use only by the Aaronic priesthood (Exodus 28:30), which has been done away with by the work of Christ (Hebrews 7:12). Yet Joseph Smith was noted for the use of an occult seer stone. According to Mormon history (CHC 1:129), while digging for a well Smith found a "chocolate-colored, somewhat egg shaped stone." He believed this stone was prepared by God, through which we would receive revelations. But as we have seen, some of these revelations contained false prophecies, which are a sure indication of a false prophet (Deuteronomy 18:22).

Mormon researcher Rev. Wesley Walters discovered papers in the sheriff's office in Norwich, New York, confirming that Joseph Smith was a money digger and seer of hidden treasures.[47] LDS apologist Dr. Hugh Nibley admitted, "...if the authenticity of the court record could be established it would be the most devastating blow to Smith ever delivered."[48] Subsequently, Mormon scholars have reluctantly admitted that the records are indeed authentic. LDS historian Marvin S. Hill wrote, "There may be little doubt now, as I have indicated elsewhere, that Joseph Smith was brought to trial in 1826 on a charge, not exactly clear, associated with money digging...."[49] Indeed, Smith's mother acknowledged that Josiah Stowell sought Smith's help because he heard Smith possessed "certain keys, by which he could discern things invisible to the natural eye."[50] LDS historian B. H. Roberts acknowledged that Stowell sought Smith because he had "heard of Joseph Smith's gift of seership" (CHC 1:82). In an affidavit by Joseph Smith's father-in-law, Isaac Hale, he testified that "the manner in which he pretended to read and interpret, was the same as when he looked for the money-diggers, with the stone in his hat, over his face, while the Book of Plates were at the same time hid in the woods."[51]

Since Joseph Smith was not very successful with his seer stone when hunting for treasure, as demonstrated by the court record of his arrest, there is no reason to believe that his alleged use of it to translate the Book of Mormon was anything less than a fraud. Even Apostle Bruce McConkie noted the similarities to a crystal ball and the potential of demonic deception through such means. He wrote: "In Imitation of the true order of heaven whereby seers receive revelations from God through Urim and Thummim, the devil gives his revelations to some of his followers through peep stones or crystal balls" (MD 565-66, 1966 edition).

Summary of Differences

The following chart illustrates the unsurpassable gulf between the evangelical and Mormon views of Scriptures.

	Evangelical Scriptures	Mormon Scriptures
Origin	Divine	Human
Nature	Infallible	Not infallible
Confirmation	Supernatural	Not supernatural
Use of Occult	Forbidden	Utilized
Changes	Not substantial	Substantial
Reliability	Highly reliable	Unreliable
Prophecies	Never failed	Often failed
Completeness	Closed canon	Open canon

It is not difficult to see how wide the divide is between Mormons and evangelicals on the doctrine of Scripture. In fact they differ on every major point. There is no significant commonality at all. The only way there could ever be harmony between them is if Mormonism would officially repudiate all the alleged revelations of Joseph Smith and accept that the Bible alone is the final written revelation of God to His people. Since this is not likely, there can be no common revelatory ground on which to stand with Mormons. Since they have repudiated one of the great fundamentals of the

Christian faith, they have no legitimate claim to the name "Christian" but are appropriately labeled a cult.

Chapter Notes

1. Some evangelicals claim there are private revelations but do not believe they are normative. The view that extrabiblical revelations are normative is not evangelical.
2. See Norman L. Geisler and William E. Nix, *General Introduction to the Bible,* revised and expanded (Chicago: Moody, 1986), ch. 5.
3. Some have used Joseph's cup of divination in Genesis 44:5,15 as biblical support for the use of objects of divination, but this is misdirected for several reasons. First, there is no evidence in the text that Joseph ever used this cup for divination. It was probably only mentioned as part of his plan to enhance his brothers' awe of him. Second, if Joseph did use it, then he too is to be condemned. He would not be the first Old Testament saint to sin (cf. Abraham, David, and Solomon). The Bible often *records* events it does not *approve.* Third, nowhere does this text give divine approval of Jospeh's alleged use of this cup. Fourth, such a practice would be clearly contrary to other teaching of Scripture (cf. Deuteronomy 18).
4. Colin J. Hemer, *The Book of Acts in the Setting of Hellenistic History* (Winona Lake, IN: Eisenbrauns, 1990).
5. Sir William Ramsay, *St. Paul the Traveller and the Roman Citizen* (New York: G.P. Putnam's Sons, 1896).
6. Simon Greenleaf, *The Testimony of the Evangelists* (Grand Rapids: Baker Book House,1984; 1874 reprint).
7. Richard L. Anderson, *Fourteenth Annual Symposium of the Archaeology of Scripture* (Brigham Young University, 1963), pp. 52-59.
8. Archibald T. Robinson, *Introduction to Textual Criticism of the New Testament* (Nashville: Broadman, 1925), p. 22.
9. See Michel L. Robinson, trans., "Tractate Sanhedrin," in the *Babylonian Talmud,* VII-VIII, 24.
10. See Geisler and Nix, *Introduction,* ch. 15.
11. Ibid.
12. St. Augustine, *The City of God,* 19:36-38.
13. Roger Beckwith, *The Old Testament Canon of the New Testament Church and Its Background in Early Judaism* (Grand Rapids: Eerdmans, 1986), p. 387.
14. See Geisler and Nix, *Introduction,* p. 431.
15. Ibid., p. 295.
16. See Norman L. Geisler and Abdul Saleeb, *Answering Islam: The Crescent in the Light of the Cross* (Grand Rapids: Baker, 1993), ch. 9.
17. See Norman L. Geisler, *Miracles and the Modern Mind* (Charlotte, NC: Impact, 1997) and N.L. Geisler, *Signs and Wonders* (Charlotte, NC: Impact, 1997).
18. See Geisler and Nix, *Introduction,* pp. 181-85.
19. Keith Marston, *Missionary Pal: Reference Guide for [Mormon] Missionaries & Teachers* (Salt Lake City: Publisher's Press, 1976), p. 26.
20. Geisler and Nix, *Introduction,* ch. 22.
21. Stephen E. Robinson, *How Wide the Divide?* (Downers Grove, Il: IVP, 1997), p. 206, note 17.

22. Orson Pratt, *Orson Pratt's Works* (Liverpool, 1851), pp. 46-47.
23. John A. Widtsoe, *Joseph Smith—Seeker After Truth* (Salt Lake City: Deseret, 1951), p. 251.
24. Reed C. Durham, *A History of Joseph Smith's Revision of the Bible*, a Ph.D. dissertation (BYU, 1965), pp. 22-23.
25. Cited by Jerald and Sandra Tanner, *The Changing World of Mormonism* (Chicago: Moody), p. 386.
26. Durham, "History," pp. 64-65.
27. Richard P. Howard, *Restoration Scripture—A Study of Their Textual Development* (Independence, MO: Herald, 1969), p. 122.
28. *Gospel Principles* (Salt Lake City: Church of Jesus Christ of Latter-day Saints, 1988), pp. 49-51.
29. To admit, as does Stephen Robinson in *How Wide the Divide?* that it is a fruadulent translation but then claim that God spoke through it anyway stretches credulity to the breaking point. First, this degrades the character of God. Second, it impugns the character of Joseph Smith, who claimed he was *translating* it when he was not.
30. See Michael Marquardt, *The Book of Abraham Papyrus Found* (Salt Lake City: Modern Microfilms, 1975).
31. Tanner and Tanner, *Changing World*, p. 105.
32. David Whitmer, "An Address to All Believers in Christ," 1887, p. 27.
33. Citations in Tanner and Tanner, *Changing World*, pp.102-03
34. Ibid.
35. Marvin S. Hill, *Dialogue: A Journal of Mormon Thought*, Winter 1972, pp. 83-84.
36. Tanner and Tanner, *Changing World*, p. 107.
37. Cited by ibid., p. 110.
38. John Whitmer, *John Whitmer's History* (Salt Lake City: Modern Microfilm), ch. 6.
39. Mark Twain, *Roughing It*, p. 110.
40. See H. Michael Marquardt, *The Use of the Bible in the Book of Mormon* (Utah Lighthouse Ministry, Box 1884, Salt Lake City, UT 84110).
41. Whitmer, *History*, pp. 30-36
42. Ibid.
43. Tanner and Tanner, *Changing World*, p. 132.
44. Joseph Smith in *Times and Seasons* (Nauvoo, IL, 1839-46), 5:613-14.
45. Apostle LeGrand Richards in a letter to Morris L. Reynolds, July 14,1966.
46. *Times and Seasons*, 5:613-14.
47. Tanner and Tanner, *Changing World*, p. 72.
48. Hugh Nibley, *The Myth Makers* (Salt Lake City: Bookcraft, 1961), p. 142.
49. Marvin S. Hill in *Dialogue: A Journal of Morman Thought*, Winter 1972, pp. 77-78.
50. Cited by Lucy Smith, *Biographical Sketches of Joseph Smith the Prophet* (London, 1853), pp. 91-93. Reprinted as the *History of Joseph Smith by his Mother*, ed. Preston Nibley (Salt Lake City: Bookcraft, 1954).
51. Printed in *Susquehanna Register*, May 1, 1834.

2

God

Francis J. Beckwith

According to the founding prophet of the Church of Jesus Christ of Latter-day Saints (LDS), Joseph Smith, Jr., "It is the first principle of the gospel to know for a certainty the character of God...."[1] In this chapter we will take a critical look at this first principle.

Mormon leaders often portray their faith as merely another branch of Christianity which, unlike other branches of Christianity, preaches the entirety of Christ's Gospel. However, most people, including some Mormons, are unaware of how radically the Mormon view of God differs from the picture of God that one finds in the Bible and traditional Christian theology.

Classical Christian Concept of God

In order to compare and contrast the Mormon concept of God with the biblical/Christian concept of God, we must first fully understand why Christians believe that their concept of God better captures the data of Scripture than does the LDS view.

Known as *classical theism*,[2] this view of God has long been the orthodox theistic position of all branches of the Christian church: Roman Catholic, Protestant, and Eastern Orthodox. Because there are variations within this tradition,

New Testament quotations in this chapter are from the Jerusalem Bible except as otherwise noted. Old Testament quotations are from the New Inernational Version except as otherwise noted. See copyright page.

I will present a "bare bones" version of it, mentioning, when appropriate, differing views within the tradition.

Although there are many divine attributes we could examine, for our present purposes it is sufficient to say that the God of classical Christian theism is at least 1) personal and incorporeal (without physical parts), 2) the Creator and Sustainer of everything else that exists, 3) omnipotent (all-powerful), 4) omniscient (all-knowing), 5) omnipresent (everywhere present), 6) immutable (unchanging) and eternal, 7) necessary and the only God, and 8) triune: one God, three Persons. Because volumes have been written on these attributes, we can only hope in this essay to present a brief summary of what they mean and where they are taught in Scripture.

Personal and Incorporeal

According to Christian theism, God is a personal Being who has all the attributes that we may expect from a perfect person: self-consciousness and the ability to reason, know, love, communicate, and so forth. This is clearly how God is described in the Scriptures (e.g., Genesis 17:11; Exodus 3:14; Jeremiah 29:11).

God is also incorporeal (bodiless). Unlike humans, God is not uniquely associated with one physical entity like a body. (The question of the incarnation of God the Son is dealt with in Chapter 3). For this reason, the Bible refers to God as spirit (John 4:24)[3] and Jesus says of His resurrected body, "Behold my hands and my feet, that it is I myself; handle me and see, for *a spirit hath not flesh and bones,* as ye see me have" (Luke 24:39 KJV, emphasis added). This is why the Bible also teaches that God is not a man (Numbers 23:19), that He is invisible (Colossians 1:15; 1 Timothy 1:17; Hebrews 11:27), that not even heaven and earth can contain Him (1 Kings 8:27), and that no mere human person has ever seen or can see God (John 1:18; 1 John 4:12). In addition, if God is creator and sustainer of everything else that exists as well as being omnipotent, immutable, and omnipresent (see following), it is difficult to see how such a being could be physical.

The Creator and Sustainer of Everything Else That Exists

In classical theism, all reality is contingent on God—that is, all reality has come into existence and *continues* to exist because of Him. Unlike a god who forms the universe out of preexistent matter (*ex materia*), the God of classical theism created the universe *ex nihilo* (out of nothing).

As we shall see below, the Bible refers to God as a Being who has always existed (e.g., Genesis 21:33; Exodus 3:15; Deuteronomy 33:27; 1 Chronicles 16:36; Job 36:26; Psalm 90:1-4; 102:12,24-27; 145:13; Isaiah 40:28; Romans 1:20). The Bible also teaches that everything that is *not* God or in God's mind (e.g., numbers, ideas) has not always existed. Consider the following biblical passages:[4]

> Nor is he dependent on anything that human hands can do for him, since he can never be in need of anything; on the contrary, it is he who gives everything—including life and breath—to everyone (Acts 17:25).

> For in him were created all things in heaven and on earth: everything visible and everything invisible, Thrones, Dominations, Sovereignties, Powers—all things were created through him and for him. Before anything was created, he existed, and he holds all things in unity (Colossians 1:16,17).

> All that exists comes from him; all is by him and for him. To him be the glory for ever! Amen (Romans 11:36).

> It is by faith that we understand that the world was created by one word from God, so that no apparent cause can account for the things we can see (Hebrews 11:3).[5]

> It is the same God that said, "Let there be light shining out of darkness" (2 Corinthians 4:6).

> You are our Lord and our God, you are worthy of
> glory and honor and power, because you made all
> the universe and it was only by your will that every-
> thing was made and exists (Revelation 4:11).

A number of things can be derived from these passages:
1) God has always existed; 2) the universe, including its matter, has not always existed; 3) God is the creator, sustainer,
and *sole* cause of the universe, which means that the universe
has no *material* cause; and 4) God created light out of darkness, which implies that out of nothing something was created. Conclusion: Scripture teaches that God created the
universe *ex nihilo.* Consequently, it is on God alone that
everything in the universe depends for its existence.

Omnipotent

God is also said to be omnipotent or all-powerful. This
should be understood to mean that God can do anything
that is 1) logically possible and 2) consistent with being a
personal, incorporeal, omniscient, omnipresent, immutable,
and wholly perfect creator.

Concerning the latter, these attributes are not *limitations*
of God's power, but *perfections.* They are attributes at their
highest level, which are essential to God's nature. For example, since God is perfect, He cannot sin; because He is
personal, He is incapable of making Himself impersonal;
because He is omniscient, He cannot forget. All this is supported by the Bible when its writers assert that God cannot
sin (Mark 10:18; Hebrews 6:18), cease to exist (Exodus 3:14;
Malachi 3:6), or fail to know something (Job 28:24; Psalm
139:17,18; Isaiah 46:10). Since God is a perfect Person, it is
necessarily the case that He is incapable of acting in a less
than perfect way, which would include sinning, ceasing to
exist, and being ignorant.

But this does not count against God's omnipotence,
since, as St. Augustine points out, "Neither do we lessen
[God's] power when we say He cannot die or be deceived.
This is the kind of inability which, if removed, would make

God less powerful than He is....It is precisely because He is omnipotent that for Him some things are impossible."[6]

When the classical theist claims that God can only do what is logically possible, he or she is claiming that God cannot do or create what is logically *im*possible. Examples of logically impossible entities include "married bachelors," "square circles," and "a brother who is an only child." But these are not *really* entities; they are merely contrary terms that are strung together and *appear* to say something. Hence, the fact that God cannot do the logically impossible does not in any way discount His omnipotence.

But what about Luke 1:37, where we are told that "*nothing* is impossible with God" (NIV)? Addressing this question, St. Thomas Aquinas points out that this verse is not talking about internally contradictory or contrary "entities," since such "things" are not really things at all. They are merely words strung together that *appear* to be saying something when in fact they are saying nothing.[7] Hence, *everything* is possible for God, but the logically impossible is *not* truly a *thing*.

Omniscient

God is all-knowing, and His all-knowingness encompasses the *past, present,* and *future.* Concerning God's unfathomable knowledge, the psalmist writes: "How precious to me are your thoughts, O God! How vast is the sum of them! Were I to count them, they would outnumber the grains of sand. When I awake, I am still with you" (Psalm 139:17,18). Elsewhere he writes, "Great is our Lord and mighty in power; his understanding has no limit" (147:5). The author of Job writes of God: "For he views the ends of the earth and sees everything under the heavens" (Job 28:24). Scripture also teaches that God has total knowledge of the past (Isaiah 41:22). Concerning the future, God says: "I make known the end from the beginning, from ancient times, what is still to come. I say: 'My purpose will stand, and I will do all that I please'" (Isaiah 46:10). Elsewhere Isaiah quotes God as saying that *knowledge* (not opinion or highly probable guesses) of the future is essential for deity, something that distinguished God from the many false gods of Isaiah's day:

> "Present your case," says the LORD. "Set forth your
> arguments," says Jacob's king. "Bring in your idols
> to tell us what is going to happen. Tell us what the
> former things were, so that we may consider them
> and know their final outcome. Or declare to us the
> things to come, tell us what the future holds, so we
> may know that you are gods. Do something,
> whether good or bad, so that we will be dismayed
> and filled with fear. But you are less than nothing
> and your works are utterly worthless" (41:21-24).

God's knowledge of the future is also asserted in the
New Testament teaching that God foreknows who will be
saved (see Romans 8:29; 1 Peter 1:1,2). Although there are
numerous other passages that imply and affirm God's
knowledge of the future,[8] it is interesting to note that one
can infer God's absolute knowledge of the future from His
test of a true prophet in Deuteronomy 18:22:

> If what a prophet proclaims in the name of the
> LORD does not take place or come true, that is a
> message the LORD has not spoken. That prophet
> has spoken presumptuously. Do not be afraid of
> him.

If, of course, God does not know the future and prophecy involves an extrapolation from current knowledge to a
highly probable future event, as some philosophers and theologians have claimed (e.g., Clark Pinnock writes that some
prophecies are "predictions based on God's exhaustive
knowledge of the past and present."),[9] it is within the realm
of possibility that God could make a mistake. But if it is both
true that He can make a mistake and that Deuteronomy
18:22 is normative for prophet status, then it is possible that
Yahweh can speak a prophecy which does not come to pass
and at the same time we would be perfectly correct in saying
that Yahweh had not spoken, although our judgment would
be false. In other words, in some possible world God does

not speak for God. Hence, only if God has absolute knowledge of the future does Deuteronomy 18:22 make sense.[10]

Omnipresent

It is the Bible's explicit teaching that God is omnipresent:

> Acknowledge and take to heart this day that the LORD is God in heaven above and on the earth below. There is no other (Deuteronomy 4:39).

> But will God really dwell on earth? The heavens, even the highest heaven, cannot contain you [God]. How much less this temple I have built! (1 Kings 8:27).[11]

> The temple I am going to build will be great, because our God is greater than all other gods. But who is able to build a temple for him, since the heavens, even the highest heavens, cannot contain him? (2 Chronicles 2:5,6).

> Since the God who made the world and everything in it is himself Lord of heaven and earth, he does not make his home in shrines made by human hands. Nor is he dependent on anything that human hands can do for him, since he can never be in need of anything; on the contrary, it is he who gives everything—including life and breath—to everyone. From one single stock he not only created the whole human race so that they could occupy the entire earth, but he decreed how long each nation should flourish and what the boundaries of its territory should be. And he did this so that all nations might seek the deity and, by feeling their way toward him, succeed in finding him. Yet in fact *he is not far from any of us, since it is in him that we live, and move, and exist,* as indeed some of your own writers have said (Acts 17:24-28, emphasis added).

Since God is not a physical being who takes up space, it would be wrong to think of Him as a sort of gas that fills up the universe. In that sense, He is *not* every*where*, since God is not a thing, like water or air, that can take up space. Rather, God is everywhere insofar as He is not limited by a spatiotemporal body, knows everything immediately without benefit of sensory organs, and sustains everything that exists. In others words, God's omnipresence logically follows from His omniscience, incorporeality, omnipotence, and role as creator and sustainer of the universe. Although neither identical to His creation (as in pantheism) nor limited by it (as in Mormon theism), God is immanent—spiritually and personally present at every point of the universe.[12]

Immutable and Eternal

When a Christian says that God is immutable and eternal, he is saying that God is *unchanging* and has *always existed* as God throughout all eternity. There never was a time when God was not God. The author of Malachi (3:6) quotes God as saying, "I the LORD do not change...." According to theologian Alan Gomes, "Biblically, the word 'counsel' refers to one's intention, resolution, will, or purpose. God's counsels are not subject to change, fluctuation, or failure."[13] And for this reason the Scriptures teach that God's purposes are unalterable (Hebrews 6:17). God says in Isaiah 46:10b: "My purpose will stand, and I will do all that I please." Moreover, the Scriptures tell us that there was never a time where God was not God. God is an eternal being:

> Before the mountains were born or you brought forth the earth and the world, from everlasting to everlasting you are God (Psalm 90:2).

> The LORD is the everlasting God, the Creator of the ends of the earth. He will not grow tired or weary, and his understanding no one can fathom (Isaiah 40:28).

This is what the high and lofty One says—he who lives forever, whose name is holy (Isaiah 57:15a).

Ever since God created the world his everlasting power and deity—however invisible—have been there for the mind to see in the things he has made (Romans 1:20).

To the eternal King, the undying, invisible and only God, be honor and glory for ever and ever. Amen (1 Timothy 1:17).

Although God certainly seems to change in response to how His creatures behave—such as in the case of the repenting Ninevites (see the book of Jonah)—His nature remains the same. No matter how the Ninevites would have responded to Jonah's preaching, God's unchanging righteousness would have remained the same: He is merciful to the repentant and punishes the unrepentant (see Jeremiah 18:7-10). Hence, a God who is responsive to His creatures is certainly consistent with, and seems to be entailed by, an unchanging nature that is necessarily *personal.*

The Bible teaches that God is *eternally* God. However Christian theologians and philosophers dispute whether He exists *in* time (the temporal eternity view) or *out of time* (the timeless eternity view).[14] The important point, however, is that the Bible teaches that God never changes and that He has always existed as God.

Necessary and the Only God

Since the God of the Bible possesses *all* power, there cannot be any other God, for this would mean that two beings possess all power. That, of course, is a logical absurdity, since if a being possesses all of everything (in this case, power) there is, by definition, nothing left for anyone else.[15]

Although the Bible teaches that humans at times worship some beings *as if* these beings were really gods (1 Corinthians 8:4-6), there is only one true and living God by nature:

> "You are my witnesses," declares the LORD…. "Before
> me no god was formed, nor will there be one after
> me" (Isaiah 43:10).

> This is what the LORD says—Israel's King and
> Redeemer, the LORD Almighty: I am the first and I
> am the last; apart from me there is no god. Who
> then is like me? Let him proclaim it. Let him declare
> and lay out before me what has happened since I
> established my ancient people, and what is yet to
> come…. Is there any God besides me? No, there is
> no other Rock; I know not one (Isaiah 44:6-8).

> For there is only one God, and there is only one
> mediator between God and mankind, himself a
> man, Christ Jesus (1 Timothy 2:5).[16]

Since everything that exists depends on God, and God is
unchanging and eternal, it follows that God cannot *not* exist.
In other words, He is a *necessary* being, whereas everything
else is contingent. Although there is no doubt that the Bible
teaches that God is a necessary being, Christian philosophers and theologians do not all agree on the precise meaning of God's necessity.[17]

Triune: One God, Three Persons

The doctrine of the trinity can be defined in the following way: In the nature of the one God there are three
centers of consciousness, which we call Persons, and these
three are equal. Each human person is one *who* and one
what; that is, there is one person per being. God is three
Whos and one *What*; that is, there are three Persons who are
one Being. Although the term "trinity" is not found in the
Bible, the doctrine is nevertheless taught there. (The word
"Bible" is not found in the Bible either). "Trinity" is merely
the term employed by theologians and church historians in
order to describe the phenomena of God they find in the
Bible.

The doctrine of the trinity is arrived at in much the same way as a scientific theory. A scientific theory, for the most part, is a reasoned explanation of observed (or unobserved, in some cases) phenomena in the natural world. Analogously, the doctrine of the trinity is a reasoned explanation of what we observe to be the phenomena of God in the Bible. Just like saying "H_2O is water" is not *adding* to water, saying "the God of the Bible is a trinity" is not *adding* to what the Scripture teaches about God. This is why it is odd that Brigham Young University professor Stephen E. Robinson in *How Wide the Divide?* criticizes some church creeds, which are belief-statements of what the Bible teaches, as being additions to the Bible:

> As for [the Nicene creed] being a "summary" of the biblical view, my English professors made it quite clear that a summary may not introduce arguments or assertions not already found in the material being summarized. Show me...*Trinity* in the New Testament and I have a problem, but there is no biblical passage or combination of passages that asserts what the Nicene Creed asserts. It is *not* a summary; it is an extrapolation.[18]

It is unclear what Robinson means. If he is saying that there is no passage or combination of passages in which the word "trinity" appears, then he is correct. But since no one has ever claimed that the word "trinity" appears in the Bible, Robinson attacks a straw man. On the other hand, if he is saying that there is no passage or combination of passages by which one may properly *infer* by the use of a sound argument the doctrine of the trinity, then Robinson has an obligation to show us why the numerous scholars in church history who have argued for the trinity are mistaken. He provides no such argument, but merely claims "that there is no biblical passage or combination of passages that asserts what the Nicene Creed asserts." Thus Robinson begs the question.

Suppose a friend of Robinson, in conversation with the professor, made two claims: 1) All bachelors are men without wives; and 2) Mr. Jones is a bachelor. If Robinson were to infer from both these claims that "Mr. Jones is without a wife," he would be inferring a correct conclusion. Would he be adding any new information to the two claims? Yes and no. No, in the sense that he would be only inferring from the claims the truth that is already present in the claims. He would not be creating a "new" truth. But yes, in the sense that he would be acquiring new knowledge he did not have before he drew the inference. In other words, Robinson would be more knowledgeable but there would be no new truth. That is to say, *nothing* is really being added to the two claims.

The doctrine of the trinity is arrived at in much the same way. It is an inference from truths already found in the Bible. The argument behind the doctrine can be put this way:

> Reason 1: "The Bible teaches that there is only one God."
>
> Reason 2: "The Bible teaches that there are three distinct Persons called God, known as the Father, Son, and Holy Spirit."
>
> Conclusion: "The three Persons—Father, Son, and Holy Spirit—are the one God."

Let us take a look at how each reason is biblically justified.

Premise 1: There is only one God.

With the exception of the Mormon Church, this premise is almost universally accepted by those who claim to be Christians. Since we have already seen above that the Bible teaches that there exists only one God, there is no reason to go over the point again.

Premise 2: There are three Persons called God.

The Father is called God. That there is a Person named the Father, who is called God, is acknowledged by a host of biblical passages, such as 1 Corinthians 1:3, which reads:

"May God our Father and the Lord Jesus Christ send you grace and peace." (See also Romans 1:7; 1 Peter 1:17.) Because I have found no Mormon who disputes this point, the above citation should suffice.

The Son is called God. The Bible also asserts that Jesus of Nazareth is God. As the preincarnate Word (John 1:1-14), He is known in classical Christian theology as God the Son. In John 8:56-58 Jesus calls Himself "I Am," equating Himself with Jehovah God (or Yahweh) of the Old Testament (Exodus 3:14). Christ's participation in the creation of the cosmos necessitates that He is God (John 1:3; Colossians 1:16; cf. Isaiah 44:24). These three passages, when carefully compared with one another, clearly affirm the deity of Christ. The last passage, Isaiah 44:24, states that God *alone* made all things. The first and second passages both affirm that all things were made through Christ. Therefore, if God *alone* made all things, and all things were made through Christ, it logically follows that Christ is in fact God. The text of Scripture and the force of logic leave us with no other option.

The apostle John calls both God and Jesus *the First and the Last* and *the Alpha and the Omega* (Revelation 1:17; 22:13), and hence equates Jesus with God. Other passages of the New Testament which implicitly or explicitly affirm Christ's deity include Mark 2:5-7; John 20:28,29; John 1:1-14; and Colossians 2:9. In Chapter 3 Dr. Ron Rhodes deals with the deity of Christ in much greater detail. He replies to those who deny Christ's deity and who do so by citing biblical passages that apparently conflict with the concept.

The Holy Spirit is called God. The deity of the Holy Spirit has been questioned by many religious groups that claim to be Christian. For example, the Jehovah's Witnesses (JW) state that the term "Holy Spirit" merely refers to the "invisible active force of the Almighty God that moves his servants to do his will."[19] In other words, the Holy Spirit is not only not deity, but he is also *not a person*; it is an impersonal force that God actively employs. For the JWs, the "Holy Spirit" is to God what a phaser is to Star Trek's Captain Kirk: an impersonal "it" directed by a personal being.

Therefore, it is necessary that we first show that the Bible teaches the personhood of the Holy Spirit. A sufficient condition for being a personal being is that he or she be a "rational, self-conscious" being.[20] A being is a self-conscious agent if he or she is able to engage in knowing, thinking, and communicating. The following passages clearly show that in Scripture the Holy Spirit is considered a person:

> And when he [the Holy Spirit] comes, he [the personal pronoun] will show the world how wrong it was about sin, and about who was in the right, and about judgment [communication]....But when the Spirit of truth comes he will lead you to the complete truth, since he will not be speaking as from himself but will say only what he has learned [knowing and thinking]; and he will tell you of the things to come [communicating] (John 16:8,13).

> One day while they were offering worship to the Lord and keeping a fast, the Holy Spirit said [communicating], "I [first personal pronoun] want Barnabas and Saul set apart for the work to which I have called them" (Acts 13:2).

In both these passages the Holy Spirit is described as engaging in self-conscious personal acts: He communicates, thinks, knows, and is described in personal pronouns (i.e., "he" and "I"). Furthermore, there are several other passages that portray the Holy Spirit as exhibiting attributes of personhood. For example, the Holy Spirit is described as consoling (Acts 9:31), helping us in our weakness (Romans 8:26), forbidding (Acts 16:6,7), and able to be lied to (Acts 5:3). Moreover, the Holy Spirit can be grieved (Ephesians 4:30) and insulted (Hebrews 10:29), and is said to possess a will (1 Corinthians 12:11).

The Bible also plainly teaches the *deity* of the Holy Spirit by attributing to Him characteristics that are possessed only by God. For example, the Spirit is described as e*ternal,* having no beginning and no end (Hebrews 9:14). Moreover, He is described as *omniscient* (1 Corinthians 2:10,11), *sovereign* (1 Corinthians 12:6,11), and *possessing the wrath of God* (Hebrews 3:7-12). In addition, Jesus tells us that to sin against the Holy Spirit is to commit an *eternal* sin (Matthew 12:31,32). In Acts 5:3,4 the Holy Spirit is clearly called God:

> "Ananias," Peter said, "how can Satan have so possessed you *that you should lie to the Holy Spirit* and keep back part of the money from the land? While you still owned the land, wasn't it yours to keep, and after you had sold it wasn't the money yours to do with it as you liked? What put this scheme into your mind? *It is not to men that you have lied, but to God*" (emphasis added).

Peter is equating a lie to the Holy Spirit with lying to God. In other words, to lie to the Holy Spirit is to lie to God. And since one cannot lie to a force or to an impersonal object, this passage teaches the personality of the Holy Spirit as well as His deity.

Conclusion: The three Persons—Father, Son, and Holy Spirit—are the one God.

Let us review our argument for the trinity. First, we showed that the Bible teaches that there is only one God. Second, we found that the Bible tells us that there are three Persons who are called God. Hence the inescapable conclusion: the three Persons are the one God. Theologians have called this the trinity.

To further buttress this argument, there are several places in the Bible in which the doctrine of the trinity is clearly implied. For example, concerning *Christ's resurrection,* we are told that the Father raised Jesus from the dead (1 Thessalonians 1:10), the Son raised Himself from the dead (John 2:19-22), and the Spirit raised Jesus from the dead (Romans 8:11). Yet we are told in Acts 17:30,31 that *God raised Jesus from the dead.* Therefore, either the Bible contradicts itself or the three Persons are the one God.

In *Christ's Great Commission* to preach the Gospel, He instructs His disciples to "go, therefore, and make disciples of all the nations; baptize them in the name of the Father and of the Son and of the Holy Spirit" (Matthew 28:19). It is important to note that the Greek word for "name" used in this verse is singular (*onoma*). It does *not* say "in the *names* of the Father and of the Son and of the Holy Spirit" but "in the *name*...." Also, there are definite articles ("the") before Father, Son, and Holy Spirit, emphasizing *distinct* Persons. In other words, the Father, Son, and Holy Spirit, three distinct *Persons,* have only one name. This clearly implies the triune nature of God. Furthermore, the trinity is implied in Christ's *incarnation* (Luke 1:35) and *baptism* (Matthew 3:16,17), in the *apostolic benediction* (2 Corinthians 13:14), and in *Christ's own teachings* (John 14:26; 15:26).

It should also be added that all the creeds of the great councils in Christian church history (whether Catholic, Protestant, or Eastern Orthodox) which deal with the doctrine of God, *after considering the same biblical data,* imply or affirm the triune nature of God.[21]

The Mormon Concept of God

Although the Mormon Church claims biblical influence on its theology, the Mormon doctrine of God is derived primarily from three groups of sources.[22] 1) The first group consists of works regarded by the Mormon Church as inspired scripture: The Book of Mormon (BM), the *Doctrine and Covenants* (DC), and *The Pearl of Great Price* (PGP). 2) The Mormon concept of God is also derived from Joseph Smith, Jr.'s other statements and doctrinal commentaries, such as the seven-volume *History of the Church of Jesus Christ of Latter-day Saints* (CHC). Although not regarded by the LDS church as scripture per se, Smith's extracanonical pronouncements on doctrine are accepted by the Mormon laity and leadership as authoritative for Mormon theology. 3) Authoritative presentations of the Mormon doctrine of God can also be found in the statements and writings of the church's ecclesiastical leaders, especially its presidents, who are considered divinely inspired prophets. Concerning these latter two groups of sources, the late Mormon Apostle Bruce McConkie writes, "When the living oracles speak in the name of the Lord or as moved upon by the Holy Spirit, however, their utterances are then binding upon all who hear, and whatever is said will without any exception be found to be in harmony with the standard works."[23] This is a very important point, since some Mormons will dismiss the extracanonical works as not scriptural. For example, Stephen Robinson plays down statements made by Lorenzo Snow and Joseph Smith, Jr. that affirm the Mormon view that God is a finite being who was once *merely* a man who eventually became God:

> To the scriptural passages above I would add Lorenzo Snow's epigram and Joseph Smith's statement in the funeral address for King Follett that God is an exalted man. Neither statement is scriptural or canonized in the technical sense, and neither has been explained or elucidated to the church in any official manner, but they are so widely accepted by Latter-day Saints that this technical point has become moot. Each of these quasi-official statements asserts flatly there was once a time before the beginning of creation when God was human, just as there will be a time after the final resurrection and judgment when exalted humans will be gods.[24]

Robinson's qualifications of Smith's and Snow's statements (both of which will be cited below) are not consistent with the Church's official pronouncements. For example, Henry D. Taylor, in the Mormon publication *The Ensign Magazine*, writes: "As Latter-day Saints we accept the following scriptures as the standard works of the Church: the Bible

(consisting of the Old Testament and the New Testament),
the Book of Mormon, the Doctrine and Covenants, the
Pearl of Great Price, and official statements made by our
leaders."[25] The book *Gospel Principles*, an official publication
of the LDS church, states: "In addition to these four books
of scripture, the inspired words of our living prophets
become scripture to us. Their words come to us through
conferences, Church publications, and instructions to local
priesthood leaders." [26]

Although Robinson downplays extrascriptural revelation
in one place, in another place he seems to be saying it is *more
important* than Scripture: the LDS "church's guarantee of doctrinal correctness lies primarily in the living prophet, and
only secondarily in the preservation of the written text."[27]

Additionally, I will consider the insights of contemporary
LDS scholars who have attempted to present Mormonism's
doctrine of God as philosophically coherent.[28]

Because there are so many doctrinal sources, it may
appear (with some justification) that it is difficult to determine precisely what the Mormons believe about God. For
example, the Book of Mormon (first published in 1830)
seems to teach a strongly Judaic monotheism with modalistic overtones (see Alma 11:26-31,38; Moroni 8:18; Mosiah
3:5-8; 7:27; 15:1-5), while the equally authoritative *Pearl of
Great Price* (first published in 1851) clearly teaches that more
than one God exists (see Abraham 4,5) and that these gods
are finite. This finite view of God culminated in the theology
of Joseph Smith's successor, Brigham Young, in sermons
that were considered authoritative at the time[29] but are now
disputed by Mormon authorities.[30] Young taught the doctrine that Adam, the first man, is the God of this world:

> Now, hear it, O inhabitants of the earth, Jew and
> Gentile, Saint and sinner! When our father Adam
> came into the garden of Eden, he came into it with
> a *celestial body*, and brought Eve, *one of his wives*,
> with him. He helped to make and organize this
> world. He is MICHAEL, *the Archangel*, the ANCIENT OF

DAYS! about whom holy men have written and spoken—HE *is our* FATHER *and our* GOD *and the only God
with whom* WE *have to do.* Every man upon the earth,
professing Christians or non-professing, must hear
it, and *will know it sooner or later.*[31]

Even though the Adam-God doctrine is rejected by
Mormon authorities today, it is clear that the Mormon doctrine of God, as a number of Mormon scholars have argued,
evolved from a traditional monotheism to a uniquely American polytheism.[32] This is why Mormon scholar Boyd
Kirkland writes that "Mormons who are aware of the various
teachings of the LDS scriptures and prophets over the years
are faced with a number of doctrinal possibilities." For
example, "they can choose to accept Book of Mormon theology, but this varies from biblical theology as well as from
Joseph Smith's later plurality-of-gods theology....While most
Mormons are unaware of the diversity that abounds in the
history of Mormon doctrine, many Latter-day Saints...have,
despite the risk of heresy, continued to believe or promote
publicly many of the alternative Godhead theologies from
Mormonism's past."[33]

Nevertheless, our chief concern will not be the historical
development of Mormon theism, but rather the dominant
concept of God *currently* held by the LDS Church. Although
there is certainly disagreement among Mormon scholars
concerning some precise points of doctrine, I believe it is
safe to say, based on documents the Church presently con-
siders authoritative, that current LDS doctrine teaches that
God is, in effect, 1) a contingent being, who was at one time
not God; 2) finite in *knowledge* (not truly omniscient), *power*
(not omnipotent), and *being* (not omnipresent or
immutable); 3) one of many gods; 4) a corporeal (bodily)
being, who physically dwells at a particular spatiotemporal
location and is therefore not omnipresent (as is the classical
God); 5) a being who is subject to the laws and principles of
a beginningless universe with an infinite number of entities

in it; and 6) not a trinity, but rather, there exists three separate Gods who are one in purpose but not in being.

The contemporary Mormon concept of God can best be grasped by understanding the overall Mormon worldview and how the Deity fits into it. Mormonism teaches that God the Father is a resurrected, "exalted" human being named Elohim who was at one time *not* God.[34] He was once a mortal man on another planet who, through obedience to the precepts of *his* God, eventually attained exaltation, or godhood, himself through "eternal progression." The Mormon God, located in time and space, has a body of flesh and bone and thus is neither spirit nor omnipresent as understood in their traditional meanings. Joseph Smith, Jr. asserts:

> God himself was once as we are now, and is an exalted man, and sits enthroned in yonder heavens!...I am going to tell you how God came to be God. We have imagined and supposed that God was God from all eternity. I will refute this idea, and take away the veil, so that you may see....It is the first principle of the gospel to know for a certainty the character of God, and to know that we may converse with him as one man converses with another, and that He was once a man like us; yea, that God himself, the Father of us all, dwelt on an earth, the same as Jesus Christ himself did; and I will show it from the Bible....
>
> Here, then, is eternal life—to know the only wise and true God; and you have got to learn how to be gods yourselves, and be kings and priests to God, the same as all gods have done before you, namely, by going from one small degree to another, and from a small capacity to a great one; from grace to grace, from exaltation to exaltation, until you attain to the resurrection of the dead, and are able to dwell in everlasting burnings, and sit in glory, as do those who sit enthroned in everlasting power.[35]

The Father has a body of flesh and bone as tangible as man's....[36]

The late Mormon President Lorenzo Snow explained: "As man is, God once was; as God now is, man may become."[37] Tenth President of the LDS Church, Joseph Fielding Smith, writes:

> Some people are troubled over the statements of the prophet Joseph Smith....The matter that seems such a mystery is the statement that *our Father in heaven at one time passed through a life and death and is an exalted man.* This is one of the mysteries....The Prophet taught that *our Father had a Father and so on.* Is not this a reasonable thought, especially when we remember that the promises are made to us that we may become like him?[38]

A member of the LDS First Council of the Seventy, Milton R. Hunter, writes:

> Mormon prophets have continuously taught the sublime truth that *God the Eternal Father was once a mortal man* who passed through a school of earth life similar to that through which we are now passing. *He became God*—an exalted being—through obedience to the same eternal Gospel principles that we are given opportunity to obey today.[39]

Omniscience, according to Mormon theology, is one of the attributes that one attains when reaching godhood. Mormons appear to be divided, however, on the meaning of omniscience. It seems that some Mormons believe omniscience to mean that God knows all true propositions about the past, present, and future. This view is consistent with the classical Christian view: God is all-knowing, and His all-knowingness encompasses the *past, present,* and *future.*[40]

On the other hand, the *dominant* Mormon tradition teaches that God does not know the future. This tradition affirms that only the *present* and the *past* can be known by God, since the former is occurring and the latter has already occurred. Consequently, since the future is not yet a "thing" and has not become *actual* (and hence cannot possibly be known), God *cannot* know the future. Therefore the Mormon God is *omniscient* in the sense that he knows everything that can possibly be known, but he nevertheless increases in knowledge as the future unfolds and becomes the present.[41] As the late Mormon President and prophet Wilford Woodruff once said: "God himself is increasing in knowledge, power, and dominion, and will do so worlds without end."[42] This is why Brigham Young and his counselors (both in 1860 and 1865) condemned *as false doctrine* Orson Pratt's claim that "God cannot know new truths."[43]

Once Elohim attained godhood, he then created this present world by "organizing" both eternally preexistent, inorganic matter and the preexistent primal intelligences from which human spirits are made (PGP, Abraham 3:22). Mormon scholar Hyrum L. Andrus explains:

> Though man's spirit is organized from a pure and fine substance which possesses certain properties of life, Joseph Smith seems to have taught that within each individual spirit there is a central primal intelligence (a central directing principle of life), and that man's central primal intelligence is a personal entity possessing some degree of life and certain rudimentary cognitive powers before the time the human spirit was organized.[44]

For this reason, Joseph Smith wrote that "man was also in the beginning with God. Intelligence, or the light of truth, was not created or made, neither indeed can be."[45] In other words, *man's basic essence or primal intelligence is as eternal as God's.*

The Mormon God, by organizing this world out of preexistent matter, has granted these organized spirits the opportunity to receive physical bodies, pass through mortality, and eventually progress to godhood, just as this opportunity was given him by his Father God. Consequently, if human persons on earth faithfully obey the precepts of Mormonism, they too can attain godhood like Elohim before them. And the purpose of attaining godhood is so that "we would become heavenly parents and have spirit children just as [Elohim] does."[46]

Based on the statements of Mormon authorities, some LDS scholars contend that a premortal spirit is "organized" by God the Father through "spirit birth." In this process, human spirits are somehow organized through literal sexual relations between Elohim and his wife, whereby they are conceived and born as spirit children *prior* to entering the mortal realm (although all human persons prior to spirit birth existed as intelligences in some primal state of cognitive personal existence).[47] Since God the Father of Mormonism was himself organized (or spirit-birthed) by his God, who himself is a "creation" of yet another God, and so on ad infinitum, Mormonism therefore teaches that the God over this world is a contingent being in an infinite lineage of gods.[48] Thus Mormonism is a polytheistic religion. This is why Joseph Smith asserts that he will "preach the plurality of Gods....I wish to declare I have always and in all congregations when I have preached on the subject of the Deity, it has been the plurality of Gods."[49]

Comparing the Mormon concept with the classical Christian concept of God, Mormon philosopher and BYU faculty member Blake Ostler writes that in contrast to the self-sufficient God who creates the universe

> *ex nihilo* (out of nothing), the Mormon God did not bring into being the ultimate constituents of the cosmos—neither its fundamental matter nor the space/time matrix which defines it. Hence, unlike the Necessary Being of classical theology who alone could not *not* exist and on which all else is contingent for existence, the personal God of Mormonism confronts uncreated realities which

exist of metaphysical necessity. Such realities include inherently self-directing selves (intelligences), primordial elements (mass/energy), the natural laws which structure reality, and moral principles grounded in the intrinsic value of selves and the requirements for growth and happiness.[50]

Concurring, Mormon elder B.H. Roberts, a member of the First Council of Seventy, writes:

... not even God may place himself beyond the boundary of space: nor on the outside of duration. Nor is it conceivable to human thought he can create space, or annihilate matter. These are things that limit even God's omnipotence. What then, is meant by the ascription of the attribute of Omnipotence to God? Simply that all that may or can be done by power conditioned by other eternal existences—duration, space, matter, truth, justice—God can do. But even he may not act out of harmony with the other eternal existences which condition or limit him.[51]

Mormonism therefore teaches that certain basic realities have *always* existed and are indestructible even by God. For Mormonism, God, like each human being, is merely another creature in the universe. In the Mormon universe, God is not responsible for creating or sustaining matter, energy, natural laws, personhood, moral principles, the process of salvation (or exaltation), or much of anything. Instead of the universe being subject to Him (which is the biblical view), the Mormon God is subject to the universe.

Unlike the God of Christian theism, who is omnipresent in being, the God of Mormonism is only omnipresent insofar as he is aware of everything in the universe. Since the Mormon God has a physical body, and hence is limited by time and space, his being cannot be present everywhere. As Roberts has pointed out, when a Mormon says that God is omnipresent he is asserting that God's influence, power, and knowledge are all-pervasive, but that the focal point of God's being (his body) exists at a particular place in time and space.[52] Because Mormon theology does not teach that the universe is contingent upon God to either bring it into being or to sustain its existence, there is no need for Mormon theology to hold to the classical Christian view of omnipresence.

Mormon theology denies the doctrine of the trinity. Joseph Smith, Jr. asserts: "Many men say there is one God; the Father, the Son, and the Ghost are only one God! I say that is a strange God anyhow—three in one, and one in three!...He would be a wonderfully big God—he would be a giant or a monster."[53] Mormon theology affirms *tritheism*, the belief that there exist three gods with which this world should be concerned (though Mormon theology teaches that there exist many other gods as well): Elohim (the Father), Jehovah (the Son), and the Holy Ghost.

Writes Smith: "The Father has a body of flesh and bone as tangible as man's; the Son also; but the Holy Ghost has not a body of flesh and bones, but is a personage of spirit. Were it not so, the Holy Spirit could not dwell in us."[54] The Father, Son, and Holy Ghost are "three separate individuals, physically distinct from each other," forming "the great presiding council of the universe."[55] And even the Holy Ghost is not *really* a spirit, since, according to Smith, there is no such thing as a nonphysical reality: "There is no such thing as immaterial matter. All spirit is matter, but is more fine or pure, and can only be discerned by purer eyes."[56] Mormon writings, including the LDS scriptures, are unclear about the Holy Ghost. This is why Mormon scholar Vern G. Swanson concludes his essay on this subject by saying: "In the end, there are few details from which to construct an adequate theology of God the Third....But I suspect that we will be left at some point with Brigham Young's promise that 'when we go through the veil we shall know much more about these matters than we now do.'"[57]

Although the Mormon view of Jesus is dealt with in Chapter 3, it is worth mentioning here that the preincarnate Jesus, Jehovah (or Yahweh), *does not* have a body of flesh and bone in Mormon theology. McConkie writes that "Christ is *Jehovah*; they are one and the same Person."[58] According to one LDS book, Jehovah "was the birthright son, and he retained his birthright by his strict obedience. Through the aeons and ages of premortality, he advanced and progressed until, as Abraham described it, he stood as one 'like unto God' [Abraham 3:24]. 'Our Savior was a God before he was born into this world.'"[59]

In *How Wide the Divide?* Stephen Robinson claims that "Evangelicals often accuse Latter-day Saints of believing in a limited, finite or changeable God, but there is absolutely nothing in LDS Scriptures or LDS beliefs to justify such a charge. I have never heard any such propositions stated in my church—*never!*"[60] In light of what has been covered, it is difficult to understand how a man of Professor Robinson's acumen can make such a claim. It should be noted that one of the people who endorsed *How Wide the Divide?*, David Paulsen (Richard L. Evans Chair of Religious Understanding, BYU), a colleague of Professor Robinson's, wrote a Ph.D. dissertation (University of Michigan, 1975) in which he presents the LDS view of God as a form of finite theism by citing numerous LDS authorities and then proceeds to give a philosophically sophisticated defense of Mormon finite theism. The title of the dissertation: *The Comparative Coherency of Mormon (Finitistic) and Classical Theism.* Professor Robinson would do well to consult Paulsen's well-documented and philosophically thought-provoking dissertation.

Philosophical Problems with the Mormon Concept of God

In addition to the obvious biblical problems with the Mormon concept of God, there are philosophical ones as well. In our two books, Professor Stephen E. Parrish and I deal with a number of philosophical problems with the

Mormon concept of God. In this chapter I will present two of these. Because of space constraints, however, I cannot reply to all the possible Mormon responses to these problems. For this reason, I refer the reader to the detailed replies in my two books.[61]

The Problem of an Infinite Number of Past Events

It is evident from what we have covered that Mormonism teaches that the past series of events in time is *infinite* or *beginningless.* Joseph Fielding Smith writes that Joseph Smith "taught that *our Father had a Father and so on.*"[62] Heber C. Kimball, who served as First Counselor in the Church's First Presidency, asserts that "we shall go back to our Father and God, who is connected with *one who is still farther back*; and this Father is connected with *one still further back, and so on....*"[63] Apostle and leading doctrinal spokesman Bruce R. McConkie writes that "the elements from which the creation took place are eternal and therefore had no beginning."[64]

There are several philosophical and scientific problems in asserting that the series of events in the past is beginningless. William Lane Craig has developed four arguments, two philosophical and two scientific, along these lines.[65] In this chapter I will apply Craig's second philosophical argument to the Mormon concept of God:

> Reason 1: "If the Mormon universe is true, then an infinite number of past events has been traversed."
> Reason 2: "It is impossible to traverse an infinite number."
> Conclusion: "Therefore the Mormon universe is not true."

Reason 1 is certainly true. We have seen already that the Mormons fully acknowledge that the past is infinite. And if it is infinite, then certainly an infinite number of events has been traversed to reach today. But can an infinite number actually be traversed, as reason 2 denies? It is clear that it cannot. Consider the following example.

Imagine that I plan to drive on Interstate 15 from my home in Anaheim Hills to the Mormon temple in Salt Lake City. The distance is about 700 miles. All things being equal, I would eventually arrive in Salt Lake City. But suppose the distance was not 700 miles but an *infinite* number of miles. The fact is that I would never arrive in Salt Lake City, since it is by definition impossible to complete an infinite count. An "infinite" is, by definition, *limitless*. Hence, a *traversed* distance by definition cannot be infinite. Consequently, if I *did* eventually arrive in Salt Lake City, this would only prove that the distance I traveled was not infinite after all. That is to say, since I could always travel one more mile past my arrival point, arriving at *any* point proves that the distance I traveled was not infinite.

Now let us apply this same logic to the Mormon universe. If the universe had no beginning, then every event has been preceded by an infinite number of events. But if one can never traverse an infinite number, one could never have arrived at the present day, since to do so would have involved traversing an infinite number of days. In order to better understand this, J. P. Moreland provides this example:

> Suppose a person were to think backward through the events in the past. In reality, time and the events within it move in the other direction. But mentally he can reverse that movement and count backward farther and farther into the past. Now he will either come to a beginning or he will not. If he comes to a beginning, then the universe obviously had a beginning. But if he never could, even in principle, reach a first moment, then this means that it would be impossible to start with the present and run backward through all of the events in the history of the cosmos. Remember, if he did run through all of them, he would reach a first member of the series, and the finiteness of the past would be established. In order to avoid this conclusion, one must hold that, starting from the present, it is *impossible* to go backward through all of the events in history.

But since events really move in the other direction,
this is equivalent to admitting that if there was no
beginning, the past could have never been exhaus-
tively traversed to reach the present moment.[66]

It is clear, then, that reasons 1 and 2 are true. Given the
fact that the argument is valid (it is in the valid form, *modus
tolens*), the conclusion therefore follows: *The Mormon universe is not true.* And if the Mormon universe is not true, then
the Mormon God does not exist, since his existence is completely
dependent on the existence of the Mormon universe.

The Problem of Eternal Progression with an Infinite Past

In this second objection, unlike the first, I am arguing
that even if we assume that the past series of events in time is
infinite (or beginningless), it is impossible for the Mormon
doctrine of eternal progression to be true. Although Professor Parrish and I present three arguments for this view elsewhere,[67] I will limit myself to one argument in this chapter.

We have already pointed out that Mormon theology
teaches that all intelligent beings have always existed in
some state or another and that they progress or move
toward their final eternal state. McConkie writes:

> Endowed with agency and subject to eternal laws,
> man began his progression and advancement in
> pre-existence, his ultimate goal being to attain a
> state of glory, honor, and exaltation like the Father
> of spirits....This gradually unfolding course of
> advancement and experience—a course that
> began in a past eternity and will continue in ages
> future—is frequently referred to as a course of *eter-
> nal progression.*
>
> It is important to know, however, that for the over-
> whelming majority of mankind, eternal progres-
> sion has very definite limitations. In the full sense,
> eternal progression is enjoyed only by those who
> receive exaltation.[68]

Here is the problem: If the past series of events in time is infinite, *we should have already reached our final state by now.* Yet we have *not* reached our final state. Therefore the Mormon worldview is seriously flawed. The Mormon may respond by arguing that we have not yet reached our final state because there has not been enough time for it to have transpired. But this is certainly no solution, since the Mormon's own worldview affirms that an infinite length of time has already transpired. One cannot ask for more than an *infinite time* to complete a task.

We must conclude, then, that since none of us has reached his final state—whether it be deity or some other posthumous reward or punishment—the past series of events in time cannot be infinite in the sense the Mormon Church teaches. For even if we assume that the past *is* infinite, since we have not yet reached our inevitable fate, the Mormon worldview is still false.

It seems then that even if a Mormon were not to find these philosophical arguments compelling, he would have to agree that *if* the arguments are sound, Mormonism collapses, since if the Mormon universe is false, then the entire theological system, which is contingent upon the Mormon universe being true, collapses. Thus Stephen Robinson is simply wrong in asserting that "in LDS orthodoxy, the ontological frame [i.e., the Mormon view of reality or the universe], while a vital part of our theology, is secondary to the truth of the gospel itself, yet Evangelicals and others (including many of our own people) often get this backwards."[69]

Answers to Questions

Space does not permit detailed responses to the many questions that may be raised against the position for which I have argued in this chapter. For this reason, I have chosen to answer two questions I believe most directly challenge my case. In order to cover as much material as space permits, my answers will be brief. It should be noted, however, that these and other questions have been answered elsewhere and with greater detail. I will refer the reader to those sources.

The Scriptural Proof Question

Aren't there passages in Scripture which teach the Mormon view of God? Some Mormons cite passages in the Bible which they believe prove two important doctrines of Mormon theology: 1) God has a body, and 2) many Gods exist.

God has a body. Mormons sometimes argue that the Bible teaches that God has a body of flesh and bone. They quote such passages as Deuteronomy 34:10 ("Since then, no prophet has risen in Israel like Moses, whom the LORD knew *face to face,*" emphasis added) and Exodus 33:21-23 ("Then the LORD said, 'There is a place *near me* where you may stand on a rock. When my glory passes by, I will put you in a cleft of the rock and cover you with *my hand* until I have passed by. Then I will remove *my hand* and you will see *my back;* but *my face* must not be seen,'" emphasis added). There are several problems with this use of the Bible.

First, the Mormons cannot cite these passages to defend their position, for these passages refer to the God of the Old Testament (Jehovah or Yahweh), a being who Mormons believe is the *preincarnate* Jesus, a god *before* he acquired a physical body.

Second, there are no biblical passages that either explicitly or implicitly teach that God is by nature a physical being (that is, no passage says, "God has a body of flesh and bone"), although there are passages (see above) that explicitly teach that God is by nature a spirit. Even Robinson admits that he does "not expect to find the [Mormon] view of the Godhead or the corporeality of God described clearly in the Old Testament," nor does he "argue that it was once there and has been removed," although he does maintain, and I believe incorrectly, "that the Bible makes no unambiguous statement about the materiality or immateriality of the Father, and that we may therefore think of him either as having a body or as not having body without 'contradicting' the Bible." [70]

Third, in light of both my second point as well as the force of the case I have already made for the God of classical theism being the God of Scripture, it seems that the passages Mormons cite to prove God's corporeality should be seen as either the use of physical language by the biblical authors to convey a particular meaning of God's actions in human terms or else instances in which God temporarily assumes a physical form (i.e., a theophany). After all, if God is creator and sustainer of everything else that exists as well as being omnipotent, immutable, and omnipresent, it is difficult to see how such a Being could be physical by nature. For a physical being who is limited by time, space, and other forces (which the Mormons believe about God) cannot be the creator and sustainer of everything that exists (since he didn't create everything and doesn't sustain it), omnipotent (since the universe is "bigger" than he is), immutable (since he *became* God), and omnipresent (since he is in a particular place in space and time). (For a discussion on how these attributes relate to the incarnation of God the Son, see Chapter 3.)

The classical concept of God makes better sense of the biblical text than the Mormon view. For if the Mormon argument (that the use of physical language by Biblical authors conveys that meaning) were taken to its logical conclusion then we would have to conclude that God possesses some very odd physical characteristics in addition to the human ones that Mormons are quite fond of embracing. For example, the Bible teaches that the Holy Spirit manifested Himself as a dove (Matthew 3:16), that God "will cover you with his feathers, and under his wings you will find refuge" (Psalm 91:4), that "our *God* is a *consuming fire*" (Hebrews 12:29; Deuteronomy 4:24), that God is a shepherd (Psalm 23), and that Jesus is a door (John 10:9), a loaf of bread (John 6:35,51), and a vine (John 15:1-5).

Many Gods exist. Although we have already seen that the Bible teaches that there is no being who is *by nature* God except for Jehovah (or Yahweh), there are some passages in the Bible, which Mormons sometimes cite, that seem to teach the existence of many gods. Take, for example, the following:

Then the LORD said to Moses, "See, I have made you like God [or "a god"] to Pharaoh, and your brother Aaron will be your prophet" (Exodus 7:1). God presides in the great assembly; he gives judgment among the "gods" (Psalm 82:1).

A careful look at these passages and similar ones, in their contexts, shows that they are *not* teaching that there are many gods by nature, but rather that certain individuals (like kings and prophets) are looked upon by *other people* as gods. It should be noted that in order to get Mormon theology out of the Bible you need much more than passages which say that some people were called gods. After all, the devil is called "the god of this world," and clearly the Bible is not teaching that the devil is by nature divine. What you need are passages which state that there is more than one God by nature and that the Mormon doctrine of eternal progression is true, that human beings can achieve godhood like "*all* gods" who "have gone before you."[71] In other words, what you need are passages that are inconsistent with what is already present in Scripture.

One passage that is often cited by Mormon apologists is 1 Corinthians 8:4-6:

Well then, about eating food sacrificed to idols: we know that idols do not really exist in the world and that there is no god but the One. And if there were things called gods, either in the sky or on the earth—where there certainly seem to be "gods" and "lords" in plenty—still for us there is one God, the Father, from whom all things come and for whom we exist; and there is one Lord, Jesus Christ, through whom all things come and through whom we exist.

Some Mormons mistakenly interpret this verse to mean that Paul is saying that there is one God "for us," but that there could be other gods for other worlds. But this is not at all what the verse is saying. It is saying that although there are things *called* gods—and there *seems to be* plenty of them—there is only one God *by nature*, for there is only one Being "from whom all things come and for whom we exist; and there is one Lord, Jesus Christ, through whom all things come and through whom we exist." Biblical theologian Gordon Fee comments on 1 Corinthians 8:4-6:

> Paul also recognizes the existential reality of pagan worship, and he knows that some within the Corinthian community are going to be affected by that reality. Thus he interrupts the concession with the affirmation "as indeed there are many 'gods' and many 'lords.'" He does not intend by this that the "gods" exist objectively. Rather, as verse 7 indicates, they "exist" subjectively in the sense that they are believed in.

> The formulae "one God" and "one Lord" stand in specific contrast to the "many gods" and "many lords" of the pagans. This means that the emphasis is not on the uniqueness of the godhead, although that may be assumed, but on the uniqueness of the only God.[72]

The Greek Philosophy Question

Isn't the classical view the result of Christians using Greek philosophy to interpret the Bible? Virtually every Mormon scholar who asks this question answers it in the affirmative.[73] According to Robinson, "Much traditional Christian theology has been wedded with Greek philosophical categories and assumptions."[74] There are several problems with this charge. Consider just the following, though much more could be said.[75]

First, it is not clear what Robinson means by philosophy or Greek philosophy. Surely he cannot mean that *philosophical reflection* has no place in theological reasoning, since his own assessment of traditional Christian theology is based on a philosophical judgment about the nature of knowledge and theology: Greek philosophy is bad for Christian theology. Moreover, Robinson assumes the logical law of noncontradiction when he claims that Mormonism and traditional Christianity cannot both be correct theological systems in every way. Clearly, even if one believed that Mormonism is more biblical than traditional Christianity or vice versa, it cannot be that they are both correct theological systems in every way. Even though this assessment appeals to a logical principle first formulated by the Greek philosopher Aristotle, it would be wrong to dismiss it as "good Aristotelian thinking." It is simply good thinking.

Perhaps Robinson is not attacking philosophy per se, but just *Greek* philosophy. But it is not clear what he means by "Greek" philosophy, since in one place he calls it "Platonic"[76] and in another place he calls it "Hellenistic."[77] But this is very confusing, since Platonism can mean so many things. Robinson may be referring to the thought of the historical Plato, whose philosophy, some scholars argue, had changed in his later dialogues when compared to his earlier ones. It is possible that Robinson may be thinking of the work of the neo-Platonists, including the pantheistic and mystical Plotinus, or he may mean the writings of St. Augustine, who employed Platonic language to explain many biblical ideas. Then again, Robinson may be referring to Philo, the Middle Platonists, or the Gnostics. Hellenistic thinking is even more diverse, since it includes the Platonists as well as numerous other philosophical systems, including the materialism of Democritus as well as Aristotelianism in all its different versions.[78]

Second, aside from claiming that "the God of Christian 'orthodoxy' is virtually indistinguishable from the God of the Hellenistic philosophers,"[79] Robinson does not explain why affinities with a pagan tradition would make one's concept of God necessarily false. After all, Plato wrote about the Demiurge, a godlike being who shapes "the world out of pre-existent matter."[80] He also believed that the soul preexisted before it was born mortal.[81] Democritus held that "everything in the universe (including the human soul) is composed of different combinations of solid, eternal bits of matter called atoms."[82] These beliefs are more consistent with Mormon theology than with classical Christian theology. Yet it would seem odd as well as philosophically irresponsible that Robinson should reject Mormon theology on such a basis, since truth is truth regardless of where it is found. To dismiss something true simply because it has affinities with a pagan system is to commit the genetic fallacy. Mormon scholar and elder John Widstoe recognized this: "A rational theology is founded on truth, on all truth...and 'A truth has no end.' In building a philosophy of life, a man, therefore, cannot say that some truth must be considered and other truth rejected. Only on the basis of all truth, that is, all true knowledge can his religion be built...."[83] So whether one's theology is "Platonic" or not is irrelevant; the question is whether it is *true*.

Third, the argument can be made that although Christian thinkers have used and continue to use the language of philosophy, especially Greek philosophy, to convey certain biblical truths, it is the Bible that reshaped Greek thought rather than the other way around. According to the church historian J.N.D. Kelly, "The classical creeds of Christendom opened with a declaration of belief in one God, the maker of heaven and earth." The reason for this is simple: "The monotheistic idea, grounded in the religion of Israel, loomed large in the minds of the earliest fathers; though not reflective theologians, they were fully conscious that it marked the dividing line between the Church and paganism." Kelly goes on to say that "the doctrine of one god, the Father and creator, formed the background and indisputable premise of the Christian faith. Inherited from Judaism, it was her bulwark against pagan polytheism, Gnostic emanationism and Marcionite dualism."[84] Citing the work of Etienne Gilson, Norman L. Geisler writes:

> The Greeks never identified their ultimate metaphysical principle with God. This was the unique

Judeo-Christian contribution to philosophy of religion. Thus, the reverse of the traditional objection is the case. It was the Judeo-Christian concept of self-existent, pure actuality (based on Exodus 3:14) that transformed Greek metaphysics.[85]

Reformed philosopher Cornelius Van Til provides an example, contrasting the unchangeableness (or "immutability") of Aristotle's Unmoved Mover (a "God" who does not interact with Its creatures) with the "immutability" of the God of the Bible:

> Surely in the case of Aristotle the immutability of the divine being was due to its emptiness and internal immobility. No greater contrast is thinkable between the unmoved *noesis noeeseoos* of Aristotle and the Christian God.
>
> This appears particularly from the fact that the Bible does not hesitate to attribute all manner of activity to God....Herein exactly lies the glory of the Christian doctrine of God, that the unchangeable one is the one in control of the change of the universe.[86]

So, even though both the classical Christian concept of God and Aristotle's God are "immutable," it is the Bible's testimony by which the Christian thinker ought to interpret God's immutability. In fact, many of the heresies in the early church are the result of trying to remake Christian theology so that it squares with certain Hellenistic philosophies.[87] Ironically, some rejected doctrines (such as the eternality of matter and the preexistence of the soul) whose origin can be traced to pagan philosophies are consistent with certain aspects of the *Mormon* worldview. Consider the comments of philosopher Paul Copan concerning some early church Fathers who, like present-day Mormons, believed that matter is eternal:

In my mind, it seems doubtful that an un-hellenized
Jewish student of the [Old Testament] would have
formulated something analogous to a Middle
Platonist cosmology on his own. What is clear is
that these church fathers were strongly influenced
by (Middle-) Platonism, which held firmly to belief
in eternal formless matter. Their belief in God as
an artificer was not due to Scripture's ambiguity on
the topic but because of the strength of the philosophical grid within which they operated.[88]

Fourth, as we have seen, there is no doubt that Christian
scholars through the centuries have used philosophical terminology and concepts to convey certain biblical and theological truths. And there is no doubt that Mormons have
done so as well.[89] The question, however, is whether these
truths are being accurately conveyed by the terminology and
concepts. For example, the language of "rights" does not
appear in the Scriptures, for such language has its origin in
the political philosophy of such Enlightenment thinkers as
John Locke, Thomas Hobbes, and John Stuart Mill. Nevertheless, one could say that the Bible teaches that rights exist.
For instance, the command not to steal implies a "right to
property," and the command not to murder implies a "right
to life." Thus it would not be wrong for a Christian to say
that the Bible teaches a "right to property," even though such
a right is not literally spelled out in Scripture. In other words,
the concept of rights is in Scripture though the language of
rights is not.

Many Mormons are quite active in the Right to Life
movement. In fact, I have worked with Mormons on behalf
of the unborn, and some Mormons have used my book
*Politically Correct Death: Answering the Arguments for Abortion
Rights* (Baker, 1993) in defending the prolife position. Although rights language does not literally appear in the Bible,
Robinson surely would not deny that the Bible teaches that
the unborn have a right to life.

Consequently, if Christians use the language of philosophy to convey what they believe to be the biblical concept of

God, they are justified in doing so *if* they have accurately conveyed what the Bible teaches about the nature of God. I believe I have met this burden earlier in this chapter by showing that the classical concept of God is the God of Abraham, Isaac, Jacob, and Jesus of Nazareth.

Conclusion: The Divide Is Wide

It is clear that the Christian and Mormon views of God are radically different (see chart on page 91). Although both Mormons and Christians (including evangelicals) agree that God is a personal Being, the differences are significant: 1) Christians believe that God is by nature an immaterial Being, whereas Mormons believe that God is by nature a material being; 2) Christians believe that God is the creator and sustainer of everything else that exists, whereas Mormons believe that God is merely the organizer of the world and is subject to the laws and principles of a beginningless universe; 3) Christians maintain that God is omnipotent, while Mormons believe that God's power is limited by certain forces in the universe which have always existed and thus have been around long before God became God; 4) Christians hold that God is omniscient and thus has knowledge of the past, present, and future, whereas Mormons believe that God knows the past and present but not the future and that God is increasing in knowledge (some Mormons, however, disagree on this point and hold the classical view); 5) Christians believe that God is omnipresent, while Mormons believe that God is localized in space; 6) Christians maintain that God is unchanging (immutable) and eternal, whereas Mormons hold that God is a changing being who has not always existed as God; 7) Christians claim that God is a necessary Being and the only true and living God in existence, while Mormons believe that God is a contingent being and one of many gods; and 8) Christians maintain that God is a trinity (three Persons, one Being), whereas Mormons are tritheists who believe that each member of the Christian trinity is a separate, finite, and personal God.

Yet, as was noted above, Stephen Robinson in *How Wide the Divide?* denies that much of what we have covered is really the Mormon concept of God.[90] He affirms that in addition to being corporeal the LDS "God is omniscient, omnipotent, omnipresent, infinite, eternal and unchangeable."[91] But, as we have seen, Joseph Smith, the founding prophet of Mormonism, testified that God by nature is changeable, finite, contingent, not eternally God, and corporeal, and that we too may become Gods. This view of God has been reaffirmed in official LDS Church literature as well as in pronouncements by other church prophets, including Brigham Young, Lorenzo Snow, and Joseph Fielding Smith. Because, according to Robinson, the LDS "church's guarantee of doctrinal correctness lies primarily in the living prophet, and only secondarily in the preservation of the written text,"[92] it is clear that these pronouncements and the theology that flows from them are Mormon doctrine.

But Robinson has an escape clause: "What God has said to apostles and prophets in the past is always secondary to what God is saying directly to his apostles and prophets now."[93] So if the current LDS President, Gordon Hinckley, says that God is not finite, then God is not finite, even though Joseph Smith and his successors said otherwise. In fact, Robinson speaks approvingly of the call of Hinckley's predecessor, Ezra Taft Benson, to emphasize the theology of the Book of Mormon,[94] which seems to teach a strongly Judaic monotheism with modalistic overtones, nothing like what was taught later by Joseph Smith and his successors.

Although some evangelicals might applaud this purported shift by some Mormons like Robinson, any real shift must go through Joseph Smith, Brigham Young, and numerous other church authorities and prophets. And this would not be easy, since it leaves Robinson (and like-minded Mormons) with the Mormon equivalent of the Liar's Paradox: If President Hinckley says that Smith was wrong about God's nature, would Robinson believe him? Evidently Robinson would, on the authority of none other than Joseph Smith, since the church's authority to make theological pronouncements hinges on the veracity of its founding prophet, who has passed on his authority to his successors. But if Smith can't be trusted to tell us the truth about God's nature, why should we believe Hinckley's claim to divine authority, since it, after all, is contingent upon the veracity of Joseph Smith?

In his introduction to *How Wide the Divide?* Robinson suggests that evangelicals, rather than relying on anti-Mormon literature, ought to ask Mormons what they believe. Robinson volunteers: "...I think I am the world's authority on what I believe, and I consider myself a reasonably devout well-informed Latter-day Saint."[95] Fair enough. But prior to that claim, Robinson qualifies it by saying, "I do not speak in this volume for the LDS Church, only for myself...."[96]

However, when we ask another Mormon, Joseph Smith, he tells us something contrary to what Robinson tells us, which forces one to ask Robinson the question: Does *Joseph Smith* speak for the LDS Church? If Robinson answers yes, then LDS doctrine does affirm a finite, changeable, contingent God, and Robinson is vindicated: He really doesn't speak for the church. If Robinson answers no, then the only difference between him and evangelicals is that the latter disbelieve in a larger number of things said by Joseph Smith

CHRISTIAN VIEW OF GOD	MORMON VIEW OF GOD
1. Immaterial	1. Material
2. Creator and sustainer of the universe, which He created out of nothing	2. A creature of the universe who organizes the world out of preexistent matter and is subject to the laws, forces, and principles of a beginningless and uncreated universe
3. Omnipotent	3. Not omnipotent
4. Omniscient	4. Not omniscient; increasing in knowledge*
5. Omnipresent in being	5. Localized in space
6. Unchanging and eternal	6. Changing and not eternal (as God)
7. Necessary and the only God by nature	7. Contingent and one of many gods
8. A trinity: three Persons, one eternal Being	8. Tritheistic: three persons who are three finite beings

*Contemporary Mormon authorities appear to disagree on this point.

than does Robinson. All of this means that the more interesting divide is *not* between Robinson's version of Mormonism and Christianity, but between Robinson and the founder of Mormonism.[97]

Chapter Notes

1. Joseph Smith, *History of the Church of Jesus Christ of Latter-day Saints,* 7 vols., introduction and notes by B.H. Roberts, 2d rev. ed. (Salt Lake City: The Deseret Book Company, 1978), 6:305. (Cited as CHC from now on.)

2. Classical theism refers to a family of views that express a general conception of God with some minor differences between its members. Mormonism, on the other hand, expresses an unrelated conception of God that differs from these traditions in many major ways. For an overview of classical theisms, see Thomas V. Morris, *Our Idea of God: An Introduction to Philosophical Theology* (Downers Grove: InterVarsity Press, 1991). I owe this point to Carl Mosser.

3. In personal correspondence with me, Mosser makes an important observation about John 4:24: "Some Mormon scholars take the phrase here ('God is spirit') as a predication of composition (i.e., God is made of 'spirit' but this does not preclude flesh). But the verse is a clear case of essential predication (i.e., God's essential nature is spirit). This *must* be the case because Jesus speaks these words in the context of answering the Samaritan woman's statement about Jews worshiping God in Jerusalem and the Samaritans on Mount Gerizim in 4:20. The point Jesus makes is that God is not 'located' either at Jerusalem or at Gerizim. The Samaritan woman had built a false dichotomy in her mind because she was conceiving of God as in some way 'located' in one of these two holy places and that to worship Him one had to be at the proper place. Jesus in effect says, 'God is not located either in Jerusalem or at Gerizim. God is spirit—He is not "located" anywhere. You don't need to go to the right place, you need to worship with the right attitude—in spirit and in truth.' Of course, for Jesus to make the point that God's essential nature is unlocated, 'spirit' precludes a physical body also being a part of that nature, since a body is located. In the case of the incarnation Jesus takes on a human nature (Philippians 2:7) but this does not in any way affect His divine nature, since the two are separate within His Person. Passages like Matthew 23:21 and 1 Kings 8:13 that speak of God dwelling in the temple do not nullify this because it is not God's *being* but His *glory* that dwelt in the temple; cf. Psalm 26:8."

4. For more passages that explicitly or implicitly teach this doctrine, see Augustus Hopkins Strong, *Systematic Theology: A Compendium* (Old Tappan, NJ: Fleming Revell, 1907), 374-78.

5. Since preexistent matter would be the *material* cause of the universe, and since this passage teaches that no cause except God can account for the universe, this passage clearly teaches creation *ex nihilo.*

6. Saint Augustine, *City of God* (Garden City, NY: Image Books, 1958), 5.10.

7. Thomas Aquinas, *Summa Theologica,* I, 25, 3, as contained in *Introduction to Saint Thomas Aquinas,* ed. Anton C. Pegis (New York: The Modern Library, 1948), 231.

8. For greater detail and more Scripture references than those presented here, see William Lane Craig, *The Only Wise God* (Grand Rapids: Baker Book House,

1987), 21-37; and Norman L. Geisler, *Creating God in the Image of Man?* (Minneapolis: Bethany House, 1997), 149-52.

9. Clark Pinnock, "God Limits His Knowledge," in *Predestination and Free Will*, eds. David Basinger and Randall Basinger (Downers Grove, IL: InterVarsity Press, 1986), 158.

10. For a complete presentation of this argument from the Bible's test of a prophet, see Francis J. Beckwith, "Limited Omniscience and the Test for a Prophet: A Brief Philosophical Analysis," in *Journal of the Evangelical Theological Society* 36.3 (September 1993)

11. This passage does not mean that the doctrine of the incarnation—that God became man in Jesus of Nazareth—is unbiblical. On the contrary, the passage is merely saying that God cannot be limited or contained by a finite reality, such as a temple. But the doctrine of the incarnation does not contradict that concept. The doctrine is saying that God *took on* a human nature in addition to His divine nature. The doctrine is *not* saying that God's being was limited or contained by human nature. Hence the passage in question is consistent with the doctrine of the incarnation. For a philosophical defense of this view, see Thomas V. Morris, *The Logic of God Incarnate* (Ithaca, NY: Cornell University Press, 1986). For a biblical and theological defense of this view, see Chapter 3 of this volume (by Ron Rhodes).

12. I owe this point to Doug Groothuis.

13. Alan W. Gomes, "God in Man's Image: Foreknowledge, Freedom, and the 'Openness' of God," *Christian Research Journal* 10 (Summer 1987): 18-24

14. See Morris, *Our Idea of God*, 119-38; and Ronald H. Nash, *The Concept of God* (Grand Rapids: Zondervan, 1983), 73-83. It seems to me, however, that if God exits before (ontologically prior to) time, His being cannot be limited by it. And since He cannot change in His nature, He must be eternal (nontemporal) both before and after creation.

15. It is true that *by* His power God *grants* power to His creatures. But unlike this hypothetical other God, their limited power is always subject to His unlimited power. Thus God "possesses" all power in that all other power comes from, and is under, His power.

16. Other passages include Isaiah 45:5,18,21,22; Jeremiah 10:10; John 17:3; 1 Thessalonians 1:9.

17. See Morris, *Our Idea of God*, 107-13; and Nash, *The Concept of God*, 106-13.

18. Stephen E. Robinson in *How Wide the Divide?: A Mormon and an Evangelical in Conversation* by Craig L. Blomberg and Stephen E. Robinson (Downers Grove, IL: InterVarsity Press, 1997), 210.

19. "Let God Be True," rev. (1952), 89.

20. *Webster's New Universal Unabridged Dictionary*, deluxe 2nd edition (New York: Simon & Schuster, 1983), 1338.

21. For a collection of creeds, see John H. Leith, ed., *Creeds of the Churches*, 3rd ed. (Louisville: John Knox Press, 1982). See also J.N.D. Kelly, *Early Christian Doctrines*, rev. ed. (San Francisco: HarperCollins, 1978); Howard F. Vos, *An Introduction to Church History*, rev. ed. (Chicago: Moody Press, 1984); and James Orr, *Progress of Dogma* (Old Tappan, NJ: Fleming H. Revell, 1901).

22. This list of sources of Mormon theology is nearly identical to the one presented by Brigham Young University philosophy professor David Lamont Paulsen in his doctoral dissertation at the University of Michigan, *The Comparative Coherency of Mormon (Finitistic) and Classical Theism* (Ann Arbor, MI: University Microfilms, 1975), 66.

23. Bruce R. McConkie, *Mormon Doctrine*, 2nd ed. (Salt Lake City: Bookcraft, 1979), 765.

24. Robinson in *How Wide the Divide?*, 85-86.
25. *The Ensign Magazine* (November 1976), 63.
26. *Gospel Principles*, rev. ed. (Salt Lake City: Church of Jesus Christ of Latter-day Saints, 1995), 55.
27. Robinson in *How Wide the Divide?*, 57.
28. For example, Gary James Bergera, ed., *Line Upon Line: Essays in Mormon Doctrine* (Salt Lake City: Signature Books, 1989); Sterling M. McMurrin, *The Philosophical Foundations of Mormon Theology* (Salt Lake City: University of Utah Press, 1959); Sterling M. McMurrin, *The Theological Foundations of the Mormon Religion* (Salt Lake City: University of Utah Press, 1965); Blake Ostler, "The Mormon Concept of God," in *Dialogue: A Journal of Mormon Thought*, 17 (Summer 1984):65-93; Paulsen, *Comparative Coherency*; Kent Robson, "Omnis on the Horizon," *Sunstone* 8 (July-August 1983): 21-23; Kent Robson, "Time and Omniscience in Mormon Theology," in *Sunstone*, 5 (May-June 1980): 17-23; and O. Kendall White, Jr., *Mormon Neo-Orthodoxy: A Crisis Theology* (Salt Lake City: Signature Books, 1987), 57-67.
29. Brigham Young's statements on the Adam-God doctrine come primarily from the *Journal of Discourses*, about which the publisher said in the preface to volume 3, "The 'Journal of Discourses' is a vehicle of doctrine, counsel, and instruction to all people, but especially to the saints" (*Journal of Discourses, by Brigham Young, President of the Church of Jesus Christ of Latter-day Saints, His Two Counsellors, the Twelve Apostles, and Others*, 26 volumes, reported by G.D. Watt [Liverpool: F.D. Richards, 1854-1886], 3:iii. (Cited as JD from now on.) Brigham Young himself said that he had "never yet preached a sermon and sent it out to the children of men, that they may not call Scripture" (JD 13:95).
30. See McConkie, *Mormon Doctrine*, 18-19; and Joseph Fielding Smith, *Doctrines of Salvation*, 3 volumes, compiled by Bruce McConkie (Salt Lake City: Bookcraft, 1955), 1:91,96.
31. JD 1:50.
32. James B. Allen, "Emergence of a Fundamental: The Expanding Role of Joseph Smith's First Vision in Mormon Religious Thought," in *Journal of Mormon History*, 7(1980): 43-61; Thomas G. Alexander, "The Reconstruction of Mormon Doctrine: From Joseph Smith to Progression Theology," in *Sunstone* 5 (July/August 1980): 32-39; Boyd Kirkland, "The Development of the Mormon Doctrine of God," in Bergera, *Line Upon Line*, 35-52.
33. Kirkland, "Development," 48.
34. McConkie writes: "*Elohim*, plural word though it is, is used as the exalted name-title of God the Eternal Father..." (*Mormon Doctrine*, 224).
35. CHC 6:305-6.
36. DC 130:22.
37. Quoted by B.H. Roberts in Joseph Smith, the Prophet, *The King Follet Discourse: The Being and Kind of Being God Is; the Immortality of the Intelligence of Man*, with notes and references by the late Elder B.H. Roberts of the First Council of Seventy (Salt Lake City: Magazine Printing, 1963), 9.
38. Joseph Fielding Smith, *Doctrines of Salvation*, 1:10,12.
39. Milton R. Hunter, *The Gospel Through the Ages* (Salt Lake City: Deseret, 1958), 104.
40. See Neal A. Maxwell, "A More Determined Discipleship," in *The Ensign Magazine* (February 1979): 69-73; and Neal A. Maxwell, *All These Things Shall Give Thee Experience* (Salt Lake City: Deseret Books, 1979).
41. Ostler cites four Mormon leaders who have held views consistent with this view of omniscience: Presidents Brigham Young, Wilford Woodruff, and Lorenzo Snow as well as member of the Council of Seventy B. H. Roberts. See Ostler, "The Mormon Concept of God," 76-78.

42. Wilford Woodruff in JD 6:120.
43. According to Ostler ("The Mormon Concept of God," 76), these official pronouncements are recorded in James R. Clark, ed., *Messages of the First Presidency*, 2 vols. (Salt Lake City: Bookcraft), 2:214-23; and *Millennial Star* 26 (21 October 1865): 658-60.
44. Hyrum L. Andrus, *God, Man and the Universe* (Salt Lake City: Bookcraft, 1968), 175.
45. DC 93:29.
46. *Gospel Principles*, 14.
47. McConkie, *Mormon Doctrine*, 386-87, 516-17, 750-51.
48. CHC 6:305-12.
49. CHC 6:474.
50. Ostler, "The Mormon Concept of God," 67.
51. B.H. Roberts, *Seventy's Course in Theology: Third Year and Fourth Year* (Salt Lake City: The Caxton Press, 1910), 4:70.
52. Ibid., 4:70-71. See McConkie, *Mormon Doctrine*, 544-45.
53. CHC 6:476.
54. DC 130:22.
55. James Talmage, *A Study of the Articles of Faith* (Salt Lake City: The Church of Jesus Christ of Latter-day Saints, 1975), 237. For a sophisticated discussion of Mormon tritheism, see David L. Paulsen, "The Doctrine of Divine Embodiment: Restoration, Judeo-Christian, and Philosophical Perspectives," in *BYU Studies* 35.4 (1995-96), 7-94.
56. DC 131:7-8.
57. Vern G. Swanson, "The Development of the Concept of the Holy Ghost in Mormon Theology," in *Line Upon Line*, 98. The quote from Brigham Young cited by Swanson is from JD 8:179. In the past, some LDS writers made a distinction between the Holy Spirit and the Holy Ghost. For example, John Widtsoe writes: "The Holy Spirit is an agent, means, or influence by which the will, power, and intelligence of God, and the Godhead, personal Beings, may be transmitted throughout space.... It is a spirit of intelligence that permeates the universe and gives understanding to the spirits of men. The phenomena of existence are but expressions of this divine medium.... The Holy Ghost, sometimes called the Comforter, is the third member of the Godhead, and is a personage, distinct from the Holy Spirit" (John Widtsoe, *Evidences and Reconciliations*, Collector's Edition [Salt Lake City: Bookcraft, 1987; orig. 1960], 76).
58. McConkie, *Mormon Doctrine*, 392. It should be noted that some Mormon scholars admit that it is not always clear in Mormon literature as to whom the name "Jehovah" refers. See Boyd Kirkland, "Elohim and Jehovah in Mormonism and the Bible," in *Dialogue: A Journal of Mormon Thought* 19, (Spring 1986), 77-93; and Boyd Kirkland, "Jehovah As Father," in *Sunstone* (Autumn 1984), 36-44.
59. *The Life and Teachings of Jesus and His Apostles*, 15, as quoted in Mark J. Cares, *Speaking the Truth in Love to Mormons* (Milwaukee: Northwestern Publishing House, 1993), 78.
60. Robinson in *How Wide the Divide?*, 92.
61. See Francis J. Beckwith and Stephen E. Parrish, *The Mormon Concept of God: A Philosophical Analysis* (Lewiston, NY: Edwin Mellen Press, 1991); and Francis J. Beckwith and Stephen E. Parrish, *See the Gods Fall* (Joplin, MO: College Press, 1997), chap. 3.
62. Joseph Fielding Smith, *Doctrines of Salvation*, 1:12. Joseph Smith declares, "Hence, if Jesus had a Father, can we not believe that *He* had a Father also?" (CHC 6:476). See also McConkie, *Mormon Doctrine*, 577.
63. JD 5:19.

64. McConkie, *Mormon Doctrine*, 77.
65. William Lane Craig, *The Kalam Cosmological Argument* (New York: Macmillan Publishing Co., 1979).
66. J. P. Moreland, *Scaling the Secular City* (Grand Rapids: Baker Book House, 1987), 29.
67. Beckwith and Parrish, *The Mormon Concept of God*, 59-63.
68. McConkie, *Mormon Doctrine*, 238-39.
69. Robinson in *How Wide the Divide?*, 19.
70. Ibid., 79.
71. Joseph Smith in CHC 6:306.
72. Gordon Fee, *The First Epistle to the Corinthians*, NICNT (Grand Rapids: Eerdmans), 372-73, 374.
73. Consider just the following citations, though many more could be marshaled: Daniel C. Peterson and Stephen C. Ricks, *Offenders for a Word* (Salt Lake City: Aspen Books, 1992), 42; Ostler, "The Mormon Concept of God," 89; McMurrin, *The Philosophical Foundations of Mormon Theology*, 15; McMurrin, *The Theological Foundations of the Mormon Religion*, 41; David L. Paulsen, "Early Christian Belief in Corporeal Deity: Origen and Augustine as Reluctant Witnesses," in *Harvard Theological Review* 83:2 (1990): 105-07; and Robson, "Omnis on the Horizon," 23.
74. Robinson in *How Wide the Divide?*, 88.
75. See, for example, Gerald Bray, *The Doctrine of God: Contours of Christian Theology* (Downers Grove, IL: InterVarsity Press, 1993); Ronald H. Nash, *Christianity and the Hellenistic World* (Grand Rapids: Zondervan, 1984); Richard A. Muller, "Incarnation, Immutability, and the Case for Classical Theism," in *Westminster Theological Journal* 45 (1983); and Geisler, *Creating God in the Image of Man?*, 95-97.
76. Robinson in *How Wide the Divide?*, 92.
77. Ibid., 17.
78. For an overview of these schools of thought, see Nash, *Christianity and the Hellenistic World*; and Kelly, *Early Christian Doctrines*.
79. Robinson in *How Wide the Divide?*, 92.
80. Kelly, *Early Christian Doctrines*, 16.
81. Ibid.
82. Nash, *Christianity and the Hellenistic World*, 31.
83. John Widtsoe, *A Rational Theology As Taught by the Church of Jesus Christ of Latter-day Saints* (Salt Lake City: Deseret, 1929), 8, as quoted in Floyd Ross, "Process Philosophy and Mormon Thought," *Sunstone* 7.1 (January-February 1982), 19.
84. Kelly, *Early Christian Doctrines*, 83, 87.
85. Geisler, *Creating God in the Image of Man?*, 96. The work of Gilson's cited by Geisler is *God and Philosophy* (New Haven: Yale University Press, 1941), chap. 1.
86. Cornelius Van Til, *An Introduction to Systematic Theology* (Nutley, NJ: Presbyterian and Reformed, 1974), 210-11, as quoted in Muller, "Incarnation, Immutability, and the Case for Classical Theism," 30.
87. See Paul Copan, "Is *Creation Ex Nihilo* A Post-Biblical Invention?: An Examination of Ferhard May's Proposal," in *Trinity Journal* 17NS (1996); Kelly, *Early Christian Doctrines*; and Muller, "Incarnation, Immutability, and the Case for Classical Theism," 28-29.
88. Copan, "Is *Creation Ex Nihilo* A Post-Biblical Invention?," 92.
89. For example, some thinkers, including Mormons, have noticed strong conceptual similarities between Mormon theism and other finite theisms and philosophical positions, such as nominalism, classical materialism, and process philosophy. See, for example, McMurrin, *The Philosophical Foundations of Mormon Theology*; McMurrin, *The Theological Foundations of the Mormon*

Religion; Paulsen, *Comparative Coherency;* Ross, "Process Philosophy and Mormon Thought;" and Garland E. Tickmeyer, "Joseph Smith and Process Theology," in *Dialogue: A Journal of Mormon Thought* 17 (Autumn 1984).

90. What follows is adapted from my review of *How Wide the Divide?* "With a Grain of Salt," *Christianity Today* (November 17, 1997), 57-59.

91. Robinson in *How Wide the Divide?*, 77.

92. Ibid., 57.

93. Ibid., 59.

94. Ibid., 68-69.

95. Ibid., 14.

96. Ibid.

97. I would like to thank several colleagues who read the original version of this manuscript and offered valuable comments and suggestions: the other authors of this volume, plus Kevin Bywater (Summit Ministries) and Douglas Groothuis (Denver Seminary). A very special thanks to Carl Mosser, a graduate student at Talbot School of Theology (Biola University), whose theological insight and wide-ranging knowledge of Mormon literature helped improve the quality of argument in this chapter.

3

Christ

Ron Rhodes

Jesus asked one of His disciples, "Who do you say I am?" This is one of the most important questions of all history. Christianity stands or falls on the identity and work of Jesus Christ.

Today one of the theological battlegrounds in the religious world is the doctrine of Christ. Scripture very plainly warns about those who preach another Jesus (Matthew 7:21-23; 2 Corinthians 11:4). The Mormon Church illustrates the need for this warning. Measured against the barometer of Scripture (2 Timothy 3:16), the Mormon Jesus is clearly "another Jesus."

As a backdrop to understanding the deviations of the Mormon view of Jesus, we will first examine the historic orthodox view of Jesus. We will then focus our attention on specific aspects of Mormon Christology with a view to demonstrating just how wide the divide is between the biblical Jesus and the Mormon Jesus.

The Christian View of Jesus Christ

John's Gospel, which is authenticated by numerous and early manuscripts (see Chapter 1), is brimming with evidences for the deity of Christ. Because the Mormon Jesus is a temporal being who came into existence at a point in time (literally *procreated* by a Heavenly Father and a Heavenly Mother), it is appropriate that we begin our discussion in

John, for this Gospel forcefully demonstrates the eternal nature of Christ as God.

John lays the foundation for his Gospel with the opening words: "In the beginning was the Word, and the Word was with God, and the Word was God" (1:1). In this verse Jesus is called "the Word" because He is the full expression or revelation of God.

Bible expositors have often noted that the phrase "in the beginning" in John 1:1 points us back to the creation account in Genesis 1:1, where we read, "*In the beginning* God created the heavens and the earth." John's "beginning" is identical to the Genesis "beginning." It is noteworthy that the Septuagint, a Greek translation of the Hebrew Old Testament that predates Christ, used the exact same Greek words for "in the beginning" as are used in John 1:1.

But what specifically does "in the beginning" refer to? Scripture seems to indicate that the universe was not created *in* time, but that time itself was created *along with* the universe.[1] In other words, time was not already in existence when God created the world. The world was created *with* time rather than *in* time. Back of the beginning mentioned in Genesis 1:1 (and John 1:1) lay a beginningless eternity.[2]

It is important to grasp this concept, because John tells us that "in the beginning [when time began] *was* the Word." The verb *was* that is used here is an imperfect tense in the Greek. This indicates *continued existence.* The imperfect tense reaches back indefinitely beyond the instant of the beginning. Thus Jesus did not come into being at a specific point in eternity past, but at that point at which all else began to be, *He already was.* No matter how far back we go in eternity past, we will never come to a point at which we could say of Christ, as the early Christian heretic Arius once did, that "there was a time when He was not."

Because Christ is the *eternal* Word, all that can be said of God can be said of Him. John is not merely saying that there is something divine about Jesus; he is affirming that He is *eternal* God, and doing so emphatically.

In keeping with the fact that Jesus is the eternal "Word" is His eternal identity as Yahweh. We see this in John 8:58, where Jesus told some Jewish critics, "Before Abraham was born, I am!" Jesus here points back to Exodus 3:14, where God reveals His name to be "I AM."

Knowing how much the Jews venerated Abraham, Jesus in John 8:58 deliberately contrasted the created origin of Abraham with His own eternal, uncreated nature. It was not simply that Jesus was older than Abraham, although His statement certainly says that too, but that His existence is a different kind than was Abraham's. Indeed, Abraham was created and finite; he came into being at a point in time. By contrast, Christ's existence never began; He is uncreated and infinite, and is therefore eternal.[3] In Jesus "we see the timeless God, who was the God of Abraham and of Isaac and of Jacob, who was before time and who will be after time, who always is."[4]

The name "Yahweh," which occurs some 5300 times in the Old Testament, is connected with the Hebrew verb "to be." The name thus conveys the idea of eternal self-existence. Yahweh never came into being at a point in time, for He has always existed. He was never born; He will never die. He does not grow older, for He is beyond the realm of time. To know Yahweh is to know the Eternal One.

A comparison of the Old and New Testaments provides powerful testimony to Jesus' identity as Yahweh. Support for this is found, for example, in Christ's crucifixion. In Zechariah 12:10 Yahweh is speaking prophetically: "They will look on me, the one they have pierced." Though Yahweh is speaking, this is obviously a reference to Christ's future crucifixion. We know that "the one they have pierced" is Jesus, for He is described this same way by the apostle John in Revelation 1:7.

The Greek translation of the Old Testament known as the Septuagint provides us with additional insights on Christ's identity as Yahweh. It renders the Hebrew phrase for "I AM" (God's name) in Exodus 3:14 as *ego eimi.* On a number of occasions in the Greek New Testament, Jesus used this term as a way of identifying Himself as God. For example, in John 8:24 Jesus declared: "If you do not believe that I am [*ego eimi*] He, you will die in your sins" (NKJV). The original Greek for this verse does not have the word *He*. The verse literally reads: "If you do not believe that I AM, you shall die in your sins."

Then, according to verse 28, Jesus told the Jews: "When you lift up the Son of Man, then you will know that I am [*ego eimi*] He" (NKJV). Again, the original Greek reads: "When you lift up the Son of Man, then you will know that I AM" (there is no *He*). Jesus purposefully used the phrase as a means of pointing to His identity as Yahweh.

It is also highly revealing that Old Testament passages about Yahweh were directly applied to Jesus in the New Testament. For instance, Isaiah 40:3 says: "In the desert prepare the way for the Lord [*Yahweh*]; make straight in the wilderness a highway for our God [*Elohim*]." Mark's Gospel tells us that Isaiah's words were fulfilled in the ministry of John the Baptist preparing the way for Jesus Christ (Mark 1:2-4).

Still another illustration is Isaiah 6:1-5, where the prophet recounts his vision of Yahweh "seated on a throne, high and exalted" (verse 1; cf. verse 3). He witnessed angels proclaiming, "Holy, holy, holy is the LORD [*Yahweh*] Almighty; the whole earth is full of his glory" (verse 3). Later, the apostle John—under the inspiration of the Holy Spirit—wrote that Isaiah "saw Jesus' glory" (John 12:41). Yahweh's glory and Jesus' glory are equated.

Christ's deity is further confirmed for us in that many of the actions of Yahweh in the Old Testament are performed by Christ in the New Testament. For example, in Psalm 119 we are told about a dozen times that it is Yahweh who gives and preserves life. But in the New Testament, Jesus claims this power for Himself: "For just as the Father raises the dead and gives them life, even so the Son gives life to whom he is pleased to give it" (John 5:21).

In the Old Testament the voice of Yahweh was said to be "like the roar of rushing waters" (Ezekiel 43:2). Likewise, we read of the glorified Jesus in heaven: "His voice was like the sound of rushing waters" (Revelation 1:15b). What is true of Yahweh is just as true of Jesus.

It is also significant that in the Old Testament, Yahweh is described as "an everlasting light," one that would make the sun, moon, and stars obsolete (Isaiah 60:19,20). Jesus will do the same for the future eternal city in which the saints will dwell forever: "The city does not need the sun or the moon to shine on it, for the glory of God gives it light, and the Lamb is its lamp" (Revelation 21:23).

Clearly, then, Jesus is Yahweh and is coequal and coeternal with the Father and the Holy Spirit. Before time began, Christ was eternally "I AM."

Christ's Attributes of Deity

We find further evidence for the eternity and deity of Christ in the fact that He possessed all the attributes of deity.

Christ is self-existent. Christ is the uncaused First Cause, the self-existent One who brought the universe into being. As the creator of all things (John 1:3; Colossians 1:16; Hebrews 1:2), Christ Himself must be *un*created. He is endlessly self-existent.

Colossians 1:17 tells us that Christ "is before all things, and in him all things hold together." Obviously, if Christ is "before all things," He does not depend on anyone or anything outside Himself for His own existence.

Christ is immutable. That Christ is immutable simply means that He (as God) is unchangeable, and thus unchanging. This does not mean that Christ is immobile or inactive, but it does mean that He is never inconsistent or growing or developing in His divine nature.

A key passage relating to the immutability of Christ is Hebrews 1:10-12, where the Father speaks of the Son's unchanging nature: "In the beginning, O Lord, you laid the foundations of the earth, and the heavens are the work of your hands. They will perish, but you remain; they will all wear out like a garment. You will roll them up like a robe; like a garment they will be changed. But you remain the same, and your years will never end." These verses teach that even when the present creation wears out like an old garment, Jesus will remain unchanged. The reference here is to the transformation of the heavens and earth which will occur after the millennium and will introduce the eternal state (2 Peter 3:10-13). Even after those cataclysmic events the Son's years will never end.

Christ's immutability is also affirmed in Hebrews 13:8, where we are told that "Jesus Christ is the same yesterday and today and forever." It is true that in the incarnation Christ *added* a human nature, but orthodox scholars have always held that the *divine* nature of Christ remains unchanged and is therefore immutable (see also James 1:17; Malachi 3:6).

Christ is omnipresent. To say that Christ is omnipresent is to say that He is *everywhere* present. How does Christ's omnipresence (as God) relate to His human body in the incarnation? Theologian John F. Walvoord is right when he says, "The fact that Christ is omnipresent does not contradict the concept that He also has locality. While living on earth, He also was omnipresent in His deity. At the present time, Christ is at the right hand of the Father (Mark 16:19; 1 Peter 3:22) although at the same time omnipresent."[5]

Christ's omnipresence is demonstrated in several ways in the New Testament. One day Jesus saw a man named Nathaniel approaching, and Jesus said, "Here is a true Israelite, in whom there is nothing false." "How do you know me?" Nathaniel asked. Jesus answered, "I saw you while you were still under the fig tree before Philip called you." Then Nathaniel declared, "Rabbi, you are the Son of God; you are the King of Israel" (John 1:47-49). Though bodily removed from Nathaniel and his situation at the fig tree, the omnipresent Lord was with him all the time.

Jesus promised His disciples that "where two or three come together in my name, there am I with them" (Matthew 18:20). Obviously, there are people all over the world who gather in Christ's name, and the only way He could be present with them all is if He is truly omnipresent.

After giving the disciples the Great Commission (to bring the Gospel to all nations), Jesus assured them: "Surely I am with you always, to the very end of the age" (Matthew 28:20). With disciples taking the Gospel all over the world, the only way Christ would be with them all at the same time would be if He were everywhere present (see Ephesians 1:23; 4:10; Colossians 3:11).

Christ is omniscient. All those who came into contact with Jesus seemed to sense that He was omniscient (all-knowing). John said that Jesus "did not need man's testimony about man, for he knew what was in a man" (John 2:25). Jesus' disciples said, "Now we can see that you know all things and that you do not even need to have anyone ask you questions" (John 16:30). After the resurrection, when Jesus asked Peter for the third time if Peter loved him, Peter responded, "Lord, you know all things; you know that I love you" (John 21:17).

Jesus knew beforehand those who would reject Him (John 6:64) and those who would follow Him (John 10:14). He knew exactly where the fish were in the water (Luke 5:4,6; John 21:6-11), and He knew just which fish contained the coin (Matthew 17:27). He knew future events (John 11:11; 18:4), including details that would be encountered (Matthew 21:2-4), and He knew that Lazarus had died without being told (John 11:14). He knows the Father *as the Father knows Him* (Matthew 11:27; John 7:29; 8:55; 10:15; 17:25).

Still another evidence for Christ's omniscience is the fact that He hears and answers the prayers of His people (Acts 7:59; 9:10-17; 1 Corinthians 16:22; 2 Corinthians 12:8; Revelation 22:20; cf. Hebrews 2:17; 4:15). Theologian Robert Reymond explains that when Jesus claimed for Himself the prerogative to hear and to answer the prayers of His disciples, He was claiming omniscience. One who can hear the innumerable prayers of His disciples—offered to Him night and day, day in and day out throughout the centuries—keep each request infallibly related to its petitioner, and answer each one in accordance with the divine mind and will would need Himself to be omniscient.[6]

Christ is omnipotent. Christ's omnipotence (the attribute of being all-powerful) is demonstrated in many ways in the New Testament. For example, Christ is said to have created the entire universe (Colossians 1:16; John 1:3; Hebrews 1:2). He sustains the universe by His own power (Colossians 1:17; Hebrews 1:3). During His earthly ministry, He exercised power over nature (Luke 8:25), over physical diseases (Mark 1:29-31), over demonic spirits (Mark 1:32-34), and over death by raising people from the dead (John 11:1-44). Moreover, Jesus' omnipotence was displayed in His own resurrection from the dead (John 2:19).

These and other attributes demonstrate beyond any doubt that Christ is eternal and unchangeable Deity.

The Incarnation of Jesus Christ

In the incarnation, the incomprehensible came to pass. The glorious Son of God forsook the splendor of heaven and became as truly a man as ourselves. Surrendering His glorious estate, He voluntarily entered into human relationships within the world. "Leaving the free, unconditioned, world-ruling absoluteness of the Divine form, the Son entered the limits of time and space of the creature."[7] Through the miracle of the virgin birth, the Son of God reached out and took to Himself a true and complete humanity without diminishing His essential deity. He united deity and humanity inseparably and eternally in one Person.

The Holy Spirit's supernatural work in Mary's body enabled Christ—eternal God—to take on a human nature (Luke 1:35). The fetal state in Mary's womb was entirely under the controlling, sanctifying ministry of the Holy Spirit.[8] And through this incarnation, a key component of the plan of salvation came to fruition (Ephesians 1:3-14). Our Savior *became flesh* with the specific purpose of dying on our behalf so that those who trust in Him could become saved and dwell with God forever.

It is important to understand that to deny either the undiminished deity *or* the perfect humanity of the incarnate Christ is to put oneself outside the pale of orthodoxy. We have already firmly established the deity of Christ above. There are also many evidences for the full humanity of Christ in Scripture. To begin with, 1 John 4:2,3a tells us: "This is how you can recognize the Spirit of God: Every spirit that acknowledges that Jesus Christ has come *in the flesh* is from God, but every spirit that does not acknowledge Jesus is not from God."

Further, Hebrews 2:14 tells us that "since the children have flesh and blood, *he too shared in their humanity* so that by his death he might destroy him who holds the power of death—that is, the devil." First Timothy 3:16 affirms that Christ *"appeared in a body,* was vindicated by the Spirit, was seen by angels, was preached among the nations, was believed on in the world, was taken up in glory." Romans 8:3 says that God sent Jesus *"in the likeness of sinful man* to be a sin offering." The apostle Paul proclaimed that "in Christ all the fullness of the Deity lives *in bodily form*" (Colossians 2:9).

Jesus' full humanity is plainly evident in the fact that He consistently displayed human characteristics. Besides growing as a normal child (Luke 2:40,52), Jesus had a physical body of flesh and bones (Luke 24:39); He experienced weariness (John 4:6), hunger (Luke 4:2), sorrow (Matthew 26:37), and weeping (John 11:35), and He needed sleep (Luke 8:23).

Christ's development as a human being was normal in every respect, with two major exceptions: Christ always did the will of God, and He never sinned. As Hebrews 4:15 tells us, in Christ "we do not have a high priest who is unable to sympathize with our weaknesses, but we have one who has been tempted in every way, just as we are—yet was without sin." Christ is utterly "holy," "blameless," and "pure" (Hebrews 7:26).

Christ's "Self-Emptying"

If Jesus Christ is truly God, then how does His deity relate to His humanity in the incarnation? This question is dealt with in Philippians 2:6-9. Paul, speaking of the incarnation, said that Christ, "being in very nature God, did not consider equality with God something to be grasped, but made himself nothing, taking the very nature of a servant, being made in human likeness" (verses 6,7).

Foundationally, the fact that Christ was said by Paul to be "in very nature God" is extremely significant. Christ in His essential being is and *always has been* eternal God—just as much as the Father and the Holy Spirit. The word "nature" in the Greek connotes that which is intrinsic and essential to a thing.[9] In the present context, the word indicates that in becoming a man, Christ did not surrender His essential deity (divine nature), but rather took upon Himself the form of a servant—a human nature.

The word "being" (in the phrase "*being* in very nature God") carries the idea of *continued existence* as God.[10] The present participle indicates that Christ, in eternity past and continuing into the present moment, has forever existed in the form of God, outwardly manifesting His divine attributes. This is the One who was conceived in the womb of Mary and took upon Himself full humanity—all the while retaining His full deity.

If Christ retained His full deity in the incarnation, then in what sense did He "make himself nothing"? I believe Christ's "making Himself nothing" involves three basic issues: the veiling of His preincarnate glory, a voluntary nonuse of some of His attributes on some occasions, and the condescension involved in taking on the likeness of men.

Veiling of preincarnate glory. It was necessary for Christ to veil the *outer appearance* of God in order to take upon Himself the form of man.[11] However, Christ never *surrendered* His glory (recall that on the Mount of Transfiguration Jesus allowed His intrinsic glory to shine forth, illuminating the whole mountainside—Matthew 17). Rather, Jesus simply *veiled* His glory in order to dwell among mortal men.

Had Christ *not* veiled His preincarnate glory, humankind would not have been able to behold Him. It would have been the same as when the apostle John beheld the exalted Christ in His glory and said, "I fell at His feet as though dead" (Revelation 1:17), or as when Isaiah beheld the glory of Christ in His vision in the temple and said, "Woe to me! I am ruined!" (Isaiah 6:5; see John 12:41).

Voluntary nonuse of some divine attributes. Second, Christ's "making Himself nothing" involved His submission to a voluntary nonuse of some of His divine attributes on *some* occasions in order for Him to accomplish His objectives. Christ could never have actually *surrendered* any of His attributes, for then He would have ceased to be God. But He could (and did) voluntarily cease using some of them during His time on earth in order to live among men and their limitations (see, for example, Matthew 24:36).

It is critical to recognize that during His three-year ministry, Jesus did in fact exercise the divine attributes of *omniscience* (He was all-knowing—John 2:24; 16:30), *omnipresence* (He was everywhere present—John 1:48), and *omnipotence* (He was all-powerful, as evidenced by miracles such as raising people from the dead—John 11). Hence, whatever limitations Christ may have suffered when He "made himself nothing" (Philippians 2:7), He did not subtract one divine attribute or in any sense make Himself less than God.

The question that arises at this point is, *Why* was it necessary that Jesus choose not to use some of His divine attributes on some occasions? It would seem that He did this in keeping with His purpose of genuinely living among human beings and their limitations. He does not seem to have ever used the divine attributes *on His own behalf,* though certainly His attributes were gloriously displayed in the many miracles He performed.

As we examine the scriptural testimony, it seems clear that Christ never used His omniscience (all-knowingness) to make His own human path easier. He suffered all the inconveniences of living in biblical times even though in His divine omniscience He had full knowledge of every human device that would ever be conceived of for human comfort.[12]

Nor did Christ use His omnipotence (the quality of being all-powerful) to make His path easier. Though Jesus as God could have just willed himself from Bethany to Jerusalem and He would have been instantly there, He instead traveled by foot like every other human and experienced fatigue in the process. "In a word, He restricted the benefits of His attributes as they pertained to His walk on earth and voluntarily chose not to use His powers to lift Himself above ordinary human limitations."[13]

Condescension of becoming a man. Third, and most important, Christ's "making Himself nothing" involved the condescension of taking on the *likeness* (literally "form" or "appearance") of men—that is, unglorified humanity—and taking on the *form* (that is, the "very essence" or "very nature") of a bondservant. Christ was thus truly human. This humanity was one that was subject to temptation, distress, weakness, pain, sorrow, and limitation. Yet at the same time it must be noted that the word "likeness" suggests *similarity but difference.* Though His humanity was genuine, He was different from all other humans in that He was sinless.[14] Nevertheless, becoming a man represented a great *condescension* on the part of Christ.

The incarnation hence involved a gaining of *human* attributes and not a giving up of *divine* attributes. That this is meant by Paul is clear in his affirmation that in the incarnation Christ was "taking the very nature of a servant," "being made in human likeness," and "being found in appearance as a man" (Philippians 2:7,8). As theologian J. I. Packer put it, "He was no less God then [in the incarnation] than before; but He had begun to be man. He was not now God *minus* some elements of His deity, but God *plus* all that He had made His own by taking manhood to Himself."[15]

The Union of Christ's Human and Divine Natures

Though Jesus in the incarnation had both a human and a divine nature, He was only one Person, as indicated by His consistent use of "I," "me," and "mine" in reference to Himself. Jesus never used the words "us," "we," or "ours" in reference to His human-divine Person. The divine nature of Christ never carried on a verbal conversation with His human nature. But the Father, who shared the same divine nature, *did* converse with the Son.

The Son of God, who before the incarnation was one in person *and* nature (wholly divine), became (in the incarnation) two in nature—divine *and* human—while remaining one Person. The eternal Son of God, who had already been a Person for all eternity past, joined Himself not with a human *person* but with a human *nature* at the incarnation. Jesus did not become two persons when He attained two natures. In other words, at the virgin conception, Christ did not at that time acquire personhood, for He *already* was a Person. He simply took upon Himself a human nature.

Moreover, it is important to understand that at the incarnation the Person of Christ became *forever after* wedded to a human nature. He did not discard His humanity or any part of it at His death, resurrection, or ascension (see 1 Timothy 2:5).

Seemingly contradictory qualities. One of the most complex aspects of the relationship of Christ's two natures is that, while the attributes of one nature are never attributed to the other, the attributes of both natures are properly attributed to His one Person. Thus Christ at the same moment in time had what seem to be contradictory qualities. He was finite and yet infinite, weak and yet omnipotent, increasing in knowledge and yet omniscient, limited to being in one place at one time and yet omnipresent. In the incarnation, the Person of Christ is the partaker of the attributes of *both* natures, so that whatever may be affirmed of either nature—human or divine—may be affirmed of the *one* Person.

Though Christ sometimes operated in the sphere of His humanity and in other cases in the sphere of His deity, in all cases what He did and what He was could be attributed to His one Person. Thus, though Christ in His human nature knew hunger (Luke 4:2), weariness (John 4:6), and the need for sleep (Luke 8:23), just as Christ in His divine nature was omniscient (John 2:24), omnipresent (John 1:48), and omnipotent (John 11), *all of this was experienced by the one Person of Jesus Christ.*

The relation of the human and divine natures. How could two different natures—one infinite and one finite—exist within one Person? As one theologian asked, "Would not one nature be dominated by the other? Would not each nature have to surrender some of its qualities in order for each to coexist beside each other? Could Jesus Christ be truly God and truly man at the same time?"[16]

The answer is that in the one Person of Christ the two natures are united without mixture and without loss of any essential attributes, and the two natures maintain their distinct identity without transfer of any property or attribute of one nature to the other.[17] As theologian Robert Lightner put it:

> In the union of the human and divine in Christ each of the natures retained its own attributes. Deity did not permeate humanity, nor did humanity become absorbed into deity. The two natures retain their complete identity even though they have been joined together in a personal union. Christ is thus theanthropic (God-man) in person. Embracing perfect humanity made Him no less God, and retaining His undiminished deity did not make Him less human.[18]

> In the joining of the human and divine natures in the one person of Christ, it is critical to recognize that there was no mixture to form a third compound nature. The human nature always remains human, and the divine nature always remains divine. To rob the divine nature of God of a single attribute would destroy His deity, and to rob man of a single human attribute would result in destruction of a true humanity. It is for this reason that the two natures of Christ cannot lose or transfer a single attribute.[19]

By virtue of the divine attribute of immutability (which says that God cannot change), we may rightly argue that it would have been virtually impossible for Christ's divine nature to alter or change (James 1:17; Hebrews 13:8), or to merge with finite humanity, as Stephen Robinson and other Mormons maintain.[20] To do so would have required that God change His very nature.

Why Did Jesus Come?

Jesus taught that His mission in being born as a man was to provide a substitutionary atonement on the cross. By so doing, He provided a *total* salvation ("eternal life") for human beings which they had no hope of procuring for themselves. (I say "total" in contrast to the Mormon view, which adds human works to salvation.)

Jesus affirmed that it was for the very purpose of dying that He came into the world (John 12:27). Moreover, He perceived His death as being a sacrificial offering for the sins of humanity (He said His blood "is poured out for many for the forgiveness of sins"—Matthew 26:26-28). Jesus took His sacrificial mission with utmost seriousness, for He knew that without Him, humanity would certainly perish (John 3:16-18) and spend eternity apart from God in a place of great suffering (Matthew 10:28; 11:23,24; 23:33; 25:41; Luke 16:22-28).

Jesus therefore described His mission this way: "The Son of Man did not come to be served, but to serve, and to give his life a ransom for many" (Matthew 20:28 KJV). "The Son of Man came to seek and to save what was lost" (Luke 19:10). Indeed, "God did not send his Son into the world to condemn the world, but to save the world through him" (John 3:17).

In John 10, Jesus compares Himself to a good shepherd who not only gives His life to save the sheep (John 10:11) but lays His life down of His own accord (John 10:18). This is precisely what Jesus did at the cross (Matthew 26:53): He laid His life down to atone for the sins of humanity.

The Words of the Biblical Jesus

Jesus' teachings—whether dealing with salvation, the kingdom of God, or ethics—were always presented as being ultimate and final. He never wavered in this. He unflinchingly placed His teachings above those of Moses and the prophets—and in a Jewish culture at that!

The Lord Jesus always spoke in His own authority. He never said, "Thus saith the Lord..." as did the prophets; He always said, "Verily, verily, *I say* unto you...." He never retracted anything He said, never guessed or spoke with uncertainty, never made revisions, never contradicted Himself, and never apologized for what He said. He even asserted that "heaven and earth will pass away, but my words will never pass away" (Mark 13:31), hence elevating His words directly to the realm of heaven.

Jesus' teachings had a profound effect on people. His listeners often seemed to surmise that these were not the words of an ordinary man. When Jesus taught in Capernaum on the Sabbath, the people "were amazed at his teaching, because his message had authority" (Luke 4:32). After the Sermon on the Mount, "the crowds were amazed at his teaching, because he taught as one who had authority, and not as their teachers of the law" (Matthew 7:28,29). When some Jewish leaders asked the temple guards why they hadn't arrested Jesus when He spoke, they responded, "No one ever spoke the way this man does" (John 7:46).

One cannot read the Gospels long before recognizing that Jesus regarded Himself and His message as inseparable. The reason Jesus' teachings had ultimate authority was because He was (is) God. The words of Jesus were the very words of God! Indeed, what mere *human* teacher would dare speak words like the following to his peers?

- If anyone is thirsty, let him come to me and drink. Whoever believes in me, as the Scripture has said, streams of living water will flow from within him (John 7:37,38).

- Peace I leave with you; my peace I give to you. I do not give to you as the world does (John 14:27).

- I am the bread of life. He who comes to me will never go hungry, and he who believes in me will never be thirsty (John 6:35).

- Come to Me, all you who labor and are heavy laden, and I will give you rest (Matthew 11:28 NKJV).

- I have come that they may have life, and that they may have it more abundantly (John 10:10 NKJV).

To give His words the stamp of divine authority, Jesus often performed a miracle immediately following a teaching. For example, after telling the paralytic that his sins were forgiven, Jesus healed him to prove He had the divine authority to forgive sins (Mark 2:1-12). After telling Martha that He was "the resurrection and the life," He raised her brother Lazarus from the dead, thereby proving the veracity and authority of His words (John 11:1-44). After rebuking the disciples in the boat for having too little faith, He stilled a raging storm to show they had good reason to place their faith in Him (Matthew 8:23-27).

The Works of the Biblical Jesus

John's Gospel always refers to the miracles of Jesus as "signs." This word emphasizes the *significance* of the action rather than the marvel itself (John 4:54; 6:14; 9:16). These signs were strategically performed by Jesus to *signify* His true identity and glory.

Recall that when John the Baptist was in prison, he sent his disciples to ask Jesus, "Are you the one who was to come, or should we expect someone else?" (Matthew 11:2,3). Jesus replied to them, "Go back and report to John what you hear and see: The blind receive sight, the lame walk, those who have leprosy are cured, the deaf hear, the dead are raised, and the good news is preached to the poor" (Matthew 11:4,5). By saying this, Jesus was reminding John that these signs were precisely what was predicted of the Messiah (Isaiah 29:18-21; 35:5,6; 61:1).

John's Gospel tells us that Jesus' signs were performed in the presence of His disciples to ensure that there was adequate *witness* to the events that transpired (John 20:30). "Witness" is a pivotal concept in this Gospel. The word occurs some 47 times in this Gospel, and the reason for this is clear: *The signs performed by Jesus were thoroughly attested.* There were *many* witnesses. Therefore, the signs cannot be simply dismissed or explained away! John's Gospel has presented *indisputable evidence* in the signs that Jesus is the Christ and the Son of God.

It is not our goal here to examine every miracle or "sign" performed by Jesus. Suffice it to say that in the process of proving His identity, Jesus demonstrated His control of nature (such as calming a storm—Matthew 8:23-27), He healed many people of bodily afflictions (such as an invalid—John 5:1-15), and He raised people from the dead (such as Lazarus—John 11). These are things that mere mortals cannot do.

John's Gospel tells us that "Jesus did many other miraculous signs in the presence of his disciples, which are not recorded in this book. But these are written that you may believe that Jesus is the Christ, the Son of God, and that by believing you may have life in his name" (John 20:30,31). In each miracle Jesus performed—whether it involved controlling the realm of nature, healing people of physical afflictions, or raising people from the dead—He distinguished Himself from weak and mortal man and attested to His true identity as Messiah-God.

The Death and Resurrection of Jesus Christ

After Jesus died on the cross, His body was buried in accordance with Jewish burial customs. He was wrapped in a linen cloth, and about a hundred pounds of aromatic spices—mixed together to form a gummy substance—were applied to the wrappings of cloth around His body.

After His body was placed in a solid rock tomb, an extremely large stone was rolled by means of levers against the entrance. This stone would have weighed up to four tons

(8000 pounds). It is not a stone that would have been easily moved by human beings.

Roman guards were then stationed at the tomb. These strictly disciplined men were highly motivated in their duties. Fear of cruel punishment by the Roman government produced flawless attention to duty, especially in the night watches. These Roman guards would have affixed the Roman seal on the tomb, a stamp representing Rome's sovereign power and authority.

All this makes the situation at the tomb following Christ's resurrection highly significant. The Roman seal had been broken, an offense that carried an automatic penalty of crucifixion upside down for the person who did it. Moreover, the large stone was moved a substantial distance from the entrance, as if it had been picked up like a pebble and plucked out of the way. The Roman guards had also fled. Since the penalty in Rome for a guard leaving his position was death, we can assume they must have had a substantial reason for fleeing!

We learn the details of what happened in Matthew 28:1-6:

> After the Sabbath, at dawn on the first day of the week, Mary Magdalene and the other Mary went to look at the tomb. There was a violent earthquake, for an angel of the Lord came down from heaven and, going to the tomb, rolled back the stone and sat on it.

> His appearance was like lightning, and his clothes were white as snow. The guards were so afraid of him that they shook and became like dead men. The angel said to the women, "Do not be afraid, for I know that you are looking for Jesus, who was crucified. He is not here; he has risen, just as he said."

Jesus Christ rose bodily from the dead. The biblical evidence for this is abundant:

- The tomb was empty, since the physical body in it had been raised and had departed (Luke 24:3).

- The risen Jesus showed His disciples "his hands and side" (John 20:20; cf. Luke 24:39,40).

- He ate on four different occasions (cf. Luke 24:41-43; John 21:10-14; Acts 10:41).

- He bodily appeared to more than 500 people at the same time (1 Corinthians 15:6).

- He made numerous other appearances to credible witnesses over a period of 40 days (Acts 1:3).

From an evidentiary viewpoint, the resurrection of Jesus Christ is one of the best-attested events of all history.[21] And, of great importance to the present study, the resurrection confirmed the truth of all that Jesus said while He was on earth (Matthew 28:6), including the fact that He is *eternal* God (John 8:58) and that He accomplished a total and complete salvation for humankind (John 19:30).

The Mormon View of Jesus Christ

Stephen Robinson in the recent book *How Wide the Divide?* argues that the only authoritative Scriptures from which we should derive (and critique!) Mormon doctrines (such as the doctrine of Christ) are the Bible, the Book of Mormon, *Doctrine and Covenants,* and *The Pearl of Great Price.* It is interesting to observe, however, that many Mormons disagree with Robinson on this. For example, the 1992 edition of the LDS book *Gospel Principles* tells us: "In addition to these four books of scripture, *the inspired words of our living prophets become scripture to us.* Their words come to us through conferences, Church publications, and instructions to local priesthood leaders."[22] (See Chapter 1.)

While most Latter-day Saints probably did not consider the sermons of Mormon prophets to be Scripture, Brigham

Young nevertheless once said, "I have never yet preached a sermon and sent it out to the children of men, that they may not call Scripture."[23] He also said, "I say now, when they [my sermons] are copied and approved by me they are as good Scripture as is couched in this Bible, and if you want to read revelation read the sayings of him who knows the mind of God."[24]

This being the case, the deviant teachings of the Mormon prophets are not so easily dismissed as Robinson would have it. If indeed the words of the Mormon prophets have been considered "Scripture" by Mormons, then their words about Jesus Christ are fair game for biblical scrutiny. In what follows, I shall deal with Mormon Christology as represented both by Mormon Scriptures *and* the teachings of Mormon prophets and leaders.

To begin, Mormon apologist Gilbert W. Scharffs has claimed that "Latter-day Saints are Christians because they emphatically believe in Christ, use His name in their official church title, and believe in the Bible and the Book of Mormon, which testify repeatedly of the reality of Christ and the truth of His teachings....Mormons are Christians. Christians are those who accept Christ as their Savior."[25]

But do Mormons believe in the Jesus of the *Bible*? According to official Mormon teaching, Jesus Christ was "begotten" or *procreated* as a spirit-child of the Father (Elohim) and a "Heavenly Mother." Jesus, as a spirit-son, then progressed in the spirit world until he became a God.[26] Christ, "by obedience and devotion to the truth...attained that pinnacle of intelligence which ranked Him as a God."[27]

In the Mormon volume *The Life and Teaching of Jesus and His Apostles*, we read of Jesus:

> He was the birthright son, and he retained that birthright by his strict obedience. Through the aeons and ages of premortality, he advanced and progressed until, as Abraham described it, he stood as one "like unto God" [Abr. 3:24]. "Our Savior was a God before he was born into this world."[28]

Prior to his incarnation, Jesus was the Jehovah of the Old Testament.[29] The Mormon *Bible Dictionary* says that "Jehovah is the premortal Jesus Christ."[30] However, Jehovah (Jesus) is viewed as being distinct from Elohim, who is the Father and is the greater of the two.

Now while Mormons teach that the Heavenly Father (Elohim) and the Heavenly Mother had *many* spirit children,[31] Jesus was allegedly the first and highest of their spirit children. The Church's official *Gospel Principles* tells us, "The first spirit born to our heavenly parents was Jesus Christ."[32] *Doctrine and Covenants* affirms that "Christ, the Firstborn, was the mightiest of all the spirit children of the Father."[33] James E. Talmage notes further that "among the spirit-children of Elohim the firstborn was and is Jehovah or Jesus Christ to whom all others are juniors."[34] Mormons commonly refer to Jesus as "our elder brother."

Of course, this ultimately means that Jesus Christ is not truly unique. The only real difference between Jesus and us is that Jesus was the *firstborn* of Elohim's children, whereas we, in our alleged preexistence, were "born" later. It appears, then, that the important distinction between Jesus (Jehovah) and God's other premortal offspring is merely one of *degree*, not of *kind*.[35]

Related to all this is the fact that, in Mormon theology, Lucifer is the spirit-brother of Jesus. "As for the Devil and his fellow spirits, they are brothers to man and also to Jesus and sons and daughters of God in the same sense that we are."[36]

Lucifer, Jesus' spirit-brother, allegedly did not like it when Jesus was appointed to be the Savior of the world. "The appointment of Jesus to be the Savior of the world was contested by one of the other sons of God. He was called Lucifer, son of the morning. Haughty, ambitious, and covetous of power and glory, this spirit-brother of Jesus desperately tried to become the Savior of mankind."[37]

According to Mormonism, Lucifer offered to go to earth and be the Savior. But he wanted to force everyone to be saved and do everything himself. Because Jesus desired to give man "free agency" (so man could prove his worthiness for exaltation), the Father chose Jesus' plan over Lucifer's. This allegedly made Lucifer angry, and he rebelled against his Father's preferential treatment. He persuaded one-third of the existing spirits in heaven to take sides and rebel also. This, in Mormonism, is known as "the war in heaven," and is the reason that group was cast out of heaven to become the devil and his demons.[38]

In any event, Mormons teach that when it came time for Jesus to be born on earth as the "Savior," He was begotten through sexual relations between a flesh-and-bone Heavenly Father and Mary—the only earthly offspring so conceived. Mormon authorities argue that Jesus as the "Son" of God was "begotten" of the Father, and these terms are to be taken *literally*. As Mormon theologian Bruce McConkie put it, "Christ was begotten by an Immortal Father in the same way that mortal men are begotten by mortal fathers."[39]

> God the Father is a perfected, glorified, holy man, an immortal Personage. And Christ was born into the world as the literal Son of this Holy Being; he was born in the same personal, real and literal sense that any mortal son is born to a mortal father. There is nothing figurative about his paternity; he was begotten, conceived, and born in the normal and natural course of events, for he is the Son of God, and that designation means what it says.[40]

Lest anyone suppose that this is the speculative viewpoint of a few Mormon leaders, consider the following.

Mormon apostle Orson Pratt said that "the fleshly body of Jesus required a Mother as well as a Father. Therefore, the Father and Mother of Jesus, according to the flesh, must have been associated together in the capacity of Husband and Wife: hence the Virgin Mary must have been, for the time being, the lawful wife of God the Father."[41]

Mormon apostle James E. Talmage likewise stated that "Jesus Christ is the Son of Elohim both as spiritual and bodily offspring; that is to say, Elohim is literally the Father of the spirit of Jesus Christ and also of the body in which Jesus Christ performed His mission in the flesh."[42]

Mormon president Ezra Taft Benson agreed:

> [There is] no question as to the paternity of Jesus Christ. God was the Father of Jesus' mortal tabernacle, and Mary, a mortal woman, was His mother.... The Church of Jesus Christ of Latter-day Saints proclaims that Jesus Christ is the Son of God in the most literal sense. The body in which He performed His mission in the flesh was sired by that same Holy Being we worship as God, our Eternal Father. Jesus was not the son of Joseph, nor was He begotten by him.... He was the Only Begotten Son of our Heavenly Father in the flesh—the only child whose mortal body was begotten by our Heavenly Father.[43]

Hence, according to Mormon doctrine, Jesus was begotten not by the Holy Spirit (though, we are told by Stephen Robinson, the Holy Spirit was involved in some mysterious way)[44] but by the Father (Elohim). *Doctrines of Salvation* affirms that "Christ is not the Son of the Holy Ghost, but of the Father."[45]

Such a doctrine naturally raises questions about the virginity of Mary. Mormon prophet Brigham Young claimed that Mary had more than one husband: "The man Joseph, the husband of Mary, did not, that we know of, have more than one wife, but Mary, the wife of Joseph, had another husband—that is, God the Father."[46]

Surprisingly, Mormon theologians maintain that even though the Father had sexual relations with Mary, she *remained* a virgin. Against every conventional understanding of the term, Bruce McConkie fancifully argues that a "virgin" is a woman who has had no sexual relations with a *mortal* man. Because God the Father was an *immortal* man, Mary remained a virgin after having relations with him. He says:

"Our Lord is the only mortal person ever born to a virgin, because he is the only person who ever had an immortal Father."[47]

At one time Mormon Church leaders taught that Jesus too had a marriage relationship. In fact, we are told, Jesus was married to both Mary and Martha; he was a *polygamist*. Early Mormon apostle Orson Hyde explains it this way:

> It will be borne in mind that once on a time, there was a marriage in Cana of Galilee; and on a careful reading of that transaction, it will be discovered that no less a person than Jesus Christ was married on that occasion. If he was never married, his intimacy with Mary and Martha, and the other Mary also whom Jesus loved, must have been highly unbecoming and improper to say the best of it.[48]

This is most certainly related to the Mormon requirement for exaltation (i.e., attaining the goal of godhood) outlined in *Doctrine and Covenants* section 132—that is, there can be no exaltation to the fullness of the blessings of the celestial kingdom outside of the marriage relation.[49] Apparently this must have applied even to Jesus.

Problems with the Mormon View

There are obviously many problems with the Mormon view of Jesus Christ. Space prohibits a detailed critique of every aspect of Mormon Christology, but below is a summary critique of the more serious problems which demonstrate just how wide the divide is between Mormonism and Christianity.

Jesus Was Not Procreated

Mormons teach that Jesus was literally procreated by ("begotten of") the Father—both spiritually and physically. As James Talmage put it, "Jesus Christ is the Son of Elohim both as spiritual and bodily offspring; that is to say, Elohim is literally the Father of the spirit of Jesus Christ and also of the body in which Jesus Christ performed His mission in the flesh."[50]

Many Mormons, including Stephen Robinson,[51] appeal to Psalm 2:7 in an attempt to prove that Jesus was begotten of the Father. However, Acts 13:33,34 makes such a view impossible, for this passage teaches that Jesus' resurrection from the dead by the Father *is a fulfillment* of the statement in Psalm 2:7, "You are my Son; today I have become your Father."[52] A basic interpretive principle is that *Scripture interprets Scripture*. The best way to find out what Psalm 2:7 means is to let Scripture *tell* us what it means. And according to Acts 13:33,34 the verse deals not with the Father's alleged procreation of Jesus but rather Jesus' resurrection from the dead.

Another verse Mormons appeal to in support of the idea that Jesus is "begotten" of the Father is John 3:16, which in the King James Version reads: "For God so loved the world that he gave his *only begotten Son*, that whosoever believeth in him should not perish, but have everlasting life" (emphasis added). The New International Version translates "only begotten" as "one and only," and indeed, this is what the original Greek communicates. The Greek word *monogenes* means "unique" or "one of a kind." It does not communicate procreation or derivation. Jesus is the *unique* or *one and only* "Son of God" in the sense that He has the same nature as the Father—a *divine* nature.

While all evangelicals hold that Jesus was eternally God, most evangelicals believe that Jesus was also *eternally* the Son of God. Ancient Semitics and Orientals used the phrase "son of…" to indicate likeness or sameness of nature and equality of being.[53] Hence, when Jesus claimed to be the Son of God, His Jewish contemporaries fully understood that He was making a claim to be God in an unqualified sense (John 5:18).[54] This is why, when Jesus claimed to be the Son of God, the Jews insisted: "We have a law, and according to that law he [Christ] must die, because he claimed to be the Son of God" (John 19:7). Recognizing that Jesus was identifying Himself as God, the Jews wanted to put Him to death for committing blasphemy.

Evidence for Christ's eternal Sonship is found in the fact that He is represented as *already being* the Son of God before His human birth in Bethlehem (John 3:16,17). Hebrews 1:2 says God created the universe *through* his "Son"—implying that Christ was the Son of God *prior* to the Creation. Moreover, Christ *as the Son* is explicitly said to have existed "before all things" (Colossians 1:17; compare with verses 13,14). Jesus Himself, speaking as the Son of God (John 8:54-56), asserts His eternal preexistence before Abraham (verse 58).[55]

Aside from the issue of the eternal Sonship of Christ, it is highly revealing that even the Book of Mormon points to the eternal nature of Jesus Christ. Second Nephi attributes to Jesus the declaration: "Behold, I am God.... I am the same yesterday, today, and forever.... I, the Lord your God, have created all men.... I am the same yesterday, today, and forever" (27:23; 29:7,9).

Mosiah 3:5,8 likewise says:

> For behold, the time cometh, and is not far distant, that with power, the Lord Omnipotent who reigneth, *who was, and is from all eternity to all eternity,* shall come down from heaven among the children of men, and shall dwell in a tabernacle of clay, and shall go forth amongst men, working mighty miracles, such as healing the sick, raising the dead, causing the lame to walk, the blind to receive their sight, and the deaf to hear, and curing all manner of diseases.... *And he shall be called Jesus Christ,* the Son of God, the Father of heaven and earth, the Creator of all things from the beginning; and his mother shall be called Mary (italics added).

How are we to respond to the Mormon claim that since Jesus is called the "firstborn," he is literally the first son born to Elohim, "the mightiest of all the spirit children of the Father"?[56] In addition to its literal sense, Greek scholars agree that the word firstborn (Greek *prototokos*) can mean "first in rank, preeminent one, heir."[57] The word carries the idea of positional preeminence and supremacy. Christ is the "firstborn" not in the sense that he is the first spirit-son born to Elohim, as Mormons hold, but in the sense that He is positionally preeminent over creation and is supreme over all things.[58] The backdrop is that among the ancient Hebrews, the word *firstborn* referred to the son in the family who was in the preeminent position, regardless of whether or not that son was literally the first son born to the parents. This "firstborn" son would not only be the preeminent one in the family, but he would also be the "heir" to a double portion of the family inheritance.

Addressing what the term "firstborn" came to mean to those living in biblical times, scholar F. F. Bruce comments:

> The word firstborn had long since ceased to be used exclusively in its literal sense, just as *prime* (from the Latin word *primus*—"first") with us. The Prime Minister is not the first minister we have had; he is the most preeminent.... Similarly, *firstborn* came to denote [among the ancients] not priority in time but preeminence in rank.[59]

This meaning of "firstborn" is illustrated in the life of David. David was the youngest (*last*-born) son of Jesse. Nevertheless, Psalm 89:27 says of him, "Also I will make him My firstborn, the highest of the kings of the earth" (NKJV). Though David was the *last* son born into Jesse's family, David is called the "firstborn" because of the preeminent position God was placing him in.[60]

We find another example of this meaning of "firstborn" in comparing Genesis 41:50,51 with Jeremiah 31:9. Manasseh was actually the first son born to Joseph, and Ephraim was born to Joseph some time later. Nevertheless, Ephraim is called the "firstborn" in Jeremiah 31:9 because of his preeminent position.[61] He was not *born* first, but he was the *firstborn* because of his preeminence.

Likewise, Ishmael was 13 years older than Isaac, but it was Isaac who became the firstborn. Further, though Esau was born first, Jacob became the firstborn.[62] Clearly, the term "firstborn" here refers not to the first one born but to the preeminent one in the family. This is the sense it carries in Colossians 1, where Christ is portrayed as preeminent over all creation (as the "firstborn"), because He is also the creator of all things (Colossians 1:16). By divine right, all of creation belongs to Him, and He is hence preeminent over it.

Jesus Is Not the Spirit-Brother of Lucifer

The Bible, of course, does *not* teach that Jesus Christ was the spirit-brother of Lucifer (or the spirit-brother of all human beings). Colossians 1:16 specifically tells us that the entire angelic realm—including the angel Lucifer—was created by Jesus Christ: "For by Him all things were created that are in heaven and that are on earth, visible and invisible, whether thrones or dominions or principalities or powers. All things were created through Him and for Him" (NKJV). The words "thrones," "dominions," "principalities," and "powers" were words used by rabbinical Jews in biblical times to describe different orders of *angels* (see Romans 8:38; Ephesians 1:21; 3:10; 6:12; Colossians 2:10,15). Apparently there was a heresy flourishing in Colosse (which Paul addressed) that involved the worship of angels. In the process of worshiping angels, Christ had been degraded. In order to correct this grave error, Paul emphasizes in this verse that Christ is the One who created all things—*including all the angels*—and hence He is supreme and is *alone* worthy to be worshiped.[63]

We know from Scripture that Lucifer is a created angelic being—a "cherub" (Ezekiel 28:13-19; cf. Isaiah 14:12-15). Since Lucifer was an angel, and since Christ created all the angels, it is very clear that Christ is not a "spirit-brother" of Lucifer. Christ is not of the created realm; rather, He Himself is the creator. Lucifer and Christ are of two entirely different classes—*creature* and *creator*.

We see Christ's distinction from the angels (and *all other* creatures) stressed throughout Scripture. For example, the whole focus of the first three chapters of the book of Hebrews is to demonstrate the superiority of Jesus Christ, including His superiority over the *prophets* (1:1-4), over the *angels* (1:5–2:18), and over *Moses* (3:1-6).[64] How is this superiority demonstrated? Christ is shown to be God's ultimate revelation (verse 1); He is the creator and sustainer of the universe (verses 2,3); and He has the very nature of God (verse 3). None of these things could be said of mere creatures—prophets, angels, or Moses.

Then, in Hebrews 1:6, we are specifically told that, far from being in the same class as angels, Christ is worshiped (*proskuneo*) *by* the angels. This is exactly the same word used of worshiping God the Father (see Revelation 4, 5). Mark 3:11 indicates that even the demons (fallen angels) fell down before Jesus when they saw Him and addressed Him as the Son of God.[65]

Jesus Is Both Jehovah and Elohim

In the recent book *How Wide the Divide?* Stephen Robinson claims, "Latter-day Saints believe that *before* the incarnation of Jesus—during the Old Testament period—the God described in Scripture as Jehovah or Yahweh was God the Son (Jesus Christ), at that time still a spirit who had not yet entered into the flesh."[66] What this book fails to point out is that Mormons believe that while Jesus was Jehovah in the Old Testament, the Father was Elohim in the Old Testament. In other words, Jehovah and Elohim are viewed as two distinct Gods, with Elohim being the greater of the two. As the Mormon *Bible Dictionary* put it:

> When one speaks of God, it is generally the Father who is referred to; that is, *Elohim*. All mankind are his children. The personage known as *Jehovah* in Old Testament times, and who is usually identified in the Old Testament as LORD (in capital letters), is the Son, known as Jesus Christ, and who is also a God...he being the eldest of the spirit children of Elohim.[67]

This Mormon doctrine can easily be debunked by verses in the Bible which demonstrate that Elohim and Jehovah are one and the same God. For example, in Genesis 27:20 Isaac tells his son, "The LORD [*Jehovah*] your God [*Elohim*] gave me success" (inserts added).

Likewise, the Almighty Himself declares in Exodus 3:6,7: "'I am the God [*Elohim*] of your father, the God [*Elohim*] of Abraham, the God [*Elohim*] of Isaac and the God [*Elohim*] of Jacob.' At this, Moses hid his face, because he was afraid to look at God [*Elohim*]. The LORD [*Jehovah*] said, 'I have indeed seen the misery of my people in Egypt. I have heard them crying out because of their slave drivers, and I am concerned about their suffering.'" Again, Elohim and Jehovah are seen to be the same God.

Similarly, Jeremiah 32:18 says: "You show love to thousands but bring the punishment for the fathers' sins into the laps of their children after them. O great and powerful God [*Elohim*], whose name is the LORD [*Jehovah*] Almighty."

In keeping with the above, we read in Deuteronomy 6:4: "Hear, O Israel: The LORD our God, the LORD is one." This was a Jewish affirmation of faith in ancient days known as the *Shema*. Notice how Jehovah and Elohim are equated in this verse: "Hear, O Israel: The LORD [*Jehovah*] our God [*Elohim*], the LORD [*Jehovah*] is one." Clearly there is no way to make this verse fit with the Mormon idea that Elohim is the Father and Jehovah is Jesus.

Further, there are clear passages in the Bible where Jesus is individually referred to as Elohim, thereby disproving the Mormon claim that only the Father is Elohim and Jesus is Jehovah. For example, we read in Isaiah 40:3: "A voice of one calling: 'In the desert prepare the way for the LORD [*Jehovah*]; make straight in the wilderness a highway for our God [*Elohim*].'" This entire verse was written in reference to the future ministry of Christ, according to John 1:23, and represents one of the strongest affirmations of Christ's deity in the Old Testament. Within the confines of a single verse Christ is called both Jehovah and Elohim.

Christ is also referred to as Elohim in Isaiah 9:6: "For to us a child is born, to us a son is given, and the government will be on his shoulders. And he will be called Wonderful Counselor, Mighty God [*Elohim*], Everlasting Father, Prince of Peace."

Elohim—a common name for God in the Old Testament (used about 2570 times)—literally means "Strong One." Elohim is portrayed in the Old Testament as the powerful and sovereign governor of the universe, ruling over the affairs of humankind. As related to God's sovereignty, the word *Elohim* is used to describe Him as the "God of all the earth" (Isaiah 54:5), the "God of all mankind" (Jeremiah 32:27), the "God of heaven" (Nehemiah 2:4), and the "God of gods and Lord of lords" (Deuteronomy 10:17).[68] It is therefore highly significant that this name is used of Jesus Christ (Isaiah 9:6; 40:3).

The "Greater-in-Nature" Question

In John 14:28 Jesus said to the disciples, "If you loved me, you would be glad that I am going to the Father, for the Father is greater than I." Many Mormons, such as Stephen Robinson, argue that this verse adds further support to the Mormon contention that Jesus and the Father are not "eternally co-equal."

In response, we must point out that Jesus in John 14:28 is not speaking about His nature or His essential being (Christ had earlier said "I and the Father are one" in this regard—John 10:30), but is rather speaking of His lowly position in the incarnation.[69] Simply put, Christ is "equal" to the Father in regard to His Godhood but "inferior" to the Father in regard to His manhood. The Father was seated upon the throne of highest majesty in heaven; the brightness of His glory was uneclipsed as He was surrounded by hosts of holy beings perpetually worshiping Him with uninterrupted praise. Far different was it with His incarnate Son—despised and rejected of men, surrounded by implacable enemies, and soon to be nailed to a criminal's cross. It is from *this* perspective that Jesus could say that the Father is "greater" than He is.

It is important to recognize the distinction between the Greek words for "greater" (*meizon*) and "better" (*kreitton*).[70] Jesus specifically said "the Father is *greater* than I," not "the Father is *better* than I." The word "greater" is used to point to the Father's greater *position* (in heaven), not a greater *nature.* (Had the word "better" been used, this would indicate that the Father has a better nature than Jesus.) But this word is used in Hebrews 1:4 in regard to Jesus' superiority over the angels. The word "better" in this verse indicates that Jesus is not just higher *positionally* than the angels; rather, He is higher than the angels *in His very nature.* Jesus is different (better) *in kind* and *in nature* from the angels.

This distinction between "greater" and "better" can be illustrated in the President of the United States.[71] The President is in a higher position than the rest of us. Therefore the President is "greater" (*meizon*) than the rest of us. However, the President is still just a human being—and hence he is not "better" (*kreitton*) than the rest of us.

Here is the important point: Jesus did not ever use the word "better" regarding His relationship with the Father, for He is not inferior or lower in nature than the Father. Rather, Jesus used the word "greater," which points to the Father being higher in position. During the time of the incarnation, Jesus functioned in the world of humanity, and this of necessity involved Jesus being positionally lower than the Father.

Jesus' "Oneness" with the Father

In John 10:30 Jesus told a group of Jews, "I and the Father are one." What did Jesus mean by this? Mormons like Stephen Robinson answer by pointing to John 17:21,22, where Jesus prayed to the Father that the disciples "may all be *one,* just as you, Father, are in union with me and I am in union with you, that they also may be in union with us...that they may be *one* just as we are *one*" (italics added).[72] It is of great significance, we are told, that Jesus used the same Greek word for "one" (*hen*) in all of these instances.

Obviously, Mormons say, Jesus was not praying that all of the disciples would become a single entity. Instead, He was praying that they would have *unity of thought and purpose,* just as He and the Father had. James Talmage argues, "The unity of the Godhead was a oneness of perfection in purpose, plan, and action, as the scriptures declare it to be, and not an impossible union of personalities, as generations of false teachers had tried to impress."[73]

Contrary to what Mormons say, the context is *always* determinative in how any given word is to be interpreted in a sentence. The English word *trunk* can refer to the front of an elephant, the back of a car, the bottom of a tree, the middle of a man, or a large storage box. In different contexts, the same word can carry different nuances of meaning. One must keep this in mind in interpreting the Greek word for "one" (*hen*).

While the word *hen* by itself does not have to refer to more than unity of purpose, the context of John 10 is clear that much more than this is meant.[74] How do we know this? The answer is found in how the Jews understood Jesus' affirmation that "I and the Father are one." They immediately picked up stones to put Him to death. They understood Jesus to be claiming to be God in an unqualified sense. Indeed, according to verse 33, the Jews said: "For a good work we do not stone You, but for blasphemy; and because You, being a man, *make Yourself God*" (NKJV, italics added). The penalty for blasphemy, according to Old Testament law, was death by stoning. Notice that Jesus did not say, "Oh, no, you misunderstand. I am only claiming unity of purpose with God." He let their interpretation stand, despite the threat to His life, because their interpretation was exactly what He was intending to communicate.

Related to this issue of "oneness" is the doctrine of the Trinity. Mormons argue that there is no biblical evidence for the evangelical understanding of the Trinity, which says there is one God with three coequal and coeternal Persons who are "one in being."[75]

The Scriptures consistently support the idea that God is one in *essence* (Deuteronomy 6:4; 1 Timothy 2:5), but three in *Persons* (Matthew 28:19; 2 Corinthians 13:14). God has one *nature*, but three *centers of consciousness*. That is, there is only one *what* in God, but there are three *whos*. There is one *it*, but three *"I"s*. This is indeed a mystery, but not a contradiction. It would be contradictory to say that God was only one Person, but also was three Persons, or that God is only one nature, but that He also has three natures. But to declare, as evangelical Christians do, that God is one essence eternally revealed in three distinct Persons is not a contradiction at all.

A grammatical analysis of Matthew 28:19 is highly revealing. The verse says: "Go therefore and make disciples of all the nations, baptizing them in the *name* of *the* Father and *the* Son and *the* Holy Spirit" (emphasis added). The word *name* in Matthew 28:19 is singular in the Greek, indicating that there is one God. But there are three Persons within the Godhead, each with a definite article (indicating distinctness)—*the* Father, *the* Son, and *the* Holy Spirit. The verse does not say "in the *names* [plural] of the Father, Son, and Holy Spirit," nor does it say "in the name of the Father, the name of the Son, and the name of the Holy Spirit." Nor does it say "in the name of Father, Son, and Holy Spirit" (omitting the definite articles). It says "in the *name* [singular, asserting the *oneness* of God] of *the* Father, *the* Son, and *the* Holy Spirit" (each distinct from the others as Persons).

But the context of John 17:21—where Jesus prayed that the disciples may be *one* "just as you [Father] are in me and I am in you"—*is entirely different*. In this context, the Greek word for "one" refers to unity among people in the midst of their diversity. Believers *then as now* had a tendency to be divisive over various issues. Hence Christ prayed for their unity. Among other things, this kind of unity can be expressed in the proper exercise of spiritual gifts among believers (Ephesians 4:3-16) as well as in praying for one another and exhorting one another (2 Corinthians 1:11; Hebrews 10:25).

The Two Natures of Christ

Stephen Robinson in the book *How Wide the Divide?* makes reference to the "unbiblical doctrine of the two natures in Christ, which was added to historic Christianity by the Council of Chalcedon in A.D. 451."[76] While the Chalcedon Creed does teach the doctrine of the two natures of Christ, this creed does not constitute the origin of the doctrine. Contrary to Mormons, this doctrine is not something that is foreign to Scripture; it is derived *directly from its pages.* The doctrine of the two natures of Christ most coherently integrates the two lines of teaching in Scripture that Jesus is *fully God* and *fully human.* Evangelicals believe in this doctrine *on scriptural authority alone.* The Creed is simply a restatement of biblical truth in concise form. (For more on creeds, see Dr. Beckwith's discussion in Chapter 2.)

Throughout Scripture we find constant witness to the fact that the incarnate Christ possessed both a human and a divine nature. Jesus in the incarnation was both a man (Hebrews 2:14) and eternal God (John 8:58). In His human nature Jesus was 30 years old during the time of His ministry (Luke 3:23), but in His divine nature He was eternal (John 1:1,2). In His human nature Jesus was hungry and tired (Matthew 4:2; 8:24; Mark 15:21; John 4:6), but in His divine nature He was omnipotent (Matthew 8:26,27; Colossians 1:17; Hebrews 1:3). In His human nature Jesus had a physical body that was limited to one place at a time, but in His divine nature Jesus was omnipresent (Matthew 28:20). In His human nature Jesus was limited in knowledge (Mark 13:32; Luke 2:52), but in His divine nature He was omniscient (John 2:25; 16:30). In His human nature Jesus died (Luke 23:46; 1 Corinthians 15:3), but in His divine nature He did not die but rather was able to raise Himself from the dead (John 2:19; 10:17,18).

If any "new concepts" about Jesus have been added to Scripture, it is done not by the creeds but rather by Joseph Smith and other Mormon leaders who transform the divine and majestic Jesus into a mere creature who was the spirit-brother of Lucifer (as well as the spirit-brother of all human beings) and who was born on earth through the sexual relations of the Father and Mary.

The Atonement of Jesus Christ

Mormons do speak of Christ accomplishing atonement,[77] but they do not mean by these words what Christians mean (see Chapter 5). In Mormon terminology, Jesus' atonement deals with Adam's transgression. Jesus "atoned for Adam's sin, leaving us responsible only for our own sins."[78] Their second Article of Faith affirms: "We believe that men will be punished for their own sins, and not for Adam's transgression."[79] Hence, salvation begins with Jesus' atonement, but each person must complete the process by doing good works. The official *Gospel Principles* manual tells us that Jesus "became our savior and he did his part to help us return to our heavenly home. It is now up to each of us to do our part and to become worthy of exaltation."[80]

According to Mormon theology, the result of Jesus' atonement is that all humankind will be resurrected. Jesus was able to overcome physical death for us. He "opened the door of immortality for all to walk through. He paid the price for us to rise from the grave. Through His own willful sacrifice—the infinite and eternal atonement—we all shall live again."[81] Hence Jesus wiped out permanent physical death. Because of what He accomplished, we will all be resurrected.

The above obviously bears little resemblance to the atonement described in the Bible. Scripture portrays the death of Christ as dealing with the sins of *all* humanity, not merely the transgression of Adam. Isaiah 53:6 says, "We all, like sheep, have gone astray, each of us has turned to his own way; and the LORD has laid on him the iniquity *of us all.*" In John 1:29 we read, "The next day John saw Jesus coming toward him and said, 'Look, the Lamb of God, who takes away the sin *of the world.*'" First John 2:2 says, "He is the atoning sacrifice for our sins, and not only for ours but also for the sins *of the whole world.*"

Jesus' mission was to provide a substitutionary atonement on the cross—and this atonement covered the sins of all humanity. By so doing, Jesus provided a *total* salvation ("eternal life," not just resurrection from the dead) for human beings which they had no hope of procuring for themselves (Matthew 26:26-28; John 12:27). It is by believing in Him alone—*with no works involved*—that one appropriates the gift of salvation made possible by Jesus (John 3:16,17). (See the discussion of the atonement in Chapter 4.)

A Different Jesus

Are Mormons Christians in the sense that the *Bible* defines Christians? As argued in this chapter, the answer must be no. Since biblically defined Christians believe in one personal, transcendent God, one incarnate Christ (fully divine *and* fully human), the completed atonement, and a gospel of grace through faith alone (no works), Mormons cannot be categorized as true Christians. A secular dictionary might lump everyone who claims to follow "Christ" into the Christian camp, but Christ Himself does not allow for this. Indeed, Jesus taught that "the way" was narrow and that we should not assume that all who call Jesus "Lord" are really Christians (Matthew 5:20; 7:13-23; John 14:6).

The discerning Christian recognizes that though the Mormons acknowledge Jesus as "Lord," they so redefine "Lord" that they completely change its meaning from that found in the Bible. The Mormon "Lord Jesus" did not eternally exist as God but rather *became* a God at a point in time. The Mormon "Lord Jesus" is not the Creator-God who is worthy of our worship.[82]

Theologian Gordon Lewis appropriately responds to the Mormon claim to follow Jesus this way:

> If the Christ of a Mormon is not the one true God (John 17:3) who is eternal (John 1:1; Hebrews 1:8-12; 5:6; 13:8), the object of worship is a creature and worship itself becomes idolatry. If the Christ of a Mormon is a spirit-child who has been procreated—like countless other spirit children by the flesh-and-bone Father and one of his wives—then

he is not uniquely of the same nature as the Father, as the Bible and the historic church teach. If the [Mormon] Christ is our finite brother, not different in kind from us, he is therefore not uniquely Immanuel—"God with us" (Matthew 1:23). The Christ of the Bible is the unique God-man—incarnate, crucified, and risen once-for-all. Only if He was infinite God in human flesh could His blood have infinite value for the justification of all the billions of people who have ever sinned.[83]

The Scriptures grant the right to be called "Christian"

Two Views of Jesus Christ		
	Evangelical	**Mormon**
Relation to Time	Eternally God	Preexistent, not eternally God
Meaning of "Firstborn"	Preeminent over all creation; not procreated	Procreated as first spirit-child
Identity	Unique Son of God	Spirit-brother of Lucifer and all humankind
Divine Names	Jehovah *and* Elohim	Jehovah, but not Elohim
Human Conception	The Holy Spirit overshadowed Mary	Begotten of Father through physical relations with Mary
Trinity	Father, Son, and Holy Spirit are one in nature and distinct in personhood	Three distinct beings
Atonement	For all humankind's sin	For Adam's transgression
Basis of Salvation	Atonement of Christ alone	Atonement plus works

only to those who receive Jesus (John 1:12) as the eternal (not just preexistent) Word who was continuously and personally *with* the one true God (verse 1) and *was* the one true God (verse 1) who became flesh (verse 14).[84] Hence the Mormon attempt to appear "Christian" based on their commitment to Christ "the Lord" backfires, for theirs is "another Jesus" who is not Christian at all (2 Corinthians 11:4).

Chapter Notes

1. Harold B. Kuhn, "Creation," in *Basic Christian Doctrines*, ed. Carl F. Henry (Grand Rapids: Baker Book House, 1983), p. 61.
2. Louis Berkhof, *Manual of Christian Doctrine* (Grand Rapids: Wm. B. Eerdmans Publishing Co., 1983), p. 996.
3. Robert Bowman, *Jehovah's Witnesses, Jesus Christ, and the Gospel of John* (Grand Rapids: Baker Book House, 1989), p. 99.
4. John F. Walvoord, *Jesus Christ Our Lord* (Chicago: Moody Press, 1980), pp. 42-43.
5. Ibid., p. 28.
6. Robert Reymond, *Jesus Divine Messiah: The New Testament Witness* (Phillipsburg, NJ: Presbyterian and Reformed Publishing Co., 1990), p. 122.
7. Erich Sauer, *The Triumph of the Crucified* (Grand Rapids: Wm. B. Eerdmans Publishing Company, 1977), p. 13.
8. Robert G. Gromacki, *The Virgin Birth: Doctrine of Deity* (Grand Rapids: Baker Book House, 1984), p. 73.
9. Charles C. Ryrie, *Basic Theology* (Wheaton, IL: Victor Books, 1986), p. 261.
10. Walvoord, *Jesus Christ*, p. 138.
11. Ibid., p. 143.
12. Ibid., p. 144.
13. Ibid.
14. Robert P. Lightner, *The Bible Knowledge Commentary: New Testament*, ed. John F. Walvoord and Roy B. Zuck (Wheaton, IL: Victor Books, 1983), p. 654.
15. J. I. Packer, *Knowing God* (Downers Grove, IL: InterVarsity Press, 1979), p. 50.
16. Ibid., p. 106.
17. Walvoord, *Jesus Christ*, p. 115.
18. Robert P. Lightner, *Evangelical Theology* (Grand Rapids: Baker Book House, 1986), p. 82.
19. Walvoord, *Jesus Christ*, p. 115.
20. Craig Blomberg and Stephen Robinson, *How Wide the Divide?* (Downers Grove, IL: InterVarsity Press, 1997), p. 83.
21. William Lane Craig, *Assessing the New Testament Evidence for the Historicity of the Resurrection of Jesus* (Lewiston, NY: E. Mellen Press, 1989); William Lane Craig, *Reasonable Faith: Christian Truth and Apologetics* (Wheaton, IL: Crossway Books, 1994); Gary R. Habermas, *The Historical Jesus: Ancient Evidence for the Life of Christ* (Joplin, MO: College Press Publishing Co., 1996); Gary R. Habermas and Antony G.N. Flew, *Did Jesus Rise from the Dead?* (San Francisco: Harper & Row, 1987).
22. *Gospel Principles* (Salt Lake City: Church of Jesus Christ of Latter-day Saints, 1992), p. 55.

23. *Journal of Discourses* (London: Latter-day Saints' Book Depot, 1854), 13:95.
24. Ibid., 13:254.
25. Gilbert W. Scharffs, *The Truth About "The God Makers"* (Salt Lake City, UT: Publishers Press, 1986), pp. 6-20.
26. Robert M. Bowman, "How Mormons Are Defending Mormon Doctrine," in *Christian Research Journal*, Fall 1989, p. 24.
27. Bruce R. McConkie, *Mormon Doctrine* (Salt Lake City: Bookcraft, 1966), p. 129.
28. *The Life and Teaching of Jesus & His Apostles*, p. 15; cited in Mark J. Cares, *Speaking the Truth in Love to Mormons* (Milwaukee: Northwestern Publishing House, 1993), p. 78.
29. Note that the *preexistence* is known as our "First Estate"; *mortality* is known as our "Second Estate."
30. "Bible Dictionary," in *The Holy Bible, Authorized King James Version with Explanatory Notes and Cross References to the Standard Works of the Church of Jesus Christ of Latter-day Saints* (Salt Lake City: The Church of Jesus Christ of Latter-day Saints, 1990).
31. James Talmage, *A Study of the Articles of Faith* (Salt Lake City: The Church of Jesus Christ of Latter-day Saints, 1982), pp. 472-73.
32. *Gospel Principles*, p. 11.
33. *Doctrine and Covenants* (Salt Lake City: The Church of Jesus Christ of Latter-day Saints, 1990), 93:21-23.
34. Talmage, *Articles*, p. 471.
35. *Doctrine and Covenants*, 93:21.
36. John Henry Evans, *An American Prophet* (New York: Macmillan, 1933), p. 241.
37. McConkie, *Mormon Doctrine*, p. 193; see the Book of Moses.
38. Mosiah 4:3.
39. McConkie, *Mormon Doctrine*, pp. 546-47.
40. Ibid., p. 742.
41. Orson Pratt, *The Seer* (Washington, D.C.: n.p., 1853-54), pp. 158-59.
42. Talmage, *Articles*, p. 466.
43. Ezra Taft Benson, *The Teachings of Ezra Taft Benson* (Salt Lake City: Bookcraft, 1988), p. 7.
44. Blomberg and Robinson, *How Wide*, p. 135.
45. Joseph Fielding Smith, *Doctrines of Salvation* (Salt Lake City: Bookcraft, 1975), 1:18-20.
46. Brigham Young, *Desert News*, October 10, 1866; cited in Jerald and Sandra Tanner, *The Changing World of Mormonism* (Chicago: Moody Press, 1981), p. 180.
47. McConkie, *Mormon Doctrine*, p. 745.
48. Orson Hyde, *Journal of Discourses*, 13:259.
49. *Doctrines of Salvation*, 2:65.
50. Talmage, *Articles*, p. 466.
51. Blomberg and Robinson, *How Wide*, p. 139.
52. David A. Reed and John R. Farkas, *Mormons Answered Verse by Verse* (Grand Rapids: Baker Book House, 1993), p. 53.
53. Ryrie, *Basic Theology*, p. 248.
54. Benjamin Warfield, *The Lord of Glory* (Grand Rapids: Baker Book House, 1974), p. 77.
55. I am indebted to Robert Bowman for these evidences.
56. *Doctrine and Covenants*, 93:21-23.
57. Cf. Reymond, *Divine Messiah*, p. 247.
58. See Geoffrey W. Bromiley, *Theological Dictionary of the New Testament*, Abridged in One Volume (Grand Rapids: Eerdmans Publishing Company, 1985), p. 968; *The Complete Word Study New Testament*, ed. Spiros Zodhiates (AMG Publishers, 1991), p. 647.

59. F.F. Bruce, in *Inerrancy*, ed. Norman L. Geisler (Grand Rapids: Zondervan Publishing House, 1979).

60. Reed and Farkas, *Mormons Answered*, p. 97.

61. Paul G. Weathers, "Answering the Arguments of Jehovah's Witnesses Against the Trinity," in *Contend for the Faith*, ed. Eric Pement (Chicago: EMNR, 1992), p. 138.

62. Ray Stedman, *Hebrews* (Downers Grove, IL: InterVarsity Press, 1992), p. 29.

63. See Marvin R. Vincent, *Word Studies in the New Testament*, vol. 3 (Grand Rapids: Eerdmans, 1975), pp. 469-70; Kenneth S. Wuest, *Wuest's Word Studies*, vol. 1 (Grand Rapids: Eerdmans, 1973), p. 184.

64. David Reed, *Jehovah's Witnesses Answered Verse by Verse* (Grand Rapids: Baker Book House, 1992), p. 48.

65. Stedman, *Hebrews*, p. 29.

66. Blomberg and Robinson, *How Wide*, p. 78.

67. "Bible Dictionary" in LDS *Holy Bible*, p. 681.

68. Ryrie, *Basic Theology*, p. 46.

69. Leon Morris, *The Gospel According to John* (Grand Rapids: Wm. B. Eerdmans Publishing Co., 1971), p. 658.

70. Walter Martin and Norman Klann, *Jehovah of the Watchtower* (Minneapolis: Bethany House Publishers, 1974), pp. 162-64.

71. Ibid., p. 164.

72. Blomberg and Robinson, *How Wide*, p. 130.

73. James Talmage, *Jesus the Christ* (Salt Lake City: Deseret Book Co., 1962), p. 374.

74. Robert M. Bowman, *Why You Should Believe in the Trinity* (Grand Rapids: Baker Book House, 1989), p. 88.

75. Blomberg and Robinson, *How Wide*, p. 129.

76. Ibid., p. 83.

77. Ibid., p. 16.

78. LeGrand Richards, *A Marvelous Work and a Wonder* (Salt Lake City: Deseret Book Company, 1958), p. 98.

79. *Articles of Faith* 2.

80. *Gospel Principles*, p. 19.

81. *Church News*, March 18, 1989, p. 16.

82. Gordon R. Lewis, "A Summary Critique" of Robinson, *Are Mormons Christians?* in *Christian Research Journal*, Fall 1992, p. 34.

83. Ibid., p. 34.

84. Ibid., p. 35.

4

Salvation

Phil Roberts

"What must I do to be saved?" (Acts 16:30) is life's most important question. The answer to it in the perspective of every religious system will determine one's present state of happiness as well as one's eternal destiny, whether heaven or hell. Both Mormonism and evangelicalism give their own response to this question, but as will be demonstrated in this chapter, their two answers are vastly different.[1] First of all, we will overview the Christian/evangelical answer to this most crucial and vital of issues. This will be done in four basic parts: 1) man's problem or need; 2) the work of Christ in response to man's need; 3) man's response to Christ's work; 4) eternal consequences. This same outline of these four points in Mormonism will follow. A summary will then conclude this chapter.

The Evangelical View

Evangelical theologian James I. Packer has commented eloquently on the importance of evangelicals' commitment to a biblical view of salvation and its expression to the world:

> Evangelicals have always seen the question of salvation as one of supreme importance, and their witness to the way of salvation as the most precious gift they bring to the rest of the church. This

Scripture quotations in this chapter are from the New King James Version except as otherwise noted. See Copyright page.

conviction rests not on the memory of the conversion of Paul or Augustine or Luther or Wesley or Whitefield or any other evangelical hero, but on the emphasis with which the Bible itself highlights salvation as its central theme.[2]

Evangelicals look to the Bible and the Bible alone for the answer (see Chapter 1). "Believe on the Lord Jesus Christ, and you will be saved, you and your household" (Acts 16:31). This response of the apostle Paul and his missionary companion, Silas, in the opinion of evangelicals, says all that needs to be said about the issue of salvation.

In an evangelical's perspective, the form and practice of baptism, church membership, good works, or denominational duty do not determine whether or not a person has salvation. Neither do any of these things determine one's *class* of salvation (versus telestial, terrestrial, or celestial in Mormon thinking). While works and service may determine a certain level of reward in the life to come, this possibility is not a matter of great theological debate for evangelicals.[3] One issue is certain, however: Never is heavenly reward seen to be tied to a church or denominational identity, or to meeting certain service requirements within a group, as it so clearly is in Mormonism.

Receiving salvation is a matter of one putting his or her personal belief and trust in Jesus Christ as the atoning sacrifice for his or her sin. (For example, see John 1:11,12; John 3:16,36). It is by God's love and grace alone that salvation was accomplished when Christ died on the cross. There He suffered the just punishment for the whole world (2 Corinthians 5:14-21). When we by simple faith accept that gift of God (Romans 6:23), He through the Holy Spirit indwells our lives, forgives our sin, and guarantees us a home in heaven.

While the fact of God's love is not simplistic, it is simple in terms of what we must do to appropriate salvation: believe and believe alone. While some evangelicals of the infant-baptism tradition may argue that the covenant of salvation may apply salvation to the children of believers prior to their age of accountability, no evangelicals would diminish the necessity of faith for salvation on behalf of all consenting Christians. The thief on the cross (Luke 23:39-43) was able to know the fullness of salvation when he believed in Jesus. For Bible-based believers those same terms and conditions have not changed.

Man's Need

The biblical drama unfolds with the telling of the creation. It is clear that the apex of God's work is the special creation of humankind—male and female—into whom He breathed the breath of life. God created both sexes in His image. The *imago dei* (image of God) was never thought to be by mainstream Christian and Bible-based theologians a physical resemblance but rather a moral and spiritual possession of God's essential goodness, righteousness, and ability to experience personal intimacy. Included as well was man's ability to decide between right and wrong, to decide to obey or disobey God Himself. Renowned theologian Carl F.H. Henry has stated that God's image exists "formally in man's personality (moral responsibility and intelligence) and...in his knowledge of God and of his will for man."[4]

From the creation account the Bible moves from the sublime to the tragic. The next focus of Scripture is the fall of mankind (Genesis 3). Eve was tempted by Satan, in the form of a serpent, to disbelieve God's restriction not to eat of "the tree of the knowledge of good and evil." She trusted Satan instead, hence questioning God's own veracity and truthfulness. In effect, she called the only wise God a liar. This act was a terrible transgression not only of God's law but of His character as well. God was left no choice but to respond in judgment. That judgment included for Adam and Eve then and for all humans now:

1) a broken relationship with God (Genesis 3:8-10).
2) broken and often mutually accusatory relationships with each other (Genesis 3:11-13).

3) personal anguish and physical, emotional, and material suffering (Genesis 3:16-19).

4) the reality of present and eternal separation from God (Genesis 3:22-24).

A quick read of the morning newspaper, or watching the evening newscast, or observing marred broken personal relationships in every human being's experience, coupled with the natural and obvious tendency to sin and an absence of God in every heart, ought to be enough to convince any person of the fall's horrible reality and of mankind's great need of grace.

In opposition to Mormon theology, as will be seen, Adam and Eve's fall was tragic and disastrous. It was in violation to God's direct will and command. In no way could it be viewed as a fall toward glory (Romans 3:23). Only through the cross of Christ will this tragedy be reversed.

Christ's Work

In Scripture, as reflected in evangelical theology, grace—God's grace—is the root, foundation, and superstructure of salvation. This position is in opposition to Mormonism, where grace comes into play "after all we can do."[5] In the Bible, grace is of the essence of new life in Christ. What is grace? Interestingly, the Greek word for grace, *xapis* or *charis,* is the same word transliterated into English as *charity.* And what is charity but someone with proper power and resources doing for the helpless what they cannot do for themselves?

After all, we are talking about salvation. God saved, redeemed, and restored helplessly lost sinners when they were without ability to help themselves. The Bible, the sole Scripture of the Christian faith, never speaks of "the eternal self-improvement plan" or of "God's 12-step program for heavenly progression." Rather, it is God's rescue of the lost as they by faith agree and believe in His grace. Grace is—

1) the motivation of God's saving acts: Ephesians 1:5-7; Revelation 13:8.

2) the basis for God's forgiveness: Psalm 94:17,18; Daniel 9:18.

3) the condition for salvation: Romans 4:16; Ephesians 2:8,9; Titus 3:7.

4) the basis of eternal rewards: 1 Peter 5:10.

5) the basis of God's call of His people to service: 2 Timothy 1:1,9; Galatians 1:15.

6) the dominant element in the work of Christ: Romans 5:2,8.

7) the basis for answered prayer and divine assistance: Hebrews 4:16; 2 Samuel 24:14.

Any system of theology and salvation that lessens the role of God's mercy deserves the anathema of Paul's inspired condemnation expressed in Galatians 1:8: "But even if we or an angel from heaven should preach to you a gospel contrary to that which we preached to you, let him be accursed" (RSVB).

The root of God's grace and His loving response to Adam and Eve's sin can be found in the early chapters of Genesis as their rebellion has just been revealed. God provided for them clothes of animal hides to cover their newly created sense of shame and guilt (Genesis 3:21). He also promised that the fruit of Eve would eventually destroy the power of Satan (Genesis 3:15). Throughout the Old Testament, animal sacrifices continued in both the tabernacle of the Israelites and later in their temple in Jerusalem. These were a foreshadowing of what would be the fulfillment and reality of God's provision full of grace—the cross and self-giving death of Jesus Christ. Scripture raises and answers this most vital question: "For if the blood of goats and bulls and the ashes of a heifer sprinkling those who have been defiled, sanctify for the cleansing of the flesh, how much more will the blood of Christ, who through the eternal Spirit offered Himself without blemish to God, cleanse your conscience from dead works to serve the living God?" (Hebrews 9:13,14 NASB).[6]

So critical and all-essential is Christ's work on the cross that Anglican evangelical John Stott says that "it lies at the centre of the historic, biblical faith" and is of itself the "greatest and most glorious of all subjects."[7] It expresses and manifests God's saving love to a helpless people deserving of God's wrath and judgment. "Much more then, having now been justified by His blood, we shall be saved from the wrath of God through Him" (Romans 5:9 NASB).

The above promise was fulfilled in the Person of Jesus Christ. Jesus was the eternal Word of God. He was God.[8] He was incarnated in the virgin Mary by the supernatural and spiritual work of the Holy Spirit. Jesus lived a sinless and perfect life, always pleasing His heavenly Father (John 8:29). And while He taught the most perfect ethic and moral principles, unsurpassed in the teachings of all other religion leaders, His real purpose for coming to earth was to die on a Roman cross of crucifixion.

The cross forms the essence of the Christian theology of salvation, for there the totality of sin was atoned for (2 Corinthians 5:21). Certain priestly or sacerdotal traditions, such as Catholicism or Eastern Orthodoxy, may claim that it is only through participation in the life and sacraments of the church that the power of the cross may be experienced, but in evangelicalism the traditional Protestant and biblical principle of *solo Christo* or Christ alone is upheld. By faith in the substitutionary sacrificial death of Christ, our sins were suffered for by Jesus so that we can be completely set free from their penalty. One descriptive biblical word for the consequences of sin is "debt." Just as someone might pay a debtor's obligation, setting him free from its burden, so Christ suffered in our place when crucified on the cross. He was made sin for us (2 Corinthians 5:21). In the wonder of grace, Jesus, who knew no sin, suffered for our sin so that in Him we might be forgiven and set free from the curse and penalty of sin.

This view of salvation argues that the work of Christ alone atones for sin. Because of what Jesus did for us, human merit counts for nothing in terms of salvation (Hebrews 1:3; 10:12-14). Yes, even a guilty criminal or a thief on a cross may be forgiven of each and every sin. Such forgiveness is not based on human deserts, but on Christ's work. A guilty and condemned criminal or a self-righteous but unforgiving and ill-deserving hypocrite may be saved completely and totally. Because Jesus died for each and every sin of the world, no one stands outside the possibility of complete redemption. He may save any person and take him or her straight to heaven into the very presence of God Himself.

Some doubters may argue that such an approach is scandalous. Indeed it is to the unbeliever (1 Corinthians 1:18). The biblical writers commented eloquently on this fact and Jesus Himself taught a parable to that end.[9] He said that a vineyard owner (Matthew 20:1-16) paid equally all of his contract workers the same amount, a denarius (about a day's wages), to all who worked that day or any part of it for him. But because both the vineyard and the money was his, he was free to bestow on the hired hands as he wished. So it is with God's salvation. It is available to the religious and irreligious, the moral and the immoral.

God's grace through the cross and redemption of Christ is essential for everyone's salvation. Without it no one would be saved, because the Bible clearly states that all of humanity falls short of God's glory, righteousness, and standards of morality (Romans 3:23; 6:23). Such an understanding of Christ's work and His cross has inspired a world of literature, poetry, and music. It caused John Newton in the eighteenth century to write these classic words:

> Amazing grace, how sweet the sound,
> That saved a wretch like me;
> I once was lost but now am found;
> Was blind, but now I see.

Man's Response

What does man need to do? Believe and have faith in the Person of Jesus Christ! Yes, faith is clearly commanded of the Lord for each and every person. We can search the Bible

in vain in an attempt to find anything related to denominational or religious identity linked to salvation. Yet a key part
of Mormonism and its teachings is that the highest level of
salvation clearly depends on becoming a temple-worthy member of the LDS Church. Hell (in the usual evangelical sense
of eternal punishment) is reserved for apostates from that
Church. The Bible, however, elucidates only inner qualities
of faith and belief which are of such a significant nature that
they produce outward and visible moral and spiritual
results. What are the biblical dimensions of genuine belief?

1. *Faith.* The Bible, particularly the New Testament, is
replete with the words *believe, accept, trust, faith.* A quick look
at a Bible dictionary or concordance will demonstrate this
truth. So important is faith or belief that the Bible states that
the "just shall live by faith" (Galatians 3:11; Hebrews 10:38,39)
and that the father of Israel, Abraham, was made righteous
because of his faith (Genesis 15:6; Romans 4:3).

Why is faith primary and essential to salvation? Because,
more than any other quality, it reflects confidence in its
object—in this case God Himself. Faith believes that God is
true to His word, that His deeds are righteous, and that His
commands are to be followed. Hence, while faith or belief is
primarily intellectual and abstract, it will always result in
works. The epistle of James makes it clear, therefore, that
faith must result in works (James 2). But never are works to
be equated with faith. To believe in Jesus Christ means to
accept His sacrifice of Himself so that He will be the Lord of
our lives.[10]

James argues not for faith and works together, as if they
are identical twins in the process of salvation, but rather for
a faith that works. Biblical faith will result in changed lives
(2 Corinthians 5:17). In another place the argument is
made that a person "is 'justified' (declared righteous before
God) by faith alone, but not by a faith that is alone."[11]

This concept is what Christian theologians have called
"justification by faith." Because a person is willing to accept
God's work in Christ and to accept it alone as the reason for
his forgiveness and reconciliation before God, his sins are

removed as far as the east is from the west (Psalm 103:12).
He is, in fact, justified. The biblical languages themselves
(Hebrew, *sadeq*, Greek, *dikaioo*) in their root meanings for
justify mean "to pronounce, accept, and treat as just; not
penally liable."[12]

As the gifted Puritan thinker Jonathan Edwards so suc-
cinctly phrased it:

> It is by works that our course appears to be good;
> but by faith our cause not only appears to be good,
> but becomes good; because thereby we are united
> to Christ.[13]

2. *Repentance.* This is an ancillary aspect of faith. But because it is often linked with belief in the Bible, we will examine briefly the relationship between the two.[14] Anyone with
military experience understands repentance. Repen-tance is
simply an about-face. Classical theologians were often careful to differentiate here between the biblical concept of
metanoia as a change of mind or that of behavior. In order to
point out the difference between belief and its results or
works, much was made of the fact that repentance meant
initially *a change of mind*.[15] Secondly, it means (as a result of
mental change) *behavioral alteration*. The primary nature of
that change is a desire to leave one's sin and return to the
Lord—to be united with the Lord God and His Son, Jesus
Christ, even as the prodigal returned to his father (Luke
15:11-32).

Repentance is never to be considered in its biblical context as being contradictory but complementary to faith.
Because faith means a trusting in and a coming to Christ—
"the spotless lamb" and "Holy One of God"—"the response
of faith implies a refutation of all that belongs to unrighteousness."[16] This is repentance; it is a turning from unrighteousness to Christ because of our faith in Him who offers us
the righteousness of God. Repentance is a genuine expression of the fruit of a believing heart. In this sense there can
be no true repentance without faith, and no genuine faith
without repentance.

3. *Confession.* "If you confess with your mouth the Lord Jesus...you will be saved" (Romans 10:9). "Whoever confesses Me [Jesus] before men, him I will also confess before My Father who is in heaven" (Matthew 10:32). Here too, genuine faith involves confession.

To acknowledge the saving work and Person of Jesus Christ is to bring faith to its fruition and fully to unite one to Christ. How can faith be genuine without a full expression of one's identity with Christ? How more perfectly is this to be done than openly, audibly, and credibly as a believing heart cries out to Jesus? This view reflects biblical wordage and their meanings (Hebrew, *gada*; Greek, *homologeo*) which convey the idea of "acknowledgment and praise of God's character and glorious works, often with expression of man's confession of faith in God and in his Son, Jesus Christ."[17]

Confession is never to be considered a saving work. It is rather the fulfillment and physical manifestation of saving faith. Did not Jesus Himself say "By your words you will be justified, and by your words you will be condemned" (Matthew 12:37)? Baptism, in the truest New Testament sense, was the place for confession because baptism itself was a physical manifestation or confession of faith. When Peter was asked at Pentecost "What must we do to be saved?" his response of "Repent, and be baptized every one of you in the name of Jesus Christ for the forgiveness of your sins" (Acts 2:38 RSVB) was completely consistent with the place that Christian theology places on faith and on baptism as a form of confession.

Just as a modern evangelist might call people to respond to an altar call in open profession of faith in Christ, Peter and New Testament evangelists called them to confession in the context of and through the mode of baptism. Notably, every New Testament candidate for baptism before he was baptized confessed that "Jesus is Lord" (Romans 10:9-13). Confession and baptism are genuine expressions of saving faith. They reflect the fullness of faith as Christians stand up and are counted for Christ. Never are those from a biblical perspective considered a work of righteousness (Titus 3:6,7).

Eternal Consequences

Evangelicals acknowledge only two places of eternal destiny—heaven or hell.[18] Why? Because these are the only two existences mentioned in the Bible. Therefore, as people who follow only the Holy Scripture of Old and New Testaments, evangelicals can speak only of what the Bible speaks.

Jesus spoke often of the afterlife, mentioning heaven and hell frequently. Importantly, He is recorded in the Bible as speaking twice as much of hell as He did of heaven.[19] Obviously Jesus understood the horrors of an eternity separated from God. He was seemingly even more anxious to warn people of that fate than to excite the redeemed with the prospects of heavenly bliss.

What was often unclear in the Old Testament the Lord Jesus Christ made startlingly clear and vivid in the New Testament.

Jesus spoke of hell as "everlasting fire" (Matthew 25:41), as "fire and brimstone" (Revelation 21:8), as "the bottomless pit" (Revelation 9:1,2), and as a place which is characterized by "wailing and gnashing of teeth" (Matthew 13:42). While theologians often debate whether the sufferings as described are literal or figurative, the terrible images described instill an awful picture of what life will be like without God in the world to come.

For the purpose of this chapter, it is important to clarify who it is that the Bible speaks of as being consigned to that place. Is it people who have failed to live up to the dictates of a particular church or movement? Mormonism makes the claim that apostates from their church will be sent to perdition or outer darkness.[20] Is that what the Bible teaches? Far from it.

Jesus Himself taught that the "everlasting fire" was prepared for "the devil and his angels" (Matthew 25:41). As well, He consigned there unbelievers, "evildoers," and false professors—those who claimed in this life to have known Jesus as Lord but in actuality had no saving relationship to Him (cf. Matthew 7:19-23; 25:41; 13:38; 23:29-33). Unbelief, rebellion against a holy God, and the consistently evil lifestyle that comes from such rebellion are the only hallmarks of hell's occupants. Importantly, nothing in the Bible is ever mentioned of lapsing from a particular church or movement (cf. 1 Corinthians 6:9-10; Galatians 5:19-21; Ephesians 5:3-5; Revelation 21:7,8; 22:14,15; John 3:18,36).

Voices are sometimes raised that hell is too severe a punishment. But we must remember that all sin, as Joseph confessed (Genesis 39:9), is against a holy and all-perfect God. It is an affront to His character and expresses rebellion to His very Person. Therefore God sets the terms of retribution. Apart from His grace and forgiveness, every person deserves hell. On the day of judgment this fact will be openly admitted by everyone (cf. Romans 3:19,20; 2:1-3).

Heaven is God's bestowal of grace on those who love Him and His Son, Jesus Christ, and who trust Him for their salvation (cf. John 3:16-36; Matthew 19:28; 1 Corinthians 15:22-24; Revelation 21:1-5). In essence, heaven is being in the presence of God and Jesus, enjoying their blessings for eternity. The cross was clearly God's judgment against all sin. For those who accept this fact, they have passed from death into life. It is scriptural that responsibilities will be assigned in heaven. The Bible, though, in God's wisdom, does not describe them in any detail.

The book of Galatians condemns any "gospel" which elevates morality or religiosity as a rival or alternative way to God or God's presence. As we shall now see, the gospel of Joseph Smith and of Mormonism makes great the divide between it and genuine Christian salvation.

The Mormon Doctrine of Salvation

When a member of the Church of Jesus Christ of Latter-day Saints is asked the question "What must I do to be saved?" what is his answer? And when he answers that question, does it differ from what the Bible declares? At issue is whether or not the LDS Church may be called truly Christian. A more personal concern then becomes whether Mormons themselves are saved and certain about their own salvation. If Mormonism teaches a different Gospel than that presented in the Bible, then there is no sure and certain hope for them. They are still left in their sin.

A Different Gospel

The answer to the question "Does Mormonism teach a different Gospel?" is answered clearly and directly by the Church of Jesus Christ of Latter-day Saints itself. It is the basic and fundamental teaching of the LDS Church that the "revelations" given to Joseph Smith in the Book of Mormon, the *Doctrine and Covenants*, and *The Pearl of Great Price*, as well as in the practice and rituals of the Mormon Church itself, contain the fullness of the Gospel. The very first revelation issued in the *Doctrine and Covenants* states:

> Wherefore, I the Lord, knowing the great calamity which should come upon the inhabitants of the earth, called upon my servant Joseph Smith, Jr., and spake unto him from heaven, and gave him commandments; and also gave commandments to others, that they should proclaim these things unto the world…that faith also might increase in the earth; *that mine everlasting covenant might be established that the fulness of my gospel* might be proclaimed by the weak and the simple unto the ends of the world.[21]

Likewise in his testimony, which is contained in the preface to the foundational book of Mormonism, the Book of Mormon, Joseph Smith commented on his supposed encounter with the angel Moroni. In being addressed by the angel, Joseph was given instruction regarding the significance of the golden plates:

> He [Moroni] said there was a book deposited, written upon gold plates, giving an account of the former inhabitants of this continent, and the source from whence they sprang. He also said that the **fulness of the everlasting Gospel** was contained in it, as delivered by the Savior to the ancient inhabitants.[22]

The ancient scriptural truths which were discussed in the first part of this chapter were not sufficient for Mormons. They were thought to be incomplete and less than full. There was a need, according to Joseph Smith, for a "fuller" Gospel to be revealed and taught. If the Gospel contained in the pages of the New Testament, however, is not complete, why is it that the apostle Paul would give such a dire and serious warning as he delivered in Galatians 1:8?

The principle that Paul underscores here is that the Gospel contained in Holy Scripture is complete and perfect in and of itself. It does not need revision, nor should it be added to or altered in any shape, form, or fashion. To add to it is to disgrace God's already-complete revelation and to jeopardize the eternal destiny of numerous persons who may miss heaven by embracing a false and alternative Gospel. Stephen Robinson claims that the Gospel of Mormonism sheds "additional light" (100-watt-bulb) and is superior to the light (40, 60, maybe even 80 watts) of the Bible.[23] As this chapter will demonstrate, Mormonism does not complete the New Testament Gospel at all, but instead introduces a spurious evangel. It is in fact not an evangel at all (see Galatians 1:6; 2 Corinthians 11:4). It offers another, broader way to salvation (see Matthew 7:13,14) that belittles the primacy and importance of grace. It insists that one must become a member in the Church of Jesus Christ of Latter-day Saints to have available to him a "progression" toward a more complete salvation. That same person must become a faithful member in that Church and become "temple worthy" to achieve a "celestial marriage" and to reach exaltation and godhood.

Perhaps even more foundational to Joseph Smith's claim to possess a fuller Gospel was his total castigation and opposition to the contemporary Christian churches of his day, including those of the Protestant/Reformational tradition. Three denominations (Presbyterian, Methodist, and Baptist) that laid much of the foundation of contemporary evangelicalism were particular targets of his venom and opposition.

In his formational vision of the spring of 1820, Joseph claimed that the three above groups were "zealous in endeavoring to establish their own tenets and disprove all others."[24] Approaching God through prayer and claiming the promise of James 1:5 to ask God for wisdom, God the "Heavenly Father" along with Jesus Christ appeared to Joseph in a body of flesh and bones. Heavenly Father told him to listen to his "Beloved Son." Further, when Jesus did speak He told Joseph to "join none of them, for they were all wrong...all their creeds were an abomination in his sight;...those professors [or believers/members] were all corrupt."[25] Jesus, he said, also told him that "they teach for doctrines the commandments of men."[26] Joseph stated that it "had never entered into my heart that all were wrong." Clearly Smith was drawing a proverbial line in the sand in claiming that heretofore the doctrines believed, preached, taught, embraced, and loved by Christians everywhere, particularly Protestants, were abominations before God.

Since Joseph Smith's "Gospel" was restored through additional revelations, it is obviously a "different gospel" (see Galatians 1:8; 2 Corinthians 11:4). Having claimed a new evangel, he then posited the theory of the "great apostasy." He then attempted to discredit further both Christian truth claims and the biblical doctrines inherited and preached throughout 18 centuries of Christian history.

The Great Apostasy

The Mormon doctrine of the great apostasy first taught by Joseph Smith had several key features. Beginning while the apostles were still alive, "some members taught ideas from their old pagan or Jewish beliefs instead of the *simple* truths taught by Jesus."[27] Then followed persecution, when the apostles were killed one by one and "surviving apostles could not meet to choose and ordain men to replace those who were dead." Soon only local organizations "prevailed" and "the perfect organization" (i.e., the Mormon conceptualized organization) "no longer existed and confusion resulted."[28]

These developments opened the door for confusion and "the destruction of the Church was complete...pagan beliefs dominated the thinking of those called Christians." It was a very different church than that organized by Jesus. Members of that church, Mormons claimed, slipped into the terrible error of believing that "God was a being without form or substance."[29] In other words, the LDS Church accused the early Christians of believing what the Bible says about God— that He is spirit and cannot be contained to a spatial/physical form or body.[30]

Additionally, an understanding of God's love was lost, as well as the idea that Christians are literal spiritual children of God. No one knew the "purpose of life," for "the priesthood and revelation were no longer on the earth." There were no apostles or other priesthood leaders with power from God, and there were no spiritual gifts. Both in America and elsewhere in the world, "it was the Church of Jesus Christ no longer; it was a church of men."[31] Total apostasy had occurred and would remain until Joseph Smith reconstituted the Church of Jesus Christ on April 6, 1830.

It must be understood that Mormons do not claim simply a limiting of the church and truth during this period, but a total loss of it:

> It was lost—the gospel with its powers and blessings—sometime after the Savior's crucifixion and the loss of his apostles. The laws were changed, the ordinances were changed, and the everlasting covenant was broken that the Lord gave to his people....There was a long period of centuries when the gospel was not available to people on this earth.[32]

Bible-based Christians and students of church history understand generally the ebb and flow of Bible truths throughout history. At times the simple and profound truths of the Gospel seemed to have almost faded from the life of the church. Corruption, religious wars, and heresies ensued and helped to cloud Scripture. But no well-informed theologian or Christian would claim that the Gospel at any point had totally disappeared from the earth! More importantly the Bible itself was always present with the church. When people searched its pages, they were exposed to its truth, which often brought revival and renewal to the people of God, such as in the time of the Reformation.

Mormonism must prove that what the early church taught was what the LDS Church presently teaches in order to prove that an apostasy of the type they have described actually occurred. No non-LDS New Testament or church history scholar would substantiate their claim.[33] No "plain or precious parts" are missing from the Scriptures, and nothing like the theological system of Mormonism ever existed in the early church.[34] In fact, it is impossible to identify the intricate priesthood and temple organization of the LDS Church as "the simple truths taught by Jesus."[35] Behind that proposition is the Mormon wish for people to accept the notion of a complete and total apostasy of the church for over 1700 years. But to the contrary, Jesus promised that He would build His church and that the gates of hell would not prevail against it (Matthew 16:18). To accept the Mormon view of the apostasy is to reject the direct promise and prophecy of Jesus Christ.

The Restoration

Having made the claim that the true Gospel had been eradicated from the face of the earth, and the church of Jesus along with it, Joseph Smith laid the foundation of the unbiblical notion that the one true church is the Church of Jesus Christ of Latter-day Saints. In his mind it was to be the purpose of that Church to teach and dispense the new Gospel according to Joseph Smith. The Church would contain a priesthood system, temples for "sacred" and secret ceremonies, and a hierarchy and reward system to encourage allegiance and loyalty. In return, the Church would offer the possibility of "temple-worthy" Mormons achieving the celestial kingdom and obtaining godhood.

According to Latter-day Saint authority, "the great apostasy...necessitated a restoration of the gospel in the last days."[36] The Christian faith at the time of the formation of the LDS Church was "perverted...and adulterated until it was congenital to the wicked heart," according to Brigham Young, successor as prophet and President of the Church to Joseph Smith.[37] The first step to restoration was the appearance of "the Father and the Son," both in bodies of flesh and bone, to Joseph Smith. This event took place near Palmyra, New York, in the spring of 1820. Next, in 1823, Moroni told him of the golden plates, which in 1827 Smith claimed he recovered and began to translate. These plates contained the "fulness of the everlasting Gospel." Smith was later allegedly visited by John the Baptist, who bestowed on him and Oliver Cowdery, his colleague, "the Aaronic Priesthood" and its authority.[38]

The authority of that priesthood contained "the keys of the ministering of angels, and of the gospel of repentance, and of baptism by immersion for the remission of sins."[39] Smith was arrogating to himself and his religion the claim of the power of the Gospel itself. After the alleged visit of John the Baptist came a visitation from Peter, James, and John, "the three chief apostles." They constituted, Mormonism claimed, the "First Presidency of the church in that day." They gave to Joseph "the keys of the greater priesthood" and "their power that the church could be organized on the earth."[40] But according to the Bible (Matthew 28:18-20), it is Jesus *alone* who has all authority for the church to do its ministry and mission. Yet this spurious event seemed to strengthen Joseph's claim for the validity of his Church. Smith perhaps did not even realize how contrary to biblical teaching the "authority" of Peter, James, and John was.

With these supposed events as his authority, Smith organized his Church on April 6, 1830. He later wrote that Jesus had revealed to him that it is "the only true and living church...with which I am well pleased."[41] Eventually the name "Latter-day Saints" was affixed, solidifying in Smith's thinking the notion that no other true saints existed or had existed since the time of the first apostles.

We will show more clearly what Bruce McConkie meant when he said, "Without the atonement, the gospel, the priesthood, and the sealing power, there would be no salvation." It is enough at this point to be reminded of his claim "If it had not been for Joseph Smith and the restoration, there would be no salvation. There is no salvation outside the Church of Jesus Christ of Latter-day Saints."[42]

Subsequent to the Church's formation, it was claimed that finally the true Church of Christ existed. The office of the Prophet had been reestablished, as well as that of the priesthood (apostles, seventies, patriarchs, high priests, elders, etc.), and the first principles and ordinances of the Gospel.[43] In the final analysis, the basis and organization for the promotion and propagation of a new Gospel had been created. The next step for us is to understand its positions.

The Gospel of Mormonism

1. Man's problem and need. Like a counterfeit 50-dollar bill which has many similar characteristics to the real thing, the Gospel of Mormonism bears similarities to the biblical Gospel. It does speak about the atonement of Jesus Christ, His suffering for sin as well as His resurrection. There are, however, crucial differences which distinguish the Mormon doctrine of the fall from true and biblical Christianity.

Adam and Eve's fall is preceded by a different understanding, according to Mormonism, of their actual existence. First, instead of Adam beginning with his physical creation, Mormonism claims he existed in a premortal state as Michael the Archangel or "the ancient of days."[44] This position has no substantiation from the Bible. The Bible claims clearly that Adam's existence began at the point of God determining to make man, male and female, and then placing them in the Garden.[45] This act marked their real beginning and contradicts their existence prior to creation.

As a result of their transgression, according to Mormonism, Adam and Eve left their purely "spiritual state" and became physical beings.[46] Again this concept is unbiblical, as God according to Scripture created Adam as a material being in whom existed the breath of life.[47]

While at a first glance of Mormon teaching it might appear that Adam and Eve did more harm than good by disobeying God's command to eat of the fruit of the tree, a closer read reveals otherwise. In fact, it appears that God Himself is put in a position of being morally duplicitous:

> The Lord gave two conflicting commandments—one to become mortal and have children, the other to not eat of the tree of knowledge of good and evil out of which mortality and children and death would result...he [Adam] chose to partake of the forbidden fruit so that the purposes of God might be accomplished by providing a probationary estate for his spirit children...he [Adam] chose the Lord's way; there was no other way whereby salvation might come unto the children of men.[48]

Once they "fell," having disobeyed or obeyed God, whichever it was, Adam and Eve "were shut out of God's presence," "suffering a spiritual death."[49] Pain and sorrow were also introduced into human experience in addition to fallen man becoming carnal, sensual, and devilish, and also becoming exposed to physical death.[50] Beyond that, though, the results of the fall were positive. First, Adam and Eve became fully mortal and were able to begin to have children.[51] They were able to "recognize and embrace good," something that, according to Mormonism, they were not able to do before.[52] There is no mention here of the blindness and prejudice toward evil that depravity brings but rather "the opportunity to obtain the joy that comes from choosing good over evil."[53] If the fall of Adam and Eve can be labeled such in Mormonism, it appears to be a fall upward into the will of God in beginning to accomplish His purpose and plan of salvation:

> If Adam and Eve had not transgressed, they would have lived forever in innocence, without children, thereby frustrating God's plan of salvation.[54]

In the perspective of Mormon theology, the fall had so many positive consequences that the horrible and destructive nature of Adam and Eve's sin is virtually forgotten. It appears that by sinning they fulfilled the will of God, an idea which axiomatically calls into question God's righteousness and holiness. Would God have willed an evil? Would He have purposed a plan of salvation that involved His purposing and planning for evil to have been done? To conceive of such a notion immediately absolves Adam and Eve of sin itself:

> I'm very, very grateful that in the *Book of Mormon*, and I think elsewhere in our scriptures, the fall of Adam has not been called a sin. It wasn't a sin.... What did Adam do? The very thing the Lord wanted him to do; and I hate to hear anybody call it sin, for it wasn't a sin. Did Adam sin when he partook of the forbidden fruit? I say to you, no, he did not.[55]

According to Mormon thinking, if the role of Adam and Eve in God's plan of salvation is understood correctly—

> ...we will realize that those who have long labeled them sinners responsible for the universal depravity of the human family are completely misguided. The truth is that Adam and Eve opened the door for us to come into mortality, a step essential to our eternal progress.[56]

By becoming mortal men and women they acquired the opportunity to achieve godhood in the celestial kingdom. Since childbearing as temple-worthy Mormons (as we shall see more clearly) is part of the process toward exaltation, their disobedience to God was a step in the right direction. "Adam was one of the greatest men who has ever lived on the earth....Adam fell, but he fell in the right direction. He fell toward the goal....Adam fell, but he fell upward."[57]

When it comes to the fall and the transgression of Adam and Eve, no more contradictory statement to biblical truth could be fabricated. The Bible says that "through one man [Adam] sin entered the world, and death through sin" (Romans 5:12). Death is a result of man's disobedience to God, not a part of God's perfect will. Salvation is a response to man's rebellion, not a complement to it. Physical death is viewed from the Bible as a curse of God upon sin, not a reward.

The fall, according to Mormonism, produced a dual nature for all of mankind. But it is not a dual nature of good and evil and right and wrong, but a dual nature of physical and spiritual dimensions. "Man has a dual nature; one, related to the earthly or animal life; the other, akin to the divine."[58] It is then his or her choice to seek to know God. There is an unimpeded potential to know God and even to become a god if the right principles are followed. The grace of God becomes less of a crucial factor. The warnings of Scripture regarding man's dark side, his lack of desire for God apart from the Holy Spirit's work, and his tendency to twist divine truth so as to worship the creature instead of the creator are lost from perspective.[59]

2. Christ's work and atonement. LDS missionaries and spokesmen often mention the atonement of Christ and His saviorship. They now frequently employ evangelical jargon and clichés. Superficially it appears as if there is little difference between a Mormon view of the cross and that of a biblically based Christian. A closer look at the LDS view of the atonement, however, demonstrates how great the divide really is.

We begin with the background of the LDS shallow and insufficient concept of the fall: Adam and Eve did not really sin; they actually were in the will of God when they ate of the forbidden fruit, although sins can be and are committed by humans. Next, remember that when an informed Mormon refers to Jesus Christ he is actually speaking of a different Jesus than the biblical Christ (see Chapter 3). The apostle Paul made clear in 2 Corinthians 11:4 that it is possible for people to talk about *a* Jesus without referring to God the Son, eternal God and creator, the Jesus of the Bible.

Mormonism has a different Jesus. He is one of many gods. He was the firstborn spiritual child of God Elohim and was "begotten" literally by the Mormon God in a physical relationship with Mary. The Jesus of Mormonism and the Jesus of the Bible are two different and distinct persons. For a biblically based Christian it is impossible to accept the idea that atonement for the sins of the world can be made by a Christ who is less than the eternal God. How can Jesus make sufficient atonement for the sins of the world if He is essentially like us and is basically our spiritual big brother?

Here is the outline of the Mormon view of Christ's work in the atonement.

a. God governs the universe by righteous law. His justice therefore demands that a penalty be paid for every sin. Since all mankind has sinned and are fallen, we are subject to God's justice, which requires the punishment of sin.[60]

b. Jesus alone possessed the attributes necessary to perform an atonement. He had no personal sin himself and was the "only begotten" son of god. (See Chapter 3.) An important question for Mormon theology here is: How is it that Jesus possessed "no personal sin" if he is/was a spiritually begotten child of God like everyone else? Is it by virtue of his being firstborn that this was possible? Seemingly his nature and person varies little if any from ours, according to Mormon teaching.

c. Through his divine attributes and the power of "Heavenly Father," Jesus accomplished an "infinite and eternal" atonement. Jesus submitted himself to "Father's" will and descended below all things in "taking upon himself the sins of all the children of God."[61] Beginning in Gethsemane and ending at the tomb, Christ made atonement for sin.

d. His atonement "affects worlds without number" and will save all of God's children except "sons of perdition."[62]

e. The agony of Christ's atonement secured a resurrection for all the children of God." "Little children" are redeemed through his work as well as all "who repent."[63]

f. People must do the *full will of God* if they are to receive the *full benefit* of the atonement.[64] If they do not keep God's commandments, they must suffer for their own sins.

A careful reading of Mormon statements regarding the atonement of Christ raises important questions and reveals various contradictions. Does Christ's atonement benefit all even though repentance is essential for experiencing those benefits? What place does faith play if people must keep God's commandments? Who are the sons of perdition who will suffer in hell?

At this point it will be helpful to discuss the Mormon concept of general/unconditional versus individual/conditional salvation.

General or unconditional salvation is the redemption or resurrection which Christ's atonement achieved. It is a salvation which is available for all people everywhere, even seemingly if they are not believers. Apostle Bruce McConkie stated:

> Unconditional or general salvation, that which comes by grace alone without obedience to gospel law, consists in the mere fact of being resurrected.[65]

Because Jesus suffered for sin and was raised from the dead (Gethsemane to resurrection), people everywhere can experience that same resurrection. Non-Mormons, it seems, will eventually be assigned to the telestial or terrestrial kingdoms, unless by proxy baptism they are promoted to the celestial kingdom. This is possible because of Christ's atonement and does not require a specific response to it themselves: The only condition placed on anyone, it appears, is that the ungodly and unrighteous must suffer sufficiently for their sins in spirit prison, otherwise—

> ...because of the fall of man came Jesus Christ, even the Father and the Son; and because of Jesus Christ came the resurrection of man. And because

of the redemption of man which came by Jesus
Christ, they are brought back into the presence of
the Lord; yea, this is wherein all men are redeemed,
because the death of Christ bringeth to pass a
redemption from an endless sleep, from which
sleep all men shall be awakened by the power of
God (Mormon 9:12-13).

According to Mormonism, without the death of Christ
there would have been no resurrection. With it, all people
may experience a resurrection and with it a form of blissful
eternity (telestial or terrestrial).[66]

There is even the claim within Mormonism that Christ's
atonement sufficed for the salvation of innumerable worlds.

Now our Lord's jurisdiction and power extend far
beyond the limits of this one small earth on which
we dwell. He is, under the Father, the Creator of
worlds without number (Moses 1:33). And through
the power of his atonement the inhabitants of
these worlds, the revelation says, "are begotten
sons and daughters unto God" (*Doctrine and
Covenants* 76:24), which means that the atonement
of Christ, being literally and truly infinite, applies
to an infinite number of earths.[67]

Christ's atonement has provided a form of salvation
"immortality" because "all people who have ever lived will be
resurrected."[68] But this concept immediately raises two questions. First, it is claimed that Jesus' atonement provides salvation in the form of immortality for all people everywhere.
But does the Bible list this as one of the purposes of Christ's
work? No. It speaks of Jesus as being the firstfruits of the resurrection (1 Corinthians 15:20), but this is the resurrection
to glory of the redeemed who have believed and put their
faith in Christ. There will also be a resurrection of the
unjust; about that the Bible is very clear: "Many of those who
sleep in the dust of the earth shall awake, some to everlasting life, some to shame and everlasting contempt."[69] It is

therefore biblically inconsistent to claim that Christ's resurrection was necessary or is necessary to guarantee and secure all people's resurrection from the dead.

Second, the benefits of salvation, according to the Bible, are always contingent on belief in Christ. There are no promises related generally to all people regardless of their faith in Christ. As will be noted in the last section of this chapter, Mormon theology threatens only the apostate from the LDS Church with the possibility of hell or outer darkness. The Bible views the universality of sinfulness with very serious consequences apart from faith in Christ. Mormonism offers a universalistic view of salvation: Christ's atonement does not just offer the potential of salvation, but offers it unconditionally to everyone—unless you leave the Church of Jesus Christ of Latter-day Saints.[70]

3. Man's response. As noted in the previous discussions, a false and truncated view of sin and fallen human nature and an inaccurate understanding of Christ's atonement has led to the Mormon view of unconditional or general salvation. It assumes that virtually all people will be saved and go on to either the telestial or terrestrial kingdoms. But how does one achieve conditional or general salvation?

Conditional salvation for the Mormon is acquisition of the highest level of heaven—the celestial kingdom. How can a person reach that goal?

At this point, what is viewed as the essential role of the Church of Jesus Christ of Latter-day Saints and that of its prophet Joseph Smith comes into play. It is believed by Mormons that when Joseph translated the golden plates and constituted the Church on April 6, 1830, he had restored the fullness of the Gospel on the face of the earth. The full truth (the Book of Mormon) and the means of practicing the teachings of the prophet in the life of his Church (the "Gospel") were now available to all who wished to participate. For a Mormon, implementing the Gospel is not just putting one's faith in Jesus Christ. Instead, the Gospel is essentially a system of commands and ordinances that one must participate in and adhere to within the membership of the LDS Church before full salvation or eternal life can be accomplished. In a very real sense Mormonism is a priestly and sacramental system of salvation that differs entirely from the biblical and evangelical truth of salvation by faith alone through Christ.

Here are the steps to the highest level of salvation in the celestial kingdom.

Step One—faith. Faith for the Mormon is paraphrased from the Bible as having "confidence in things that are not seen, but that are true."[71] The first difficulty for the Gospel of Mormonism is that it calls for faith in a Jesus who is not the Jesus of the Bible, but who is our spiritual brother from heaven, born like us as a spirit child of heavenly parents.[72] By its own definition, believing in what is true, Mormonism fails the test of faith because it asks us to accept an alternative, unbiblical Christ. But there is another vital point. Does Mormonism teach faith in Christ Himself or faith in what Christ is said to command? While the phrase "believe in Christ" is often used in Mormon literature, "faith," instead of being the singular means of salvation, is in this case merely the starting point.

Step Two—repentance. For the Mormon, repentance involves confessing and abandoning sin as well as restoring or resolving *all* damage done by one's sin.[73] This may be a noble definition, but it is not a biblical one. It assumes that a person has the ability to repair all damage caused by one's sin. And a further condition is added to repentance: You should "spend the balance of your lives trying to live the commandments of the Lord so he can eventually pardon you and cleanse you."[74] Full salvation is to be earned, according to Mormonism. A person must achieve perfection.[75]

Logically, a proselyte to the Mormon Church is thereby encouraged to obey the commands of the one true Church, "the ordinances of the Gospel." Consistent with works salvation, further steps are added to the LDS plan of salvation.

Step Three—baptism by immersion in the Mormon Church. It is here that the influence of Mormonism is unmistakable. The LDS Church claims to be the only true

Church, and that all Christian denominations are false or incomplete. Baptism, therefore, in order to be legitimate must be executed by "a duly commissioned servant or representative of the Savior."[76] This servant is to be a member of the Aaronic priesthood of the LDS Church. When baptism occurs under these circumstances, it becomes "the gateway through which we enter the celestial kingdom."[77]

Step Four—laying on of hands by a member of the Melchizedek priesthood in order to receive the Holy Ghost. The Holy Ghost is not promised as a result of faith and belief; it comes instead as a result of a Melchizedek priest bestowing it:

> The authority to bestow the Holy Ghost belongs to the Melchizedek Priesthood...the elder says "Receive the Holy Ghost," and "I confirm you a member of the Church of Jesus Christ of Latter-day Saints."[78]

Consequently a Mormon will happily speak of himself as a born-again Christian. His or her new birth was produced by baptismal regeneration in the LDS Church, not by faith in Christ.[79]

Step Five—ordination for the males only into the Melchizedek priesthood. The laying on of hands and ordination by a LDS male member makes a man a member of that same order. This step is necessary for progression to exaltation to the celestial kingdom:

> This higher priesthood is designed to enable men to gain exaltation in the highest heaven in eternity....Perfection can be gained only in and through and because of their priesthood.[80]

Also Mormons believe the "Holy Ghost" will come to a person only when he or she is faithful and desires help from the Melchizedek priesthood.[81]

Step Six—receive the temple endowments. Temple rites for both sexes of sealing, anointing, and other rituals comprise the sixth step toward "eternal life" for the diligent Mormon. These rites, which must occur within the confines of a Mormon temple and under the administration of the Mormon priesthood, clearly demonstrate the importance of Mormon temples in their plan of salvation.[82] The temples have a vital and necessary place for Mormons regarding the celestial kingdom. Through the rituals practiced in them "recipients are endowed with power from on high. They receive an education relative to the Lord's purposes and plans...and are taught the things that must be done by man in order to gain exaltation in the world to come."[83] The endowments are necessary for "preparing to return to the presence of God."[84] The various rites and rituals as well as the secret name given to temple-worthy Mormons enable them to pass the celestial guards and enter the celestial realm.

Step Seven—celestial marriage. Mormon belief maintains that "celestial marriage is the gate to an exaltation in the highest heaven within the celestial world." Once having their marriage sealed in the temple for "time and eternity," worthy Mormons may then potentially advance to godhood in the resurrection, having their spouses make it then possible for these "gods" to produce and procreate children for their own worlds.[85]

Step Eight—observing the word of wisdom. Joseph Smith taught that the use of "strong drinks"—alcoholic beverages or "hot drinks"—referring as presently interpreted to coffee and tea, both containing caffeine, would demonstrate unworthiness for exaltation.[86] Mormonism states clearly the benefits of observing the word of wisdom: "The reward is life, not only prolonged mortal life, but life eternal."[87]

Step Nine—sustain the prophet. Each prophet/ President of the LDS Church is believed to be the sole revelator and representative of God to His Church. It is essential, therefore, that every worthy Mormon support or sustain his word (message) at each church conference (April 6 and

October 6). "To reject the word of the Lord [the message of the prophet] is to reject the Lord himself," and to be unworthy of the celestial kingdom.[88]

Step Ten—tithing. "One tenth of the interest or increase of each member of the Church is payable into the tithing funds of the Church each year."[89] And "payment of an honest tithing is essential to the attainment of those great blessings which the Lord has in store for his faithful saints. Members of the church who fail or neglect to pay an honest tithing are thereby denying themselves of the receipt of these rich blessings."[90] *Doctrine and Covenants* is even more explicit: "For he that is tithed shall not be burned at his coming."[91]

Step Eleven—sacrament meetings. A sacrament meeting is the weekly Sunday gathering of local Mormons when they meet to sing, testify, and share the sacrament, in their tradition, of bread and water. Regular participation in this occasion is necessary in order to stay in the close fellowship of the Church. Such meetings are the occasion for renewing one's covenant vows begun at baptism.[92] By keeping this covenant through the observance of the sacraments, the Mormon is taught that "we will always have the Lord's spirit to be with us and that by following this pattern, believing on his name, we will gain a remission of our sins."[93]

Step Twelve—obedience to the Church. Obedience and continued participation in the Church of Jesus Christ of Latter-day Saints is essential for conditional salvation.[94] In fact hell is particularly reserved for apostates who leave the LDS Church for one reason or another and join some other religious group. This topic will be discussed in more detail later.

Unconditional or individual salvation ("eternal life" in Mormon nomenclature) is never a certainty. A Mormon may never be sure that he has fully qualified for exaltation. His hope is that he has adhered to the above 12 steps consistently and regularly enough for him to achieve the celestial kingdom.

At this stage the notion of grace enters into Mormon thinking. Second Nephi 25:23 states: "It is by grace that we are saved, after all we can do." Grace is the Mormon's last hope, not his first and only appeal, as found in the Bible. Once a Mormon has diligently applied himself to do all that the Church requires, then perhaps he may appeal to grace. This is certainly a radical departure from the biblical concept: "By grace you have been saved through faith, and that not of yourselves; it is the gift of God, not of works, lest anyone should boast."[95]

In the Mormon system, how can a person know when he has done all that he can do? More directly, who has ever done all that can be done? Cannot everyone have done something more or something else? In fact, when grace is presented as ancillary "to all that can be done," it is no longer grace. If everything that could be done has been accomplished, grace or anything else should not be needed. Rather, it appears that "grace" as applied here is only window dressing to give the Mormon plan of salvation an air of biblical authenticity.

The plan of salvation according to the conditional redemption of the Mormon Church is not a Gospel at all. It is rather a plan of Mormon works devised to bring submission and obedience to the Church of Jesus Christ of Latter-day Saints. In *Gospel Principles* a parable describing the Mormon plan of salvation is told. A debtor begs his creditor for mercy because his debts are large and long overdue. Just as the cruel creditor is ready to cast the debtor into prison, a friend intervenes. He offers to "pay the debt" for the friend. The debtor is further encouraged by the friend, "You will pay the debt to me and I will set the terms. It will not be easy, but it will be possible."[96]

The rich friend had intervened not with a free gift, but with a loan to be repaid. Is not the friend representative of the LDS Church? Each devout saint under the Mormon system is working desperately to pay off his or her obligation in order to enter the celestial kingdom. The false hope is offered that if he does all he can, at that point grace will take over.

Such a teaching is a far cry from biblical grace and salvation. It is not a Gospel of freedom through Christ, but a gospel of servitude and obligation to a religious organization.

In Matthew 18:21-35 Jesus told the story of a king who forgave his servants their large debts to him. One of the servants turned afterward and demanded from a fellow servant payment of a small debt. Unable to pay, the small debtor was thrown into prison. The point of the parable is that God's kingdom is built on true grace. We should forgive one another just as God through Christ has forgiven us. All of our transgressions were placed on Christ, our sinbearer, and we are freely forgiven as a result.

The biblical Gospel of Jesus Christ is that no debts remain to be paid. Jesus Christ suffered for our sins sufficiently on the cross so that everyone who believes in Him may be forgiven of all wrongs—past, present, and future.

4. Mormonism and eternal consequences. In contradiction to the Bible, Mormonism speaks not of two eternal destinies, heaven or hell, but of four—the celestial, terrestrial, and telestial kingdoms, plus hell or outer darkness. The extra-biblical designations are due to the claimed revelations of Joseph Smith contained in *Doctrine and Covenants*.[97] The spurious nature of these claims has already been exposed earlier in this book. Our purpose here is to show the uniqueness and unbiblical nature of Mormonism and how greatly the features of Mormon theology contrast with the truths of the Bible.

The celestial kingdom. Mormonism teaches that worthy Mormons may inherit the highest glory of the celestial kingdom. This kingdom is the place where qualifying Mormons—

- will "live eternally in the presence of Heavenly Father and Jesus Christ."
- "will become gods."
- "will have their righteous family members with them...will be able to have spirit children also" who will "have the same relationship to them as we do to our Heavenly Father."

- "will receive a fulness of joy."
- "will have everything that our Heavenly Father and Jesus Christ have—all power, glory, dominion and knowledge."[98]

Mormonism definitely teaches that worthy Mormons can become gods. They can literally receive and acquire what theologians have traditionally called the incommunicable attributes of God. To understand the radical nature of this claim, it is important to know that the communicable attributes of God—righteousness, holiness, and goodness—were those qualities possessed by Adam and Eve in the Garden of Eden. They are those qualities that God can share with mankind without being less than God.[99] Incommunicable attributes—His omniscience, omnipotence, and omnipresence and eternality—are characteristics that only God Himself can possess. Yet LDS scholar Stephen Robinson claims that Mormons can possess them.[100] How can it be that God who possesses all power can share all power without having less-than-complete power Himself. It is incomprehensible. Yet this is the claim of Mormonism. The glory, which the Bible says God cannot share with any other, Mormonism claims is possessed by those who through the celestial glory receive exaltation: "Man is the child of God, formed in the divine image...capable, by experience through ages of aeons, of evolving into a God."[101] Thus it is concluded that "through the atonement and their own faithfulness, those who obtain exaltation become gods" and "receive all things that the Father has."[102]

In addition to "worthy Mormons," children who die before the age of eight (the age of baptism in the LDS Church) and those of the non-Mormon kingdom, ("Gentiles") who are baptized by proxy in a Mormon temple after their own death will inherit the celestial kingdom. These secret ceremonies are held in over 50 temples around the world. Baptism and marriage for the dead are performed by temple-worthy Mormons for dead persons whose names have been assigned to them. They are the names of people whom

it is believed, did not have a adequate knowledge of the
gospel. Their release from spirit prison is dependent on their
acceptance of the claimed truths of the LDS Church.[103]

> We have been authorized to perform baptisms vic-
> ariously so that when they (the dead) hear the
> gospel preached and desire to accept, that essen-
> tial ordinance will have been performed.[104]

> All who hear and believe...whether living or dead,
> are heirs of salvation in the celestial kingdom of
> God.[105]

How far does such a possibility extend? Who is eligible
for proxy baptism? Every person who did not have a chance
to accept the Gospel of Mormonism in this life.[106] One star-
tling example of Mormonism's open-ended approach to
postmortem proselytization is the baptism, ordination to
priesthood, and marriage (to Eva Braun) of Adolf Hitler at
the Jordan Temple, South Jordan, Utah, on September 28,
1993.[107] If he accepted this temple work, Adolf Hitler was
promoted to paradise and is well on his way to the celestial
kingdom.

Mormonism takes considerable credit and pride in
devising a system of salvation in which there is almost universal salvation. According to their Gospel, even Adolf Hitler
might likely make it not only to a better place, but to godhood itself!

The terrestrial and telestial kingdoms. The features of
the terrestrial kingdom vary greatly from that of the celestial
realm. Nevertheless, they are generally very positive. Those
who go to the terrestrial kingdom are "they who though
honorable fail to comply with the requirements for exaltation were blinded by the craftiness of men and unable to
receive and obey the high laws of God." (*Doctrines of the
Gospel Student Manual*, page 91, Church of Latter-day Saints,
Salt Lake City, Utah, 1986). They proved "not valiant in the
testimony of Jesus." These are obviously unworthy Mormons
and/or non-Mormons who never joined the Church of Jesus

Christ of Latter-day Saints. The experiences of those going the terrestrial route include:

- enjoying the presence of the son but not the "fulness" of the Father.
- ministering to those in the telestial kingdom.
- exercising power, might, and dominion over the lower telestial kingdom.
- coming forth "after those" inheriting the "celestial kingdom have been resurrected."[108]

Who qualifies for the telestial kingdom? Those who "profess to follow Christ" "but willfully reject the gospel" (i.e., the principles and teachings of Mormonism) and reject Jesus, the prophets (i.e., the biblical prophets and the Mormon presidents), and the everlasting covenant. These people "will inherit" this level of salvation.[109] This group will also include "murderers, liars, sorcerers, adulterers, and whoremongers."[110] How will these people reach this level of redemption? Is it by faith and trust in Christ? No. The Mormon claim is that they will "become clean through their suffering."[111] This is apparently a reference to their trials in spirit prison prior to the final resurrection at the end of the millennium. The system presented here is clearly not biblical but is a form of purgatory with its source rooted in the teachings of Joseph Smith.

The Mormon teaching about hell or outer darkness is that, first of all, it will be populated primarily by "Satan and the one-third of the hosts of heaven who followed him."[112]

Rooted partly in the biblical notion of fallen angels (Revelation 12:7-9), these "hosts of heaven" are the fallen premortal spirit children of "Heavenly Father." While Mormonism makes the claim to possess a more compassionate system of eternal rewards, Mormon belief would consign to eternal condemnation one-third of the population of an infinite number of worlds. The result is an infinite number of premortal spirits in an infinite number of hells. This view of eternity is clearly incomprehensible and *infinitely* less compassionate.

In addition to these, apostates from the Church of Jesus Christ are consigned to outer darkness or hell:

> Those who in mortality have known the power of God, have made partakers of it...then later denied the truth...who deny the Holy Ghost...will have no forgiveness and will be the sons of perdition. Sons of perdition will suffer the wrath of God and partake of the second death.[113]

Thus we see that only those who have been baptized by the LDS Church, have been prayed for by a priest in the Church, and have received the Holy Ghost through the LDS priesthood are capable of committing the unpardonable sin. They are the ones who have received a burning in the bosom after having studied Mormon claims.[114] Once having experienced this subjective impulse, "you shall feel that it is right," they have then rejected it. This rejection of "truth" labels them an "apostate" or "son of perdition":[115]

> —the father saves all the works of his hands, except those sons of perdition, who deny the son after the Father has revealed him.[116]

Whatever the source of this feeling—psychosomatic, self-induced, or demonic—subjective feelings are never an adequate truth claim. Nonetheless, rejecting Mormonism after this supposed experience uniquely qualifies one for hell. That being the case, the proper conclusion is that it is far better to never join the Church of Jesus Christ of Latter-day Saints at all than to become a member and later leave the group. After all, a nonmember could at least qualify for the terrestrial or telestial levels of salvation. It would still be possible to dwell in the presence of Jesus. It would be an existence of "glory" which "surpasses all human understanding."[117] By proxy baptism, as in the case of Adolf Hitler, a person could even gain the celestial kingdom.

A cryptic passage in *Doctrine and Covenants* raises another critical issue: "...the Lord will not lay any sin to your charge...but unto that soul who sinneth shall the former sins return, saith the Lord your God."[118]

Robert Millet of Brigham Young University has argued that if a Mormon does not "comply with the further requirements of heaven" then all of his former sins will be "returned" upon him.[119] Millett argues, referring to *Doctrine and Covenants*, that if a Mormon had continued in doing righteous deeds by "obedience to the requirements of heaven...through baptism, the laying on of hands and obeying the commandments of the Lord" that person would qualify for exaltation. Thus Mormons who fail to meet the requirements of the celestial kingdom are punished by being assigned to the telestial or terrestrial realms. This perspective, once again, seems to be completely related to one's faithfulness to Mormonism.

Clearly it is the case that the eternal kingdoms of Mormonism are not biblical. Heaven is based on a reward system that presents to "worthy Mormons" the status of godhood in the celestial kingdom. Hell for mortals is reserved only for those who apostatize from the Mormon Church. Non-Mormon, "moral" people will dwell with Jesus in the terrestrial kingdom. But the Bible speaks of only one realm where Father and Son dwell in harmony with all the true saints.[120]

Summary

While the biblical/evangelical view of salvation is based on grace and is a matter of sincere trust in Christ, Mormonism pays lip service to both grace and faith. "Grace" in Mormonism is applied only after a person has done all that is possible for him to do. Mormonism is a priestly system which demands full obedience. It is not just a case of doing good deeds, for the Mormon Gospel demands allegiance to the entire system of Mormon temple rites. The temple work of baptism for the dead claims to make it possible for the unbelieving and unrepentant in this life, including Adolf Hitler, to achieve godhood. Mormonism's view of temple work for the dead destroys the centrality of faith, for those who have died have obviously seen and experienced the truth of eternal destiny. The biblical definition of faith is a willingness to believe even if one has not seen the realities in which one believes.[121]

Mormonism creates three heavens. All of them are derived from Mormon sources, and none from the Bible. Additionally, according to Mormonism those who are designated to hell are only those who have apostatized from the LDS Church. Given the view of the Church that an infinite number of worlds exist, however, there are by necessity an infinite number of souls in perdition. When the biblical Gospel is compared to the "Gospel" of Mormonism, what we see is not the filling out of gaps in Christian truth, as Stephen Robinson claims, but contrary and opposing ways of salvation. It is impossible that both can be right. For all of us who have experienced the transforming love of God and His salvation through trust in the Jesus of the Bible, there is no way to the Father but through Him! (John 14:6).

As well can it be that an infinitely gracious God would leave the world without any evidence of His grace and of the Gospel of the Lord Jesus Christ for almost 18 centuries? That is impossible to conceive and contrary to Scripture (Matthew 16:18). Charles Wesley, the poet of the eighteenth century evangelical revival, beautifully expressed the fullness of the Gospel in these lines:

> And can it be that I should gain
> An interest in the Savior's blood?
> Died He for me, who caused His pain?
> For me, who Him to death pursued?
> Amazing love! How can it be
> That Thou, my God, shouldst die for me?
> 'Tis mystery all! The Immortal dies!
> Who can explore His strange design?
> In vain the firstborn seraph tries
> To sound the depths of love divine!
> 'Tis mercy all! Let earth adore,

Let angel minds inquire no more.
No condemnation now I dread;
Jesus, and all in Him, is mine!
Alive in Him, my living Head,
And clothed in righteousness divine,
Bold I approach the eternal throne,
And claim the crown, through Christ my own.
—Charles Wesley, 1707-88

Evangelical and Mormon Views of the Doctrine of Salvation

	Evangelical Doctrine of Salvation		Mormon Doctrine of Salvation			
	Believer	Unbeliever	Faithful Mormon	Inactive Mormon	Apostate Mormon	Non-Mormon
Man's Condition	· Lost and rebellious against God	· Lost and rebellious against God	· Basically good · May commit sins · Perfection possible	· Basically good · May commit sins · Perfection no longer possible	· Basically good · May commit sins · Perfection no longer possible	· Basically good · May commit sins · Perfection not possible
Means of Salvation	Christ's work · Died for sins of all the world · Raised eternally as Lord · Incarnate as Messiah and Savior	Christ's work · Died for sins of all the world · Raised eternally as Lord · Incarnate as Messiah and Savior	Work of Christ of Mormonism · Restoration of Gospel and establishment of LDS Church	Work of Christ of Mormonism · Restoration of Gospel and establishment of LDS Church	Work of Christ of Mormonism · Negated; sins are reapplied	Work of Christ of Mormonism · Christ's atonement provides immortality for all people
Man's Response	· Faith Alone	· Unbelieving · Unrepentant	· Faith · Obedience · Baptism by LDS Priesthoods · Temple work: tithing, etc. · Word of wisdom · Celestial marriage	· Believes · Joins LDS Church · Becomes inactive	· Believes · Joins LDS Church · Rejects Mormonism after testimony of the Holy Spirit an burning of th bosom	· Post mortem belief is necessary for celestial exaltation · Terrestrial: must be morally good · No response necessary for telestial must suffer sins in spirit prison
State of Redemption	· Heaven · Paradise (prior to last judgment)	· Hell	· Celestial kingdom · Godhood	· Terrestrial or telestial kingdom	· Hell or Outer Darkness	· Celestial: possible through proxy baptism · Telestial

Chapter Notes

1. In their book *How Wide the Divide?* (InterVarsity Press, 1997), Stephen Robinson and Craig Blomberg deal with this question, but unfortunately most of the concerns raised in this chapter are not discussed.
2. Kenneth Kantzer and Carl Henry, editors, *Evangelical Affirmations* (Grand Rapids: Zondervan, 1990), pp. 111-12.
3. Cf. 1 Corinthians 3:8; 9:25; Ephesians 6:8; Colossians 3:24; Revelation 22:12.
4. See Henry's article on "Image of God" in Walter A. Elwell, editor, *Evangelical Dictionary of Theology* (Grand Rapids: Baker, 1984), p. 547.
5. Book of Mormon, II Nephi 25:23.
6. The book of Hebrews is the classical treatment of Christ's work as High Priest and sinbearer in light of the Old Testament sacrificial system.
7. John R. W. Stott, *The Cross of Christ* (Downers Grove: InterVarsity Press, 1986), p. 7.
8. John 1:1. See the chapter on Christ.
9. See 1 Corinthians 1:23. The Greek word translated as "stumbling block" is *skandalon*, from which is derived the English word "scandalous."
10. For example, see Ephesians 2:8-10.
11. Ron Rhodes and Marian Bodine, *Reasoning from the Scriptures with the Mormons* (Eugene: Harvest House, 1995), p. 335.
12. J. I. Packer, "Justification," in Elwell, *Evangelical Dictionary of Theology*, p. 593.
13. Jonathan Edwards, "Justification by Faith Alone," in *The Works of Jonathan Edwards*, vol. I (Banner of Truth, 1974), p. 650.
14. Acts 3:19; 8:22; 17:30; 26:20.
15. See the article "Repentance" in *New Dictionary of Theology*, S.B. Ferguson et al, editors, InterVarsity Press, 1988.
16. Donald Guthrie, *New Testament Theology* (Downers Grove, IL: InterVarsity Press 1981), p. 590.
17. *Evangelical Dictionary of Theology*, p. 262.
18. Paradise, as mentioned by Jesus to the thief on the cross (Luke 23:43), is mentioned three times in the New Testament (see also 2 Corinthians 12:4; Revelation 2:7) and generally refers to "a superterrestrial place of blessedness" or heaven, "being in the presence of God." See study note for Luke 23:43 in *Harper Study Bible*, Harold Lindsell, editor, Zondervan Press.
19. A quick review of heaven and hell in the four Gospels reveals this fact.
20. See pages 175–176.
21. *Doctrine and Covenants* 1:17-18, 21-23.
22. "Testimony of the Prophet of Joseph Smith" contained in the Introduction of The Book of Mormon. No pagination is listed, but the above comments are on the first page of the Introduction.
23. Blomberg and Robinson, *How Wide the Divide?*, pp. 165-66.
24. Joseph Smith, "History," in *Pearl of Great Price* 1:9.
25. Joseph Smith, "History," in *Pearl of Great Price* 1:29.
26. Ibid.
27. *Gospel Principles*, p. 105.
28. Ibid.
29. Ibid.
30. See the following Scriptures: Psalm 139:7-11; Isaiah 31:3; John 4:24; Acts 7:48; 2 Corinthians 3:17.
31. *Gospel Principles*, p. 106.
32. *Doctrines of the Gospel Student Manual: Religions 231 and 232* (Salt Lake City: Church Educational System—Church of Jesus Christ of Latter-day Saints, 1986), p. 60. Quote cited in the manual used for educating LDS youth is from Spencer W. Kimball, *The Teachings of Spencer W. Kimball*, p. 423.

33. The "great apostasy" has never been mentioned by any non-Mormon church historian. See, for example, Howard F. Vos, *Exploring Church History* (Nashville: Nelson).
34. See Chapter 1.
35. *Gospel Principles*, p. 105.
36. *Doctrines of the Gospel*, p. 61.
37. Ibid., p. 62.
38. Joseph Smith, "History," in *Pearl of Great Price* 1:66-75.
39. Ibid., 1:69.
40. *Doctrines of the Gospel*, p. 63.
41. *Doctrine and Covenants* 1:30.
42. McConkie, *Mormon Doctrine*, p. 670.
43. *Gospel Principles*, p. 113.
44. *Doctrine and Covenants* 27:11
45. Genesis 1:26-28.
46. 2 Nephi 2:22; Moses 3:5-7.
47. Genesis 2:7.
48. McConkie, *A New Witness for the Articles of Faith*, p. 47.
49. Alma 42:6-7; *Doctrine and Covenants* 29:40-41; Moses 5:4; 6:49.
50. Moses 6:48; Alma 41:11; Ether 3:2; *Doctrine and Covenants* 20:20; Moses 6:48; Alma 12:22-24.
51. Moses 4:22; 5:2-3,11.
52. Moses 5:10-11; 2 Nephi 2:11. See *Doctrines of the Gospel*, p. 19.
53. *Doctrines of the Gospel*, p. 19; 2 Nephi 2:25-27; Moses 5:10-11.
54. *Doctrines of the Gospel*, p. 19. See also 2 Nephi 2:22-24; Moses 5:10-11.
55. *Doctrines of the Gospel*, p. 20. Quoted from Joseph Fielding Smith, "Fall-Atonement-Resurrection-Sacrament," in *Charge to Religious Educators*, p. 124.
56. *Doctrines of the Gospel*, p. 19.
57. "Church News," in *Deseret News*, July 31, 1965, p. 7.
58. Ibid., p. 21. Quoted from David O. McKay, *Gospel Ideals*, pp. 347-48.
59. See, for example, Romans 1:18-32.
60. A helpful outline of the Mormon view of the atonement according to Mormonism is contained in *Doctrines of the Gospel*, chapter 9, pp. 22-26.
61. Ibid., p. 22.
62. Ibid.
63. Ibid. See *Doctrine and Covenants* 29:46-50; Alma 7:12-13; *Doctrine and Covenants* 19:15-19. While the LDS Church does not endorse the doctrine of "blood atonement," it is a curious belief and part of Mormonism doctrinal history. A helpful survey and critique is found in Jerald and Sandra Tanner, *The Changing World of Mormonism*, pp. 490-504. This doctrine illustrates how far from evangelicalism historic Mormonism has been.
64. Ibid. See also *Doctrine and Covenants* 19:15-20; Mosiah 3:19; 2 Nephi 9:21.
65. McConkie, *Mormon Doctrine*, second edition (Salt Lake City: Bookcraft, 1966), p. 669.
66. The nature of the telestial and terrestrial kingdoms will be discussed soon.
67. *Doctrines of the Gospels*, pp. 25-26. See Chapter 2 for a detailed critique of Mormon polytheism.
68. *Gospel Principles*, p. 74. See also the article in the *Encyclopedia of Mormonism* on the Atonement of Christ.
69. Daniel 12:2. See also John 5:28,29; Acts 24:14,15; Revelation 20:11-15.
70. See pp. 43-45 for the Mormon view of apostates.
71. *Gospel Principles*, p. 117.
72. See Chapter 3.
73. Much of the outline of the Mormon plan of salvation is taken from *Gospel Principles*, an official publication of the Church of Jesus Christ of Latter-day Saints.

74. *Gospel Principles*, p. 126.

75. Notably, Robert Millet's (Religion Professor at BYU) recent book on salvation is entitled *You Are Doing Better Than You Think: Perfection Is Within Reach* (Salt Lake City: Deseret Book Co., 1995).

76. James E. Talmage, *The Articles of Faith* (Salt Lake City: Deseret Press, 1976), p. 137.

77. *Gospel Principles*, p. 131.

78. Talmage, *Articles of Faith*, p. 167.

79. See John 3:1-16.

80. McConkie, *Mormon Doctrine*, p. 167.

81. *Gospel Principles*, p. 139.

82. The rites include: 1) preparatory ordinance (ceremonial washing and anointing); 2) "a course of instruction by lectures and representations"; 3) "making covenants"; 4) "a sense of divine presence" (*Encyclopedia of Mormonism*, vol. 1, p. 455).

83. McConkie, *Mormon Doctrine*, p. 227.

84. *Encyclopedia of Mormonism*, vol. 1, p. 455.

85. *Doctrine and Covenants* 131:1-4.

86. *Doctrine and Covenants* 89, G&P 192.

87. *Gospel Principles*, p. 195.

88. McConkie, *Mormon Doctrine*, p. 150.

89. Ibid., p. 796.

90. Ibid., p. 798.

91. *Doctrine and Covenants* 64:23.

92. McConkie, *Mormon Doctrine*, p. 660.

93. *Gospel Principles*, p. 155.

94. McConkie, *Mormon Doctrine*, p. 539.

95. Ephesians 2:8,9.

96. *Gospel Principles*, p. 77.

97. See *Doctrine and Covenants* 76:71-80; 88:21-30; 101:65; 105:4-5; 130:11; 131:1-2; 132:19; 137:6-8.

98. *Gospel Principles*, p. 302; see also *Doctrine and Covenants* 76.

99. See especially the chapter on God for further argumentation in this matter.

100. See *How Wide the Divide?* p. 82.

101. The First Presidency, "The Origin of Man," in *Improvement Era*, November 1909, p. 81. Cited in *Achieving a Celestial Marriage* (Salt Lake City: Church Educational System, 1992), p. 130.

102. *Doctrines of the Gospel*, p. 90, citing *Doctrine and Covenants* 76:55,58; 84:38; 132:19-20.

103. *Doctrine and Covenants* 128:5.

104. *Doctrines of the Gospel*, p. 86, cited from Boyd Packer, in Conference Report, October 1975, p. 147.

105. *Doctrines of the Gospel*, p. 85, cited in Joseph Fielding Smith, *Doctrines of Salvation* 2:133.

106. Mormons apparently do not endorse the notion of a second opportunity to receive a true witness of the spirit. Post mortem evangelism is basically confined to people who never were Mormons. This view would be consistent with apostates of the church being consigned to outer darkness.

107. This information was gleaned from the *International Genealogical Index of the LDS Church*.

108. *Doctrines of the Gospel*, p. 90; see also *Doctrine and Covenants* 76:77-91; 88:99; 45:54.

109. *Doctrines of the Gospel*, p. 90; *Doctrine and Covenants* 76:99-101,103.

110. Ibid.

111. Ibid.

112. *Doctrines of the Gospel*, p. 91; *Doctrines and Covenants* 76:25-30; 29:36-38.
113. *Doctrines of the Gospel*, p. 91; *Doctrines and Covenants* 76:31-48.
114. *Doctrine and Covenants* 76:43-44.
115. Ibid., 9:8.
116. Ibid., 76:43-44.
117. *Doctrines of the Gospel*, p. 90; *Doctrine and Covenants* 76:84-89.
118. *Doctrine and Covenants* 82:7.
119. Robert Millet, *Within Reach*. Deseret Books, Salt Lake City, 1995, p.82.
120. Acts 7:55,56; Hebrews 8:1.
121. Hebrews 11:1,2; John 20:29.

5

Terminology

Jerald and Sandra Tanner

Whenever an evangelical Christian and a Latter-day Saint engage in a doctrinal discussion they encounter the problem of terminology. LDS leaders use the standard vocabulary of Christianity but with radically different definitions. Stephen Robinson, a BYU professor, commented on this problem in the recent book *How Wide the Divide?*:

> Besides history, another obstacle to mutual understanding is terminology—our respective theological vocabularies. Latter-day Saints and Evangelicals generally employ the same theological terms, but we usually define them differently, and this quite often makes communication more difficult than if we spoke different religious languages entirely. The similarity of terms makes us *think* we are communicating, but when all is said and done both sides go away with the feeling that nothing quite added up, and this raises suspicions of deception.[1]

For example, when Christians hear Mormons refer to the Garden of Eden they may incorrectly assume that the LDS believe it was by the Tigris and Euphrates rivers. Joseph Smith, however, claimed by revelation that the Garden of Eden was in western Missouri. This would throw off the

---

Scripture quotations in this chapter are from the King James Version except as otherwise noted. See Copyright page.

entire first part of Genesis. Noah would have entered the ark in Missouri and ended up in some location in the Middle East. LDS Apostle John A. Widtsoe explained:

> Latter-day Saints know, through modern revelation, that the Garden of Eden was on the North American continent and that Adam and Eve began their conquest of the earth in the upper part of what is now the state of Missouri. It seems very probable that the children of our first earthly parents moved down along the fertile, pleasant lands of the Mississippi valley.[2]

Further on in the same book Apostle Widtsoe explained:

> When the flood came in the days of Noah, the Mississippi drainage must have increased to a tremendous volume, quite in harmony with the Biblical account. Noah's ark would be floated on the mighty, rushing waters, towards the Gulf of Mexico.[3]

It is obvious, then, that a Christian should never take for granted that his LDS friend understands common Christian terms in the biblical way.

Because the Bible has many warnings about false prophets (Matthew 24:11,24; 2 Corinthians 11:4,13; 1 John 4:1) and people teaching strange doctrines (2 Peter 2:12; Galatians 1:6-8; Hebrews 13:9), it is essential that we understand what the Bible says on various doctrines. One of the crucial issues is the nature of God. The book of Deuteronomy has a very severe warning about any prophet that would teach a false view of God: "If there arise among you a prophet, or a dreamer of dreams...saying, Let us go after other gods, which thou hast not known, and let us serve them, thou shalt not hearken unto the words of that prophet" (Deuteronomy 13:1-3). This was such a serious issue in the Old Testament that false prophets were to be put to death

(Deuteronomy 13:8-10). This chapter will demonstrate that the Church of Jesus Christ of Latter-day Saints is indeed teaching a different god and a counterfeit gospel, thus offering a false hope.

The following list of Christian terms will be defined by LDS sources and then by biblical quotes. While this is not a complete list of terminology differences, it will cover the most basic ones.

Godhead

LDS

Latter-day Saints believe that God the Father is a resurrected man who has achieved godhood. Jesus is another resurrected man who has achieved godhood. The Holy Ghost is a separate spirit being who achieved godhood but does not have a physical body. These three beings are totally separate gods. This is explained in one of Joseph Smith's revelations: "The Father has a body of flesh and bones as tangible as man's; the Son also; but the Holy Ghost has not a body of flesh and bones, but is a personage of Spirit. Were it not so, the Holy Ghost could not dwell in us" (D&C 130:22). The Mormons teach that the Father, Son, and Holy Ghost are one in purpose, not one in essence. Preceding these three Gods there would be a countless number of Gods who rule other worlds. Each of these Gods was at one time a mortal on some other world. As resurrected, exalted beings each God and his wife procreated the spirits for their earth. One of these Gods and his wife would be the Heavenly Parents of the person who became our God.

In one of Joseph Smith's last sermons he declared:

> God himself was once as we are now, and is an *exalted man*...it is necessary we should understand the character and being of God and how he *came to be so*; for I am going to tell you *how God came to be God*. We have imagined and supposed that God was God from all eternity. I will refute that idea....The

Scriptures inform us that Jesus said, As the Father hath power in Himself, even so hath the Son power—to do what? Why, what the Father did. The answer is obvious—in a manner to lay down His body and take it up again. Jesus, what are you going to do? *To lay down my life as my Father did,* and take it up again.... Here, then, is eternal life—to know the only wise and true God; and you have got to learn how to be *Gods yourselves,* and to be kings and priests to God, *the same as all Gods have done before you,* namely, by going from one small degree to another, and from a small capacity to a great one...to inherit the same power, the same glory and the same exaltation, until you arrive at the station of *a God,* and ascend the throne of eternal power, the same as those who have gone before. What did Jesus do? Why; I do the things I saw my Father do when worlds come rolling into existence. *My Father worked out his kingdom with fear and trembling,* and I must do the same; and when I get my kingdom, I shall present it to *my Father,* so that he may obtain kingdom upon kingdom, and it will exalt him in glory. He will then take a *higher* exaltation, and *I will take his place,* and thereby become exalted myself. So that Jesus treads in the tracks of his Father, and inherits what God did before; and God is thus glorified and exalted in the salvation and exaltation of all his children.[4]

At a later time Smith proclaimed:

I will preach on the *plurality of Gods....* Paul says there are Gods many and Lords many. I want to set it forth in a plain and simple manner; but to us there is but one God—that is pertaining to us; and he is in all and through all. But if Joseph Smith says there are *Gods many and Lords many,* they cry, "Away with him! Crucify him! Crucify him!"...Mankind verily say that the Scriptures are with them. Search the Scriptures, for they testify of things that these apostates would gravely pronounce blasphemy. Paul, if Joseph Smith is a blasphemer, you are. I say there are *Gods many* and *Lords many*, but to us only one, and we are to be in subjection to that one, and no man can limit the bounds or the eternal existence of eternal time.... Some say I do not interpret the Scripture the same as they do. They say it means the heathen's gods.... I have it from God, and get over it if you can. I have a witness of the Holy Ghost, and a testimony that Paul had no allusion to the heathen gods in the text.... In the very beginning the Bible shows there is a *plurality of Gods* beyond the power of refutation. It is a great subject I am dwelling on. The word Elohim ought to be in the plural all the way through—Gods. The *heads of the Gods appointed one God for us*; and when you take that view of the subject, its sets one free to see all the beauty, holiness and perfection of the Gods.... Many men say there is one God; the Father, the Son and the Holy Ghost are only one God. I say that is a strange God anyhow—three in one, and one in three! It is a curious organization.... All are to be crammed into one God, according to sectarianism. It would make the biggest God in all the world. He would be a wonderfully big God—he would be a giant or a monster.... I want to reason a little on this subject. I learned it by translating the papyrus which is now in my house.... "Intelligences exist one above another, so that there is no end to them."...If Abraham reasoned thus— If Jesus Christ was the Son of God, and John discovered that *God the Father* of Jesus Christ *had a Father*, you may suppose that *He had a Father* also. Where was there ever a son without a father? And where was there ever a father without first being a son? ...I want you to pay particular attention to

what I am saying. Jesus said that *the Father wrought
precisely in the same way as His Father had done before
Him.* As the *Father* had done before? He laid down
His life, and took it up the same as *His Father had
done before.* He did as He was sent, to lay down His
life and take it up again; and then was committed
unto Him the keys. I know it is good reasoning.[5]

B.H. Roberts, of the Quorum of Seventy, explained:

But if God the Father was *not always God,* but came
to his present exalted position by *degrees of progress*
as indicated in the teachings of the prophet, how
has there been a God from all eternity? The answer is that there has been and there now exists *an
endless line of Divine Intelligences—Deities,* stretching
back into the eternities, that had no beginning
and will have no end. Their existence runs parallel
with endless duration, and their dominions are as
limitless as boundless space.[6]

The 1985 LDS priesthood manual quoted Brigham
Young as saying:

He is our Father—the Father of our spirits—and
was *once a man* in mortal flesh as we are.... It
appears ridiculous to the world, under their dark-
ened and erroneous traditions, that God has once
been a *finite being.*[7]

LDS Apostle James E. Talmage taught:

We believe in a God who is Himself *progressive...*a
Being who has *attained* His exalted state by a path
which now His children are permitted to follow....
In spite of the opposition of the sects, in the face of
direct charges of blasphemy, the Church proclaims

the eternal truth: *As man is, God once was; as God is, man may be.*[8]

Bible

The foundation for Christian theology is the nature of God. All other doctrines are dependent on this. Jesus prayed, "And this is life eternal, that they might know thee, the only true God, and Jesus Christ, whom thou hast sent" (John 17:3). There are numerous biblical references that demonstrate that there is only one God. The God of the Bible has eternally been God, has no superiors, was never a human before becoming deity, and is a spirit. In Isaiah God Himself declared, "Ye are my witnesses, saith the LORD, and my servant whom I have chosen: that ye may know and believe me, and understand that I am he; *before* me there was *no* God formed, neither shall there be after me. I, even I, am the LORD; and beside me there is no savior" (Isaiah 43:10,11). "Thus saith the LORD the King of Israel, and his redeemer, the LORD of hosts: I am the first, and I am the last; and *beside me there is no God*" (Isaiah 44:6). "Tell ye, and bring them near; yea, let them take counsel together: who hath declared this from ancient time? Who hath told it from that time? Have not I the LORD? And *there is no God else beside me,* a just God and a Savior; *there is none beside* me. Look unto me and be ye saved, all the ends of the earth; for I am God, and *there is none else*" (Isaiah 45:21,22).

In the book of Numbers we read, "God is not a man, that he should lie, neither the son of man, that he should repent; hath he said, and shall he not do it? Or hath he spoken, and shall he not make it good?" (Numbers 23:19).

Jesus taught, "God is a Spirit, and they that worship him must worship him in spirit and in truth" (John 4:24). In Paul's letter to Timothy he wrote, "Now unto the King eternal, immortal, invisible, the only wise God, be honor and glory for ever and ever. Amen" (1 Timothy 1:17).

Throughout the New Testament we see the one God as Father, Son, and Holy Ghost. Jesus instructed his disciples, "Go ye therefore and teach all nations, baptizing them in the name of the Father and of the Son and of the Holy Ghost" (Matthew 28:19). For a more complete treatment on this subject see Chapter 2, on the nature of God.

Jesus Christ

LDS

Latter-day Saints believe that Jesus is our elder brother, born to Heavenly Parents in the Pre-existence. Jesus, Lucifer, angels, and all humans are the same species and are literally brothers and sisters. When God needed to pick a Savior for our world He chose Jesus over Lucifer. This so angered Lucifer that he led a war in heaven which led to his expulsion as the devil. In the Mormon manual *Gospel Principles* we read:

> Every person who was ever born on earth was *our spirit brother or sister* in heaven. The *first* spirit born to our heavenly parents was *Jesus Christ*...so he is *literally our elder brother*.... We needed a Savior to pay for our sins and teach us how to return to our Heavenly Father. Our Father said, "Whom shall I send?"...*Two of our brothers* offered to help. Our oldest brother, *Jesus Christ*, who was then called Jehovah, said, "Here am I, send me"....Satan, who was called *Lucifer*, also came, saying, "Behold, here am I, send me."...After hearing *both sons* speak, Heavenly Father said, "I will send the first." ...Because our Heavenly Father chose Jesus Christ to be our Savior, Satan became angry and rebelled.[9]

Jesus was one of many that helped in the creation of our world. In another LDS manual we read:

> It is true that *Adam* helped to form this earth. He labored with our *Savior Jesus Christ*. I have a strong view or conviction that *there were others also* who assisted them. Perhaps *Noah* and *Enoch*; and why

not *Joseph Smith*.... We know that Jehovah-Christ, assisted by "many of the noble and great ones" (Abr. 3:22), of whom Michael is but the illustration, did in fact create the earth and all forms of plant and animal life.[10]

Past President Joseph Fielding Smith taught:

> The Savior did *not* have a fulness at first, but *after* he received his body and the resurrection *all power was given unto him* both in heaven and in earth. Although he was *a* God, even the Son of God, with power and authority to create this earth and other earths, *yet there were some things lacking* which he did not receive until *after* his resurrection. In other words he had not received the *fulness* until he got a resurrected body.[11]

Bible

The Bible does not speak of Jesus as *a* God, but as *the* God. In Isaiah 9:6 we read, "For unto us a child is born, unto us a son is given...and his name shall be called Wonderful, Counselor, *The mighty God,* the everlasting Father, the Prince of Peace." Jesus is fully God, not a subordinate deity. When He declared to the Jews that "before Abraham was, I am," they realized He was claiming to be God. That is the reason they wanted to stone Him (John 8:58). Paul wrote to Timothy, "And without controversy great is the mystery of godliness: God was manifest in the flesh..." (1 Timothy 3:16). In Hebrews 13:8 we read, "Jesus Christ the same yesterday and today and forever." John understood this truth when he wrote, "In the beginning was the Word, and the Word was with God, and the Word was God "(John 1:1,2).

The Bible declares Jesus to be the Creator. Paul explained, "For by him were all things created, that are in heaven and that are in earth, visible and invisible, whether they be thrones or dominions or principalities or powers; *all things were created by him* and for him; and he is before all

things, and by him all things consist" (Colossians 1:16,17).
The work of creation was done solely by the Godhead. See
Chapter 3, on Jesus Christ, for a more thorough treatment
of this subject.

Holy Ghost

LDS

Mormons believe that the Holy Ghost is a separate being
from God the Father and Jesus the Son. They also make a
distinction between the Holy *Ghost* and the Holy *Spirit*. For
some unexplained reason the Holy Ghost became a God
without going through an earth existence and receiving a
physical body. Past President Joseph Fielding Smith stated:

> The Holy Ghost is the third member of the
> Godhead. He is a Spirit, in the form of a man. The
> Father and the Son are personages of tabernacle;
> they have bodies of flesh and bones. The Holy
> Ghost is a personage of Spirit, and has a spirit body
> only. As a Spirit personage the Holy Ghost has size
> and dimensions. He does not fill the immensity of
> space, and cannot be everywhere present in per-
> son at the same time.... The Holy Ghost should
> not be confused with the Spirit, which fills the
> immensity of space and which is everywhere pre-
> sent. This other Spirit is impersonal and has no
> size, nor dimension; it proceeds forth from the
> presence of the Father and the Son and is in all
> things. We should speak of the Holy Ghost as a per-
> sonage as "he" and this other Spirit as "it," although
> when we speak of the power or gift of the Holy
> Ghost we may properly say "it."...The Holy Ghost,
> as we are taught in our modern revelation, is the
> third member in the Godhead and a personage of
> Spirit. These terms are used synonymously: Spirit
> of God, Spirit of the Lord, Spirit of Truth, Holy
> Spirit, Comforter; all having reference to the Holy

Ghost. The same terms largely are used in relation
to the Spirit of Jesus Christ, also called the Light of
Truth, Light of Christ, Spirit of God, and Spirit of
the Lord; and yet *they are separate and distinct things.*
We have a great deal of confusion because we have
not kept that clearly in our minds.[12]

Bible

The New Testament shows no distinction between the
Holy *Ghost* and the Holy *Spirit.* The same Greek word *pneuma*
is translated *ghost* and *spirit* in the King James Version. Thus
in 1 Corinthians 3:16 we read, "Know ye not that ye are the
temple of God, and that the Spirit [*pneuma*] of God dwelleth
in you?" Further on in the same letter Paul writes, "What?
Know ye not that your body is the temple of the Holy Ghost
[*pneuma*] which is in you, which ye have of God, and ye are
not your own?" (1 Corinthians 6:19). Also, in 1 Corinthians
12:3 we read, "Wherefore I give you to understand that no
man speaking by the Spirit [*pneuma*] of God calleth Jesus
accursed, and that no man can say that Jesus is the Lord but
by the Holy Ghost [*pneuma*]."

Mother in Heaven

LDS

Latter-day Saints believe that when God was still a mortal
on another world he married a wife in the "new and everlasting" temple ceremony, and after their death and resurrection they progressed to godhood. In a 1909 Doctrinal
Exposition by the LDS First Presidency we read:

> All men and women are in the similitude of the
> universal Father *and Mother,* and are literally the
> sons and daughters of Deity.... Man is the child of
> God, formed in the divine image and endowed
> with divine attributes, and even as the infant son of
> an earthly father and mother is capable in due

time of becoming a man, so the undeveloped off-spring of *celestial parentage* is capable, by experience through ages and aeons, of evolving into *a God.*[13]

Past President Spencer W. Kimball taught:

Men and women [are] in the image of *heavenly parents.* God made man in his own image and certainly he made woman in the image of his wife-partner. You [women] are daughters of God. You are precious. You are made in the image of *our heavenly Mother.* [14]

Mormon Apostle Bruce R. McConkie explained:

God lives in the family unit. He is our Father in heaven—the literal and personal Father of the spirits of all men. He begat us; we are the offspring of *Heavenly Parents*: we have an *Eternal Father* and an *Eternal Mother.* We were born as spirits, and we dwelt in the presence of our *Eternal Parents*; we lived before our mortal birth. As spirits we were in all respects as we are now save only that we were not housed in mortal bodies as is the present circumstance. Christ was the Firstborn of all the heavenly host; Lucifer was a son of the morning: each of us came into being as conscious identities in our appointed order; and Christ is our Elder Brother.[15]

Bible

There is nothing in the Bible to indicate that God has a wife. First of all, there is only one God (Deuteronomy 6:4; Mark 12:29). The Godhead is the Father, Son, and Holy Ghost (Matthew 28:19). Obviously this does not include a wife. God told Isaiah, "Even everyone that is called by my name, for *I have created him* for my glory, I have formed him; yea, I have made him" (Isaiah 43:7). And further on He declares, "Thus saith the Lord, thy redeemer, and *he that formed thee from the womb,* I am the Lord that maketh *all things,* that stretcheth forth the heavens *alone,* that spreadeth abroad the earth *by myself*" (Isaiah 44:24). Notice that God formed us *alone* and by Himself. God has declared: "I am the LORD; that is my name; and *my glory will I not give to another,* neither my praise to graven images" (Isaiah 42:8).

Creation

LDS

Latter-day Saints believe that matter is eternal. God did not truly create out of nothing but organized existing matter to form worlds without number. In LDS scriptures we read, "There is no such thing as immaterial matter. All spirit is matter, but it is more fine or pure, and can only be discerned by purer eyes; we cannot see it; but when our bodies are purified we shall see that it is all matter" (D&C 131:7,8). Joseph Smith taught:

> You ask the learned doctors why they say the world was made out of nothing; and they will answer, "Doesn't the Bible say He created the world?" And they infer, from the word create, that it must have been made out of nothing. Now, the word create came from the *baurau* which does not mean to create out of nothing; it means to organize; the same as a man would organize materials and build a ship. Hence, we infer that God had materials to organize the world out of chaos—chaotic matter, which is element, and in which dwells all the glory. *Element had an existence from the time he had.* The pure principles of element are principles which can never be destroyed; they may be organized and re-organized, but not destroyed. They had no beginning, and can have no end.[16]

Bible

God alone is eternal. He created matter, time, space, and life and called them into existence. Isaiah recorded: "Thus saith the LORD, thy redeemer, and *he that formed thee from the womb,* I am the LORD that *maketh all things,* that stretcheth forth the heavens *alone,* that spreadeth abroad the earth *by myself*" (Isaiah 44:24). This is reinforced by Malachi: "Have we not all one father? Hath not *one God created us?*" (Malachi 2:10). David declared, "For all the gods of the people are idols, but the LORD made the heavens" (1 Chronicles 16:26).

Preexistence

LDS

Latter-day Saints teach that everyone had a preexistence. Our intelligence (mind) has eternally existed. Our intelligences were born as spirit-children to God and his wife in a premortal state ages before we were born here on earth. In one of Joseph Smith's revelations we read, "Man was also in the beginning with God. Intelligence, or the light of truth, was not created or made, neither indeed can be" (D&C 93:29).

According to another revelation, God told Abraham:

> I dwell in the midst of them all...for I rule in the heavens above, and in the earth beneath, in all wisdom and prudence, over all the intelligences thine eyes have seen from the beginning; I came down in the beginning in the midst of all the intelligences thou hast seen.
>
> Now the Lord had shown unto me, Abraham, the intelligences that were organized before the world was; and among all these there were many of the noble and great ones....[17]

Bible

Only the Godhead (Father, Son, and Holy Ghost) has eternal existence. We are God's creation and did not have a spiritual existence prior to our birth on earth. When Jesus declared, "Verily, verily, I say unto you, Before Abraham was, I am" (John 8:58), He was claiming to be truly God and that Abraham had a beginning. Paul writes, "And he is before all things, and by him all things consist" (Colossians 1:17). Paul's teachings in his first letter to the Corinthians would seem to rule out a prior life in heaven as spirit beings: "Howbeit that was not first which is spiritual, but that which is natural, and afterward that which is spiritual" (1 Corinthians 15:46). In Zechariah 12:1 we read that God "formeth the spirit of man within him."

Sons of God

LDS

The LDS Church teaches that we are literally the spirit children of God and his wife, born in a prior existence before coming to this earth. Bruce R. McConkie explained:

> Pre-existence is the term commonly used to describe the pre-mortal existence of the spirit children of God the Father. Speaking of this prior existence in a spirit sphere, the First Presidency of the Church...said: "All men and women are in the similitude of the *universal Father and Mother* and are *literally* the sons and daughters of Deity"; as spirits they were the "offspring of celestial parentage." ...These spirit beings, the offspring of exalted parents, were men and women, appearing in all respects as mortal persons do, excepting only that their spirit bodies were made of a more pure and refined substance than the elements from which mortal bodies are made.[18]

Bible

We are God's creation, not procreation. We become a child of God at conversion. John declared, "But as many as received him, to them gave he power to *become* the sons of God, even to them that *believe* on his name" (John 1:12).

Paul tells us, "For as many as are led by the Spirit of God, they are the sons of God.... Ye have received the Spirit of *adoption*, whereby we cry, Abba, Father" (Romans 8:14,15). Paul instructed the Galatian Christians, "Ye are all the children of God by *faith* in Christ Jesus" (Galatians 3:26).

The Fall

LDS

Latter-day Saints teach that the fall of man was a blessing. God intended Adam and Eve to fall in order to introduce mortality and physical death. They believe that Adam was given two conflicting commandments when he was told to have children and yet not eat of the fruit.

Milton R. Hunter, of the First Council of Seventy, wrote:

> ...when God placed Adam and Eve in the Garden of Eden He gave them two great commandments, namely: first, "to be fruitful, and multiply, and replenish the earth;" second, not to partake of the fruit "of the tree of knowledge of good and evil," commonly referred to as "the forbidden fruit." It was *impossible* for the first parents of the human race to obey both of God's commandments. If the first and most important one was observed, the second one of necessity must be broken. In other words, Adam and Eve could not bear children until they became mortal beings. Then why did God give them what seem to be *two conflicting commandments?* The most important reason was that they might have a choice to make and thereby exercise their free agency.[19]

Past LDS President Joseph Fielding Smith commented:

> I never speak of the part Eve took in this fall as a sin, nor do I accuse Adam of a sin.... When he ate, he became subject to death, and therefore he became mortal. This was a transgression of the law, but not a sin in the strict sense, for it was something that Adam and Eve *had to do.* I am sure that neither Adam nor Eve looked upon it as a sin, when they learned the consequences, and this is discovered in their words after they learned the consequences.... Eve said: "Were it not for our transgression we never should have had seed, and never should have known good and evil, and the joy of our redemption, and the eternal life which God giveth unto all the obedient."...We can hardly look upon anything resulting in such benefits as being a sin, in the sense in which we consider sin.[20]

LDS Apostle Bruce R. McConkie explained:

> Adam, our first parent (1 Ne. 5:11), a "son of God" (Moses 6:22), was first placed on earth as an immortal being.... There was no death, no mortality, no corruption, *no procreation.* Blood did not flow in Adam's veins, for *he was not yet mortal....* As yet the full knowledge of good and evil had not been placed before him; and, what was tremendously important in the eternal scheme of things, *he could have no children....* According to the foreordained plan, *Adam was to fall....* Adam was to introduce mortality and all that attends it, so that the opportunity for eternal progression and perfection might be offered to all the spirit children of the Father.[21]

LDS Apostle James E. Talmage wrote:

> ...our first parents are entitled to our *deepest gratitude* for their legacy to posterity—the means of winning title to glory, exaltation, and *eternal lives.* But for the opportunity thus given, the spirits of God's offspring would have remained forever in a state of innocent childhood, sinless through no effort of their own; negatively saved, not from sin, but from the opportunity of meeting sin; incapable of winning the honors of victory because prevented from taking part in the conflict. As it is, they are heirs to the birthright of Adam's descendants—*mortality,* with its immeasurable possibilities and its God-given freedom of action. From Father Adam we have inherited all the ills to which flesh is heir; but such are necessarily incident to a knowledge of good and evil, by the proper use of which knowledge *man may become even as the Gods.*[22]

Sterling W. Sill, member of the Council of Seventy, declared: "Adam fell, but he fell in the *right* direction. He fell *toward the goal....* Adam fell, but he fell *upward.*"[23]

Bible

God intended man to obey Him and to "be fruitful and multiply, and replenish the earth" (Genesis 1:28). It would be contrary to the nature of God for Him to give a command that was physically impossible for man to fulfill. Man sins because of his own desires, not because God tempts him. James tells us, "Let no man say when he is tempted, I am tempted of God; for God cannot be tempted with evil, neither tempteth he any man. But every man is tempted when he is drawn away of his own lust and enticed" (James 1:13,14). Peter instructed, "But as he which hath called you is holy, so be ye holy in all manner of conversation, because it is written, Be ye holy, for I am holy" (1 Peter 1:15,16).

The Bible does not present a picture of joy but one of judgment due to Adam's sin. Paul wrote, "Wherefore as by one man sin entered into the world, and death by sin; and so death passed upon all men, for that all have sinned" (Romans 5:12). Further on in the same epistle Paul wrote, "Let not sin therefore reign in your mortal body, that ye should obey it in the lusts thereof" (Romans 6:12).

John tells us that "all unrighteousness is sin" (1 John 5:17). In Psalm 5:4 we read, "Thou art not a God that hath pleasure in wickedness; neither shall evil dwell with thee." Habakkuk declared, "Thou art of purer eyes than to behold evil, and canst not look on iniquity" (Habakkuk 1:13).

Virgin Birth

LDS

While many members of the LDS Church do not understand their Church's teachings on the virgin birth, the statements of their leaders show a belief in a literal conception. Past President Ezra Taft Benson explained:

> A fundamental doctrine of true Christianity is the divine birth of the child Jesus. This doctrine is *not generally comprehended* by the world. The *paternity* of Jesus Christ is one of the "mysteries of godliness" comprehended only by the spiritually minded.... Thus the testimonies of appointed witnesses leave no question as to the *paternity* of Jesus Christ. God was the *Father* of Jesus' mortal tabernacle, and Mary, a mortal woman, was His mother.... The Church of Jesus Christ of Latter-day Saints proclaims that Jesus Christ is the Son of God *in the most literal sense. The body* in which He performed His mission in the *flesh* was *sired* by that same Holy Being we worship as God, our Eternal Father. Jesus was *not* the son of Joseph, nor was He begotten by the *Holy Ghost*.... He was the Only Begotten Son of our Heavenly Father in the flesh—the only child whose mortal body was begotten by our Heavenly Father.[24]

LDS Apostle Bruce R. McConkie wrote: "Christ is the Only Begotten...the Only Begotten Son...the only Son of the Father *in the flesh.* Each of the words is to be understood *literally.* Only means only; Begotten means begotten; and Son means son. Christ was begotten by an Immortal Father *in the same way that mortal men are begotten by mortal fathers.*"[25]

Further on in the same book McConkie states:

> God the Father is a perfected, glorified, holy *Man,* an immortal Personage. And Christ was born into the world as the *literal* Son of this Holy Being; he was born in the *same* personal, real, and *literal* sense that any mortal son is born to a mortal father. There is *nothing figurative* about his paternity; he was *begotten, conceived* and born *in the normal and natural course of events,* for he is the Son of God, and that designation means what it says.[26]

In the LDS *Encyclopedia of Mormonism* we read:

> For Latter-day Saints, the paternity of Jesus is not obscure. He was the *literal, biological son* of an immortal, *tangible Father* and Mary, a mortal woman.... He was not the son of the Holy Ghost; it was only through the Holy Ghost that the power of the Highest overshadowed Mary.[27]

Bible

The Bible declares God to be "spirit" (John 4:24), not a resurrected man. And a spirit does not have flesh and bones (Luke 24:39). The Bible proclaims that Jesus' conception was a miracle: "Now the birth of Jesus Christ was on this wise: When as his mother Mary was espoused to Joseph, before they came together, she was found with child of the Holy Ghost" (Matthew 1:18). Luke wrote: "And the angel said unto her, Fear not, Mary...thou shalt conceive in thy womb, and bring forth a son, and shalt call his name JESUS.... Then said Mary unto the angel, How shall this be, *seeing I know not a man?* And the angel answered and said unto her, The Holy Ghost shall come upon thee, and the power of the Highest shall overshadow thee; therefore also that holy thing which shall be born of thee shall be called the Son of God" (Luke 1:30-35).

Salvation by Grace

LDS

Latter-day Saints believe Christ's death paid for Adam's transgression and secured universal resurrection. Salvation by grace is defined as universal resurrection. Beyond this we must earn our own place in heaven. We are saved by grace *after all we can do.* Mormons also make a distinction between general salvation (resurrection) and individual salvation (exaltation). In the Book of Mormon we read, "For we labor diligently to write, to persuade our children, and also our brethren, to believe in Christ, and to be reconciled to God; for we know that it is by grace that we are saved, *after all we can do*" (2 Ne. 25:23).

LDS Apostle Bruce McConkie explained it this way.

1. *Unconditional or general salvation,* that which comes by grace alone without obedience to gospel law, consists in the *mere fact of being resurrected.* In this sense salvation is synonymous with *immortality....*

2. *Conditional or individual salvation,* that which comes *by grace coupled with gospel obedience,* consists in receiving an inheritance in the celestial kingdom of God. This kind of salvation follows faith, repentance, baptism, receipt of the Holy Ghost, and *continued righteousness to the end of one's mortal probation....* Even those in the celestial kingdom, however, who do not go on to exaltation, will have immortality only and not eternal life. Along with those of the telestial and terrestrial worlds they will be "ministering servants".... They will live "separately and singly" in an unmarried state "without exaltation, in their saved condition, to all eternity."

3. *Salvation in its true and full meaning* is synonymous with *exaltation or eternal life* and consists in gaining an inheritance in the highest of the three heavens within the celestial kingdom.... This full salvation is obtained in and through the *continuation of the family unit* in eternity, and those who obtain it *are gods*.... Many conditions must exist in order to make such salvation available to men. Without the atonement, the gospel, the priesthood, and the sealing power, there would be no salvation.... If it had not been for Joseph Smith and the restoration, there would be no salvation. There is no salvation outside The Church of Jesus Christ of Latter-day Saints.... Since all good things come by the grace of God (that is, by his love, mercy, and condescension), it follows that salvation itself—in all its forms and degrees—is bestowed because of this infinite goodness. However, one of the untrue doctrines found in modern Christendom is the concept that man can gain salvation (meaning in the kingdom of God) by grace alone and without obedience. This soul-destroying doctrine has the obvious effect of lessening the determination of an individual to conform to all of the laws and ordinances of the gospel.... *Salvation in the celestial kingdom of God, however, is not salvation by grace alone.* Rather, it is salvation by grace *coupled with obedience to the laws and ordinances of the gospel.*[28]

Bible

The Bible never equates salvation with resurrection. Resurrection merely initiates the final stage of salvation (Romans 8:23). Salvation is not universal but is based on each individual's response to God's offer of eternal life through faith in Christ. If a person has *salvation* he also has *eternal life.* Paul makes this clear in Romans 1:16: "For I am not ashamed of the gospel of Christ; for it is the power of God unto *salvation* to every one that *believeth,* to the Jew first, and also to the Greek." Hebrews 9:28 reads, "So Christ was once offered to bear the sins of many; and unto them that look for him shall he appear the second time without sin unto *salvation.*" Paul also taught, "For by grace are ye saved through *faith,* and that not of yourselves, it is the gift of God: not of works, lest any man should boast" (Ephesians 2:8,9). For a more detailed discussion, see the chapter on salvation.

Redemption

LDS

The Latter-day Saints teach that Christ's atonement redeems us from mortal death and assures us of resurrection. But individual redemption is through full obedience. Past President Joseph Fielding Smith taught:

> *Conditional redemption* is also universal in its nature; it is offered to all but not received by all; it is a universal gift, though not universally accepted; its benefits can be obtained only through faith, repentance, baptism, the laying on of hands, and *obedience to all other requirements of the gospel.*

> *Unconditional redemption* [i.e., resurrection] is a gift forced upon mankind which they cannot reject, though they were disposed....

> Redemption from the original sin is without faith or works; redemption from our *own sins* is given through faith *and works....* Man cannot, by any possible act, prevent his redemption from the fall; but he can utterly refuse and prevent his redemption from the penalty of his own sins.[29]

The LDS second Article of Faith reads: "We believe that men will be punished for *their own sins,* and not for Adam's transgression."[30]

Bible

Christ redeems us from both mortal death and spiritual death. Paul clearly taught that all those who have been redeemed will enjoy eternal life: "For the wages of sin is death; but the *gift* of God is *eternal life* through Jesus Christ our Lord" (Romans 6:23).

Again, in Ephesians Paul proclaimed, "And you hath he quickened, who were dead in trespasses and sins...and were by nature the children of wrath, even as others. But God, who is rich in mercy, for his great love wherewith he loved us, even when we were dead in sins, hath quickened us together with Christ (by grace ye are saved), and hath raised us up together, and made us sit together in heavenly places in Christ Jesus, that in the ages to come he might show the exceeding riches of his grace in his kindness toward us through Christ Jesus" (Ephesians 2:1-7).

In the book of Revelation we read about those who have been redeemed: "And they sang a new song, saying, Thou art worthy to take the book, and to open the seals thereof; for thou wast slain, *and hast redeemed us to God* by thy blood out of every kindred, and tongue, and people, and nation" (Revelation 5:9).

Gospel

LDS

In Mormonism the Gospel is defined as all the teachings and ordinances of the LDS Church. The true Gospel was taken from the earth shortly after the death of the 12 apostles and was not present on the earth until Joseph Smith restored it in 1830. Apostle McConkie wrote:

> The *gospel* of Jesus Christ is *the plan of salvation*. It embraces all of the *laws, principles, doctrines, rites, ordinances, acts, powers, authorities, and keys* necessary to save and exalt men in the highest heaven hereafter. It is the covenant of salvation which the Lord makes with men on earth

... Just as there are false teachers, false religions, false prophets and false Christs, so there are *false gospels*.... And the revealed test whereby the *true gospel* may be identified is that revelations, visions, miracles, signs, apostles, prophets, and all the gifts of the Spirit will always be found in connection with it.... The *true gospel* of Jesus Christ was restored to earth in the last days through the instrumentality of Joseph Smith. It is found *only* in The Church of Jesus Christ of Latter-day Saints.[31]

Bible

The Gospel is the good news of God's provision for our salvation. It is defined as Christ's death and resurrection as an atonement for our sins—not a church, eternal progression, or temple ordinances. Paul gives a very clear definition of the Gospel in his letter to the Corinthians: "Moreover, brethren, I declare unto you the *gospel* which I preached unto you, which also ye have received, and wherein ye stand, by which also ye are saved, if ye keep in memory what I preached unto you, unless ye have believed in vain. For I delivered unto you first of all that which I also received, how that *Christ died for our sins* according to the scriptures, and that he was *buried*, and that he *rose again* the third day according to the scriptures" (1 Corinthians 15:1-4).

Paul left us a grave warning about those who would preach any other Gospel in his letter to the Galatians: "I marvel that ye are so soon removed from him that called you into the grace of Christ unto *another gospel*, which is not another; but there be some that trouble you, and would pervert the gospel of Christ. But though we or an angel from heaven preach any other gospel unto you than that which we have preached unto you, let him be accursed" (Galatians 1:6-8).

True Church

LDS

Mormonism teaches that only the LDS Church is God's true church. After the death of the original apostles, the true church was taken from the earth. It was restored by Joseph Smith in 1830. Smith claimed that God invested the authority in him to "lay the foundation of this church, and to bring it forth out of obscurity and out of darkness, the only true and living church upon the face of the whole earth, with which I, the Lord, am well pleased" (D&C 1:30). Later Joseph Smith claimed that God revealed to him the true name of His Church: "For thus shall my church be called in the last days, even The Church of Jesus Christ of Latter-day Saints" (D&C 115:4).

LDS Apostle Bruce R. McConkie explained:

> Our Lord's *true* Church is the formal, *official organization* of believers who have taken upon themselves the name of Christ by baptism, thus covenanting to serve God and keep his commandments.... As such its affairs are administered by apostles, prophets, and other *legal administrators* appointed by Christ the King.... It is the congregation or assembly of saints who have forsaken the world by accepting the gospel, a *formal society* of converted persons and *not* the unorganized spiritual vagary termed the Christian church by sectarianism.... With the coming of the great apostasy the primitive Church was lost, and the various churches or societies which have since grown up bear no particular similarity to the original.[32]

Further on McConkie claimed:

> To *his earthly kingdom* in the dispensation of the fulness of times the Lord has given the formal name, *The Church of Jesus Christ of Latter-day Saints* (D. & C. 115:3-4). This Church is "the only true and living church upon the face of the whole earth" (D. & C. 1:30), the *only organization authorized by the Almighty* to preach his gospel and administer the ordinances of salvation, the only Church which has power to save and exalt men in the hereafter.[33]

Bible

Christ's church is not a particular organization. As born-again Christians we are all part of God's true church. God has "put all things under his [Christ's] feet, and gave him to be the head over all things to the church, which is his body, the fullness of him that filleth all in all" (Ephesians 1:22,23). Paul explains this in his first letter to the Corinthians: "For as the body is one, and hath many members, and all the members of that one body, being many, are one body, so also is Christ. For by one Spirit are we all baptized into one body, whether we be Jews or Gentiles, whether we be bond or free, and have been all made to drink into one Spirit. For the body is not one member, but many" (1 Corinthians 12:12-14).

Jesus promised that His church would never be taken from the earth: "And I say also unto thee that thou art Peter, and upon this rock I will build my church; and the gates of hell shall not prevail against it" (Matthew 16:18).

At another time Christ assured his followers, "Again I say unto you that if two of you shall agree on earth as touching anything that they shall ask, it shall be done for them of my Father which is in heaven. For where two or three are gathered together in my name, there am I in the midst of them" (Matthew 18:19,20).

Priesthood

LDS

Latter-day Saints believe that only the LDS Church has authority to baptize, ordain, and act in the name of God. They have a two-part priesthood system, the Aaronic priesthood for male teenagers and the Melchizedek priesthood for men 19 years of age or older. Past President Joseph Fielding Smith gave this description:

> *Authority* is an eternal principle operative throughout the universe.... *Priesthood* is divine authority which is conferred upon men that they may officiate in the ordinances of the gospel. In other words,

priesthood is a part of God's own power, which he bestows upon his chosen servants that they may act in his name in proclaiming the gospel and officiating in all the ordinances thereof. All such *official acts* performed by these *duly authorized servants* are recognized by the Author of our salvation. Man cannot act *legally* in the name of the Lord unless he is vested with the *priesthood,* which is divine authority. No man has the power or the right to take this honor to himself. Unless he is called of God, as was Aaron, he has no authority to officiate in any of the ordinances of the gospel; should he do so his act is not valid or recognized in the heavens.... All men who assume authority, but who have not been properly called, will have to answer for their acts in the day of judgment. *Nothing that they perform in the name of the Lord is valid, for it lacks the stamp of divine authority.* To deceive and lead others to believe that *unauthorized* acts are valid when performed in the name of the Lord is a grievous sin in the sight of God.... Only *authorized* officers may properly officiate in rites and ceremonies of the kingdom. No man has the right to assume the authority and officiate without being ordained to the ministry. To do so is an unauthorized and illegal act.[34]

In one of Joseph Smith's revelations we read:

There are, in the church, two priesthoods, namely, the Melchizedek and Aaronic, including the Levitical Priesthood. Why the first is called the Melchizedek Priesthood is because Melchizedek was such a great high priest.... All other authorities or offices in the church are appendages to this priesthood. But there are two divisions or grand heads—one is the *Melchizedek Priesthood,* and the other is the *Aaronic* or Levitical Priesthood.[35]

Bible

The Aaronic priesthood of the Old Testament was restricted to the lineage of Aaron. The Levites served under them in the temple. Even Jesus could not hold this priesthood because He descended from the tribe of Judah. Hebrews 7:14 explains: "For it is evident that our Lord sprang out of Judah, of which tribe Moses spoke nothing concerning priesthood." The priesthood of the Old Testament was brought to an end with the death of Christ. The writer of Hebrews wrote, "If therefore perfection were by the Levitical priesthood (for under it the people received the law), what further need was there that another priest should rise after the order of Melchisedec, and not be called after the order of Aaron? For the *priesthood being changed,* there is made of necessity a change also of the law" (Hebrews 7:11,12). Although Jewish high priests are mentioned in the New Testament, Jesus Christ is the Christian's only High Priest and the only one "after the order of Melchizedec." In the book of Hebrews we read, "And being made perfect, he became the author of eternal salvation unto all them that obey him; called of God an high priest after the order of Melchisedec...who is made, not after the law of a carnal commandment, but after the power of an endless life.... But this man, because he continueth ever, hath an unchangeable priesthood" (Hebrews 5:9,10; 7:16,24).

When Paul gave instructions to Timothy about leadership he did not say anything about ordaining men to either the Aaronic or Melchizedek priesthoods. Instead, the emphasis was on choosing mature Christians: "And the things that thou hast heard of me among many witnesses, the same commit thou to *faithful* men, who shall be able to teach others also" (2 Timothy 2:2).

Forgiveness

LDS

Latter-day Saints believe that God's forgiveness is granted at the end of a process of repentance and reformed behavior. LDS Apostle M. Russell Ballard explains: "The Savior's atonement provides *forgiveness* when you have repented *completely*.... Once you have forsaken your sins, never return to them, because 'unto that soul who sinneth shall the former sins return' (D&C 82:7)."[36]

Past President Spencer W. Kimball taught: "...even though *forgiveness* is so abundantly promised, there is no promise nor indication of forgiveness to any soul who does not *totally* repent.... We can hardly be too forceful in reminding people that they cannot sin and be forgiven and then sin again and again and expect forgiveness."[37]

Bible

Christ offers forgiveness the moment we turn to Him. He does not demand a period of reformed behavior before He will forgive us. When friends brought a sick man to Jesus, He immediately said, "Son, thy sins be forgiven thee" (Mark 2:5). Paul wrote to the Colossian Christians, "And you, being *dead in your sins* and the uncircumcision of your flesh, hath he quickened together with him, *having forgiven you all trespasses,* blotting out the handwriting of ordinances that was against us, which was contrary to us, and took it out of the way, nailing it to his cross" (Colossians 2:13,14). Forgiveness is given on the basis of God's grace, not man's performance. Paul declared that God has "made us accepted in the beloved, in whom we have redemption through his blood, the *forgiveness of sins,* according to the riches of *his grace*" (Ephesians 1:6,7).

Born Again

LDS

Latter-day Saints believe that to be *born again* is to be baptized into the LDS Church. Apostle Bruce McConkie explained:

> Those who go through the form of *baptism in water* and by the Spirit, under the hands of *legal administrators,* thus becoming *members of the Church,* by such

course have power given them to be *born again* in
the full sense that is required for salvation. Church
members are not born again by the mere fact of
baptism alone; rather, after baptism, they must so
live as to experience a "mighty change" in their
hearts.[38]

Bible

The Bible never equates being born again with church
membership. We are spiritually dead until our spiritual
birth. Paul instructed the Ephesian Christians, "And you
hath he quickened, who were dead in trespasses and sins"
(Ephesians 2:1). First Peter 1:23 says, "Being born again, not
of corruptible seed, but of incorruptible, by the word of
God, which liveth and abideth forever." In Paul's second letter to the Corinthians we read, "Therefore if any man be in
Christ, he is a new creature: old things are passed away;
behold, all things are become new" (2 Corinthians 5:17). We
are born of the Spirit when we trust in Christ for eternal life.
Jesus said, "Marvel not that I said unto thee, Ye must be born
again.... As Moses lifted up the serpent in the wilderness,
even so must the Son of man be lifted up, that whosoever
believeth in him should not perish, but have eternal life"
(John 3:7,14,15).

Baptism

LDS

Mormons believe that the LDS Church is the only
Church that has authority from God to baptize, and that
baptism must be performed by a person having the LDS
priesthood. LDS Apostle James E. Talmage explained:

Water baptism, then, becomes a basic principle
and the first essential ordinance of the gospel. It is
to be administered by one *having authority*; and
that authority rests in the *Priesthood* given of God.
Following baptism by water, comes the ordinance

of the bestowal of the Holy Ghost by the *authorized imposition of hands,* which constitutes the true baptism of the Spirit. These requirements, designated specifically the "first principles and ordinances of the gospel," "Mormonism" claims to be absolutely essential to membership in the Church of Christ....[39]

Apostle McConkie wrote:

> Baptism serves four purposes: 1. It is for the remission of sins.... 2. It admits the repentant person to membership in the Church and kingdom of God on earth.... 3. It is the gate to the celestial kingdom of heaven, that is, it starts a person out on the straight and narrow path which leads to eternal life.... 4. It is the means whereby the door to personal sanctification is opened....
>
> *True* water baptisms are performed by *legal* administrators who immerse the candidate in water. The symbolic representation thus adhered to bears record of the death, burial, and resurrection of Christ.[40]

Bible

While the Bible speaks of believers being baptized, it never states that baptism has to be done by someone holding a special priesthood. The emphasis is on *belief,* not on authority. The Philippian jailer asked Paul and Silas, "Sirs, what must I do to be saved?" They responded, "*Believe* on the Lord Jesus Christ, and thou shalt be saved, and thy house." We then read that he "was baptized" along with his family. They then "rejoiced, *believing* in God" (Acts 16:30-34). When Peter preached to the Jews, "they were pricked in their heart, and said unto Peter and to the rest of the apostles, Men and brethren, what shall we do? Then Peter said unto them, Repent, and be baptized every one of you in the name of Jesus Christ for the remission of sins, and ye shall receive the gift of the Holy Ghost" (Acts 2:37,38).

Dealing with Sin

LDS

When a Mormon sins after joining the LDS Church, God's forgiveness is granted at the end of a process of repentance, reformed behavior, and confession to a Priesthood leader. Past President Spencer W. Kimball wrote: "Repentance means not only to convict yourselves of the horror of the sin, but to *confess it,* abandon it, and restore to all who have been damaged to the total extent possible; then spend the balance of your lives trying to live the commandments of the Lord so he can *eventually pardon you* and cleanse you." [41]

In one of the current LDS Church manuals we read:

> Elder Kimball said: "To every forgiveness there is a condition.... There must be conviction of the sin, abandonment of the evil, *confession of the error to properly constituted authorities of the Lord....*"

> For many people, *confession* is the most difficult part of repentance. We must confess not only to the Lord but also to the person we have offended, such as a husband or wife, and to *the proper priesthood authority.* [42]

In one of Joseph Smith's revelations it is stated: "...go your ways and sin no more; but unto that soul who sinneth *shall the former sins return,* saith the LORD your GOD."[43]

Bible

God has promised to always forgive when we turn to Him. A Christian has the comfort that "if we confess our sins, he is faithful and just to forgive us our sins, and to cleanse us from all unrighteousness" (1 John 1:9). While the Bible speaks of confessing our sins to each other, it is for the purpose of joining with other believers in prayer for healing. James wrote, "And the prayer of faith shall save the sick, and the Lord shall raise him up; and if he have committed sins, they shall be forgiven him. Confess your faults one to another, and pray one for another, that ye may be healed" (James 5:15,16). There is nothing about the need to confess to a specific leader. Because we still struggle with sin, forgiveness is always of grace. David exclaimed, "Bless the LORD, O my soul, and forget not all his benefits: who forgiveth all thine iniquities, who healeth all thy diseases; who redeemeth thy life from destruction, who crowneth thee with lovingkindness and tender mercies" (Psalm 103:2-4).

Temple

LDS

Latter-day Saints claim that Joseph Smith restored the original temple ceremony. The LDS temples are used for eternal marriages for both the living and the dead, as well as for baptisms for the dead. A person must have a temple marriage in order to progress to godhood. After members go through the temple for the first time (for their own *endowments*), their future participation in the rituals will be in behalf of dead persons. Women go through the temple ordinances and proxy eternal marriages for dead women and men go through the rituals for dead men. Bruce R. McConkie explains: "From the days of Adam to the present, whenever the Lord has had a people on earth, temples and temple ordinances have been a crowning feature of their worship.... The inspired erection and proper use of temples is one of the great evidences of the divinity of the Lord's work.... Where these are not, the Church and kingdom and the truth of heaven are not."[44]

Bible

The temple in the Old Testament, with its high priest and animal sacrifices, was a foreshadowing of Christ's role as both our final High Priest and the last blood offering for sin (Hebrews chapters 5-10). There is nothing in the New Testament about "eternal marriages" and secret rituals in a

Christian temple. The Jewish temple ceremonies are clearly explained in the Old Testament (Exodus chapters 26-30) and have no relationship to the LDS temple ceremony.[45]

The New Testament teaches that God's temple is a spiritual building made up of all Christians, with Christ as the foundation (1 Corinthians 3:16). This is emphasized in Ephesians 2:19-22: "Now therefore ye are no more strangers...but fellow citizens with the saints, and of the household of God, and are built upon the foundation of the apostles and prophets, Jesus Christ himself being the chief cornerstone, in whom all the building fitly framed together groweth unto a holy temple in the Lord, in whom ye also are builded together for a habitation of God through the Spirit."

Eternal Life

LDS

Mormons believe that in order to obtain eternal life (the top level of the celestial kingdom) one must be married in the LDS temple and live a faithful Mormon life. One can go to *heaven* but not have *eternal life*. Eternal life is defined as the ability to procreate children through all eternity. The following appears in one of Joseph Smith's revelations: "In the celestial glory there are three heavens or degrees; and in order to obtain the highest, a man must enter into this order of the priesthood (meaning the new and everlasting covenant of marriage); and if he does not, he cannot obtain it. He may enter into the other, but that is the end of his kingdom; he cannot have an increase" (D&C 131:1-3).

In another revelation Joseph Smith wrote:

> And again, verily I say unto you, if a man marry a wife by my word, which is my law, and by the new and everlasting covenant...by him who is anointed, unto whom I have appointed this power and the keys of this priesthood...they shall pass by the angels, and the gods, which are set there, to their exaltation and glory...*which glory shall be a fulness*

and a continuation of the seeds forever and ever. Then shall they be *gods*, because they have no end; therefore shall they be from everlasting to everlasting, because they continue; then shall they be above all, because all things are subject unto them. Then shall they be *gods*, because they have all power, and the angels are subject unto them.... For strait is the gate, and narrow the way that leadeth unto the *exaltation and continuation of the lives* [eternal procreation].... Receive ye, therefore, my law. Broad is the gate, and wide the way that leadeth to the deaths [eternal celibacy]; and many there are that go in thereat, because they receive me not, neither do they abide in my law.[46]

LDS Apostle David Haight explained: "Immortality comes to us all as a free gift by the grace of God alone, without works of righteousness. *Eternal life*, however, is the *reward* for obedience to the laws and ordinances of His gospel."[47]

Bible

Eternal life is promised to all Christians. It is not limited to certain ones who have gone through special rituals. The Bible never mentions the necessity of temple marriage or the ability to continue to have children in heaven. Everyone in heaven has eternal life. John declared, "He that hath the Son hath *life*, and he that hath not the Son of God hath not life. These things have I written unto you that *believe* on the name of the Son of God, that ye may *know* that *ye have eternal life*, and that ye may believe on the name of the Son of God" (1 John 5:12,13; also John 5:24).

Jesus plainly taught that those who have eternal life do not live in a married state in heaven. We read in Luke 20: 35,36, "But they which shall be accounted worthy to obtain that world, and the resurrection from the dead, *neither marry nor are given in marriage;* neither can they die any more, for they are equal unto the angels, and are *the children of God,* being the children of the resurrection."

Immortality

LDS

Immortality is defined as the ability to live forever in one of three kingdoms of heaven but is not the same as eternal life. Those who only gain immortality will remain single in heaven. In Joseph Smith's revelation on marriage we read, "...if a man marry him a wife in the world, and he marry her not by me nor by my word...when they are out of the world they neither marry nor are given in marriage; but are appointed angels in heaven.... Therefore, they cannot be enlarged, but remain separately and singly, without exaltation, in their saved condition to all eternity..." (D&C 132:15-17).

LDS Apostle Bruce R. McConkie gave this explanation:

> As used in the scriptures, *eternal life* is the name given to the *kind of life* that our Eternal Father lives. The word eternal as used in the name eternal life, is a noun and not an adjective.... and has been chosen by him as the particular name to identify the kind of life that he lives.... Accordingly, *eternal life* is not a name that has reference only to the unending duration of a future life; *immortality* is to live forever in the *resurrected state*, and by the grace of God all men will gain this unending continuance of life. But only those who *obey* the fullness of the gospel law will inherit *eternal life*.... Thus those who gain eternal life receive exaltation...they ...have all power, and receive the fullness of the Father. *They are gods.*[48]

Apostle McConkie went on to explain immortality:

> Immortality is to live forever in the resurrected state with body and spirit inseparably connected. The Lord's work and glory is to bring to pass both the immortality and the eternal life of man

(Moses 1:39): all are resurrected to a state of immortality....[49]

Even those in the celestial kingdom, however, who do *not* go on to exaltation, will have *immortality only* and not *eternal life.* Along with those of the telestial and terrestrial worlds they will be "ministering servants, to minister for those who are worthy of a far more, and an exceeding, and an eternal weight of glory." They will live "separately and singly" in an unmarried state "without exaltation, in their saved condition, to all eternity."[50]

Bible

The Scriptures never make a distinction between immortality and eternal life. They amount to the same thing. Paul wrote to Timothy, "But is now made manifest by the appearing of our Savior Jesus Christ, who hath abolished death, and hath brought *life and immortality* to light through the gospel" (2 Timothy 1:10).

Hell

LDS

Mormons believe that hell is a place that exists eternally but that people stay there for only a limited time. Bruce R. McConkie explained:

> That part of the spirit world inhabited by wicked spirits who are awaiting the eventual day of their resurrection is called hell. Between their death and resurrection, these souls of the wicked are cast out into outer darkness, into the gloomy depression of sheol, into the hades of waiting wicked spirits, into hell.... Hell will have *an end....* After their resurrection, *the great majority* of those who have suffered *in hell* will pass into *the telestial kingdom;* the balance, cursed as sons of perdition, will be consigned to partake of endless woe with the devil and his angels....

Statements about an everlasting and endless hell (Hela. 6:28; Moro. 8:13), are to be interpreted in the same sense as those about eternal and endless punishment (D.&C.19:4-12; 76:44, 105). Who will go to hell? This query is abundantly answered in the scriptures.... Thus, for those who are heirs of some salvation, which includes all except the sons of perdition (D.&C.73:44), *hell has an end*, but for those who have wholly given themselves over to satanic purposes there is no redemption from the consuming fires and torment of conscience. They go on forever in the hell that is prepared for them.[51]

Bible

There are no verses indicating that people ever get out of hell. In the book of Revelation we read, "But the fearful, and unbelieving, and the abominable, and murderers, and whoremongers, and sorcerers, and idolaters, and all liars, shall have their part in the lake which burneth with fire and brimstone, which is the *second death*" (Revelation 21:8).

In the book of Matthew Jesus taught, "Another parable put he forth unto them, saying, The kingdom of heaven is likened unto a man which sowed good seed in his field; but while men slept, his enemy came and sowed tares among the wheat, and went his way.... He said unto them, An enemy hath done this.... Let both grow together until the harvest; and in the time of harvest I will say to the reapers, Gather ye together first the tares, and bind them in bundles to burn them, but gather the wheat into my barn.... The enemy that sowed them is the devil; the harvest is the end of the world; and the reapers are the angels. As therefore the tares are gathered and burned in the fire, so shall it be in the end of this world. The Son of man shall send forth his angels, and they shall gather out of his kingdom all things that offend, and them which do iniquity, and shall cast them into a furnace of fire: there shall be wailing and gnashing of teeth. Then shall the righteous shine forth as the sun in the kingdom of their Father" (Matthew 13:24-43).

In another parable Jesus talked about the inability to travel between heaven and hell: "And beside all this, between us and you there is a great gulf fixed, so that they which would pass from hence to you cannot; neither can they pass to us that would come from thence" (Luke 16:26).

Heaven

LDS

Mormons divide heaven into three kingdoms. The wicked of the world go to the telestial kingdom, good people who never joined the LDS Church go to the terrestrial kingdom, and faithful Mormons go to the celestial kingdom. Mormons usually cite 1 Corinthians 15:40,41 in support of this doctrine: "There are also celestial bodies, and bodies terrestrial; but the glory of the celestial is one, and the glory of the terrestrial is another. There is one glory of the sun, and another glory of the moon, and another glory of the stars; for one star differeth from another star in glory."

In one of Joseph Smith's revelations he described these three kingdoms:

> ...concerning them who shall come forth in the resurrection of the just—... They are they who are the church of the Firstborn. They are they into whose hands the Father has given all things [i.e., the celestial kingdom]—They are they who are priests and kings, who have received of his fulness, and of his glory; and are priests of the Most High, after the order of Melchizedek.... Wherefore, as it is written, *they are gods*, even the sons of God—...These shall dwell in the *presence of God*....

> And again, we saw the *terrestrial* world, and behold and lo, these are they who are of the *terrestrial*, whose glory differs from that of the church of the Firstborn who have received the fulness of the Father, even as that of the moon differs from the

sun in the firmament....These are they who receive of his glory, but not of his fulness. These are they who receive of the *presence of the Son*, but not of the fulness of the Father. Wherefore, they are bodies terrestrial, and not bodies celestial, and differ in glory as the moon differs from the sun....

And again, we saw the glory of the *telestial*, which glory is that of the lesser, even as the glory of the stars differs from that of the glory of the moon in the firmament. These are they who received not the gospel of Christ, neither the testimony of Jesus.... These are they who shall not be redeemed from the devil until the last resurrection, until the Lord, even Christ the Lamb, shall have finished his work. These are they who receive not of his fulness in the eternal world, but of the Holy Spirit through the ministration of the terrestrial.... These are they who are liars, and sorcerers, and adulterers, and whoremongers, and whosoever loves and makes a lie. But behold, and lo, we saw the glory and the inhabitants of the telestial world, that they were as innumerable as the stars in the firmament of heaven, or as the sand upon the seashore.... And they shall be servants of the Most High; *but where God and Christ dwell they cannot come*, worlds without end (D&C 76:51-112).

Bible

There are only two states after death: everlasting punishment and eternal life. Matthew recorded: "When the Son of man shall come in his glory...and before him shall be gathered all nations; and he shall separate them one from another, as a shepherd divideth his sheep from the goats; and he shall set the sheep on his right hand, but the goats on the left. Then shall the King say unto them on his right hand, Come, ye blessed of my Father, inherit the kingdom prepared for you from the foundation of the world.... Then shall he say also unto them on the left hand, Depart from me, ye cursed, into everlasting fire, prepared for the devil and his angels.... And these shall go away into *everlasting punishment*, but the righteous into *life eternal*" (Matthew 25:31-46).

Paul wrote, "For the wages of sin is death, but the gift of God is eternal life through Jesus Christ our Lord" (Romans 6:23).

Paul offered no hope for those who do not accept the Gospel: "And to you who are troubled rest with us, when the Lord Jesus shall be revealed from heaven with his mighty angels, in flaming fire taking vengeance on them that *know not God*, and that *obey not the gospel of our Lord Jesus Christ*, who shall be punished with *everlasting destruction* from the presence of the Lord, and from the glory of his power, when he shall come to be *glorified in his saints*, and to be admired in all them that *believe...*" (2 Thessalonians 1:7-10).

Mormons misuse 1 Corinthians 15:40, where Paul speaks of *celestial* bodies and *terrestrial* bodies. The whole chapter is dealing with the resurrection, not with levels of heaven. The word *celestial* means *heavenly* and the word *terrestrial* means *earthly*. Paul is contrasting the body we now have as mortals with the one we will have in heaven. This is explained in verse 44: "It is sown a natural body; it is raised a spiritual body."

Kingdom of God

LDS

Only those who merit the celestial kingdom will be in the kingdom of God. This kingdom is also divided into three levels. Only those going on to godhood themselves will be in the presence of God. These are the only ones who will be married and continue to procreate. In one of Joseph Smith's revelations we read:

> In the *celestial* glory there are *three* heavens or degrees; and in order to obtain the *highest*, a man must enter into this order of the priesthood

(meaning the new and everlasting covenant of marriage); and if he does not, he cannot obtain it. He may enter into the other, but that is the end of his kingdom; he cannot have *an increase....* For these angels did not abide my law; therefore, they cannot be enlarged, but remain *separately and singly,* without exaltation, in their *saved* condition, to all eternity; and from henceforth are *not gods,* but are *angels* of God forever and ever.[52]

In the LDS *Encyclopedia of Mormonism* it is stated:

Exaltation is the greatest of all the gifts and attainments possible. It is available only in the *highest degree* of the Celestial Kingdom and is reserved for members of the Church of the Firstborn. This exalted status, called *eternal life,* is available to be received by a man and wife. It means not only *living in God's presence,* but receiving power to do as God does, including the power to *bear children* after the resurrection.... Blessings and privileges of exaltation require unwavering faith, repentance, and complete obedience to the gospel of Jesus Christ.[53]

Noted LDS leader B.H. Roberts explained:

Instead of the God-given *power of procreation* being one of the chief things that is to pass away, it is one of the chief means of man's *exaltation* and glory in that great eternity, which like an endless vista stretches out before him! Through it man attains to the glory of the *endless increase of eternal lives,* and the right of presiding as priest and patriarch, king and lord over his ever increasing posterity. Instead of the commandment, "Be fruitful, and multiply and replenish the earth," being an unrighteous law, it is one by means of which the *race of the Gods* is perpetuated, and is as holy and pure as the commandment, "Repent and be baptized." Through that law, in connection with an observance of all the other laws of the gospel, man will yet attain unto the power of the Godhead....[54]

In one of LDS Apostle George Q. Cannon's sermons we read:

Every man and every woman who prays unto the Father, who is in the habit of doing so, expresses that desire in his or her prayer—that we may be counted worthy to receive *celestial glory* and *exaltation* in the *presence of God* and the Lamb. What a great thing to ask! Do we take in, as a people and as individuals, the full purport of this request! When we talk about celestial glory, we talk of the condition of *endless increase*; if we obtain celestial glory in the fullest sense of the word, then we have wives and children in eternity, we have the power of *endless lives* granted unto us, the *power of propagation* that will endure through all eternity, all being fathers and mothers in eternity; fathers of fathers, and mothers of mothers, kings and queens, priests and priestesses, and shall I say more? Yes, all becoming *gods*.[55]

Bible

As Christians we look forward to the time when *all* the redeemed will be in the presence of God. This will not be in the capacity of gods engaged in eternal procreation, but as redeemed sinners praising God. In the book of Revelation John describes a scene of worship, not self-elevation: "The four and twenty elders fall down before him...and worship him...and cast their crowns before the throne, saying, Thou art worthy, O Lord, to receive glory and honor and power; for thou hast created all things, and for thy pleasure they are and were created" (Revelation 4:10,11). In the book of

Matthew we are promised, "The Son of man shall send forth his angels, and they shall gather out of his kingdom all things that offend, and them which do iniquity, and shall cast them into a furnace of fire: there shall be wailing and gnashing of teeth. Then shall the righteous shine forth as the sun *in the kingdom of their Father*" (Matthew 13:41-43). In Paul's first letter to the Christians at Thessalonica we read, "For God hath not appointed us to wrath, but to obtain *salvation* by our Lord Jesus Christ, who died for us, that, whether we wake or sleep, we should live together *with him*" (1 Thessalonians 5:9,10). In the book of Revelation we are assured, "And I saw a new heaven and a new earth; for the first heaven and the first earth were passed away, and there was no more sea. And I John saw the holy city, new Jerusalem, coming down from God out of heaven, prepared as a bride adorned for her husband. And I heard a great voice out of heaven saying, Behold, *the tabernacle of God is with men,* and *he will dwell with them,* and they shall be his people, and *God himself shall be with them,* and be their God" (Revelation 21:1-3).

Conclusion

Clearly the LDS Church has attached totally different definitions to biblical terms. They have a God who was once a finite being, a Jesus who is our elder brother, and a Gospel requiring LDS temple marriages. However, most Mormons do not have a clear understanding of these definitions. Many truly think their beliefs are fairly close to evangelicals. Christians who try to witness to their LDS friends will need to listen carefully and ask questions to discover exactly what they understand about Mormonism and the Bible. Then they can share with them the good news that Christ alone is the answer, not a particular church. The true church is a spiritual organism (Ephesians 1:20-23; 1 Corinthians 12:12-14), not a religious organization.

Chapter Notes

1. Stephen Robinson, *How Wide the Divide?*, p. 13.
2. John A. Widtsoe, *Evidences and Reconciliations*, three volumes in one (Salt Lake City: Bookcraft, 1960), p. 127.
3. Ibid., pp. 396-97.
4. TPJS, pp. 345-47.
5. TPJS, pp. 370-74.
6. B. H. Roberts, *New Witnesses for God*, vol.1, p. 461, as quoted in *LDS Collectors Library '97*, CD-ROM.
7. Brigham Young, as quoted in *Search These Commandments; Melchizedek Priesthood Personal Study Guide* for 1985 (Salt Lake City: Church of Jesus Christ of Latter-day Saints, 1984), p. 153.
8. James E. Talmage, *Articles of Faith* (Salt Lake City: Church of Jesus Christ of Latter-day Saints, 1972), p. 430.
9. GP, pp. 11,17-1.
10. DG, pp. 16-18.
11. DG, pp. 9-10.
12. DS, vol.1, pp. 38-51.
13. EM, vol. 4, pp. 1667-68.
14. Spencer W. Kimball, *The Teachings of Spencer W. Kimball* (Salt Lake City: Bookcraft, 1982), p. 25.
15. Bruce R. McConkie, *The Mortal Messiah*, vol. 1, p. 21, as quoted in *LDS Collectors Library '97*, CD-ROM.
16. TPJS, pp. 350-52.
17. PGP, Abraham 3:21-22.
18. MD, p. 589.
19. Milton R. Hunter, *Pearl of Great Price Commentary*, p. 114, as quoted in *LDS Collectors Library '97*, CD-ROM.
20. DS, vol. 1, pp. 111-15.
21. MD, p. 268, 1979 ed.
22. AF, ch. 3, p. 70.
23. *Deseret News*, Church Section (Salt Lake City), July 31, 1965, p. 7.
24. Ezra Taft Benson, *The Teachings of Ezra Taft Benson* (Salt Lake City: Bookcraft, 1988), pp. 6-7.
25. MD, p. 546.
26. MD, p. 742.
27. EM, vol. 2, p. 729.
28. MD, pp. 669-70.
29. DS, vol. 2, p. 10.
30. PGP, The Articles of Faith, no. 2.
31. MD, pp. 331-34, 1979 ed.
32. MD, p. 133.
33. MD, p. 136.
34. DS, vol.3, pp. 80-81.
35. D&C 107:1-6.
36. *Ensign*, Nov. 1990, p. 38.
37. Spencer W. Kimball, *The Miracle of Forgiveness* (Salt Lake City: Bookcraft, 1969), pp. 353, 360.
38. Bruce R. McConkie, *Doctrinal New Testament Commentary*, vol. 1, pp. 141-42, as quoted in *LDS Collectors Library '97*, CD-ROM.
39. James E. Talmage, *The Story and Philosophy of "Mormonism,"* p. 121, as quoted in *LDS Collectors Library '97* CD-ROM.
40. MD, pp. 70-72.

41. GP, p. 126.
42. GP, p. 252.
43. D&C, 82:7.
44. MD, pp. 780-81.
45. See Jerald and Sandra Tanner, *Evolution of the Mormon Temple Ceremony, 1842-1990* (Salt Lake City: Utah Lighthouse Ministry, 1990).
46. D&C 132:19-25.
47. *Ensign*, Nov. 1989, p. 61.
48. MD, p. 237.
49. MD, p. 376.
50. MD, p. 670.
51. MD, pp. 349-51.
52. D&C 132:1-17.
53. EM, vol. 2, p. 479.
54. B. H. Roberts, *New Witnesses for God*, vol.1, p. 457, as quoted in *LDS Collectors Library '97*, CD-ROM.
55. JD, vol. 22, p. 124.

6

A Word to Our Mormon Friends

The Bible urges us to speak the truth in love (Ephesians 4:15). Throughout this book we have spoken the truth as we know it based on God's Word. This epilogue is a loving word from our hearts for our Mormon friends.[1] Of course, just speaking the truth often seems unloving, especially if it is bad news. However, as every doctor knows, it is sometimes necessary to hurt before one can heal. Before the good news of the true Gospel can be appreciated we must all hear the bad news about our sin. We have no need to be rescued unless we are drowning.

The truth, shared by Mormons and evangelicals, is that no one can get to the presence of our Heavenly Father without being absolutely perfect. But how can this kind of perfection be achieved? Since it is the sincere desire of every good Mormon, the question must be answered.

There is strong agreement by Mormons and evangelicals with the words of Jesus recorded in Matthew 5:48: "Be ye therefore perfect, even as your Father which is in heaven is perfect." In fact, 3 Nephi 12:48 reaffirms it, saying: "Therefore I should that ye should be perfect, even as I, or your Father who is in heaven is perfect."

It is important to note that the stress, even in the "inspired" translation of Joseph Smith, is on *being* perfect, not on *becoming* perfect. Indeed, in a chapter loved by Mormons,

---

Scripture quotations in this chapter are from the King James Version except as otherwise noted. See Copyright page.

James added: "For whosoever shall keep the whole law, and yet offend in one point, he is guilty of all" (James 2:10).

The Mormon Necessity of Good Works

All informed Mormons know what meeting the standards for perfection entails. The following list is taken from the priesthood manual, *To Make Thee a Minister and a Witness* (page 59). Being perfect includes: 1) personal prayers, 2) regular family prayer, 3) regular family home evening, 4) home storage, 5) regular Scripture study, 6) strict personal worthiness, 7) support of church leaders, 8) tender concern for one's wife and family members, 9) keeping the family history, 10) having patience and love, 11) honest work and integrity in one's occupation, 12) exemplary grooming and dress, 13) regular attendance at church meetings and activities, 14) regular temple attendance, 15) keeping the Word of Wisdom, and 16) having purity of thought.

According to Mormon teaching, without doing these faithfully and continually one cannot enter into the top level of the celestial kingdom and live with his or her Heavenly Father. Failure in a single point means that one has not reached absolute perfection and therefore cannot reach exaltation.

The Mormon Necessity of Repentance

What is more, LDS teaching demands complete and permanent repentance of sin in order to live with the Heavenly Father. Mormon prophet Kimball declared in *Doctrines of the Gospel* that "repentance must involve an all-out, total surrender to the program of the Lord. That transgressor is not fully repentant who neglects his tithing, misses his meetings, breaks the Sabbath, fails in his family prayers, does not sustain the authorities of the Church, breaks the Word of Wisdom, does not love the Lord nor his fellowmen" (page 41). It is worthy of note that breaking the Sabbath includes not fasting for all 24 hours of the first Sunday of the month. For "the law to the Latter-day Saints, as understood by the authorities of the church, is that food and drink are not to be partaken of for 24 hours, 'from even to even, and that the Saints are to refrain from all bodily gratification and indulgences.'"[2]

Further, genuine repentance necessary for exaltation means that one will never repeat the offense. If he does, then he loses the forgiveness he got as a result of his repentance. For the Mormon manual, *Gospel Principles* states emphatically that "those who receive forgiveness and then repeat the sin are held accountable for their former sins" (page 244).

The Mormon Necessity of Perfection

Considering the seemingly impossible standards of perfection set forth by the Mormon Church, it would seem that reaching the celestial kingdom is next to impossible. Yet Mormons believe that those who achieve exaltation will live in the family unit in the presence of God. Therefore we conclude that, according to LDS teaching, most Mormons will live as single servants in some lower level of heaven. And only a small number of people will merit outer darkness (hell).

But is this the picture presented in the Bible? Jesus repeatedly spoke of only two options: eternal life or destruction (see Matthew 7:13,14; 25:31-41). Therefore every Mormon should ponder seriously what "destruction" means and who merits it. If a Mormon is not found "perfect" in the sight of God, then he or she will face eternal separation from Heavenly Father, but only a tiny segment of society will be cast into "outer darkness" forever (which evangelicals call hell). But how is this possible? If absolute perfection, involving the keeping of all the above-stated rules of the LDS Church is necessary, then how can more than a minuscule number ever make it—if anyone?

Many Mormons suffer depression and even suicidal tendencies because of their inability to attain the standard of perfection demanded of their Church to reach the celestial kingdom. Nonetheless, official Mormon doctrine is emphatic in stating that reaching this absolute perfection is possible.

First Nephi 3:7 affirms: "I know that the Lord giveth no commandments unto the children of men, save he shall prepare a way for them that they may accomplish the things which he commandeth them." The LDS manual *Walk in His Ways B* instructs primary school teachers to "stress the concept that with God's help we can obey every commandment we receive" (pages 34-35). In fact, this concept is directly linked with perfection. An official LDS commentary on the New Testament, *The Life and Teachings of Jesus & His Apostles,* affirms: "Perfection is a word that causes different reactions from many people. Some people say, 'Perfection? Why that is impossible!' Others say, 'Perfection! I get discouraged just thinking about it!' Yet would the Lord give us a commandment that was impossible for us to keep?' " (page 67).

Past prophet Spencer W. Kimball did not hesitate to insist on absolute perfection: "Yes, I said, but we are commanded to be supermen. Said the Lord, 'Be ye therefore perfect, even as your Father which is in heaven is perfect.' (Matthew 5:48). We are gods in embryo, and the Lord demands perfection of us."[3]

The Absolute Perfection of Jesus Christ

According to the Bible which Mormons accept, all human beings are sinful and only Jesus lived an absolutely perfect life. Further, the Bible affirms that no human being can attain absolute perfection by his own works. It comes only through Christ's work for us and by faith. Jesus said in John 6:47 of the Joseph Smith "inspired" translation: "Verily, verily, I say unto you, He that believeth on me hath everlasting life." This is in the present tense ("hath")—right now by faith and not by works. This is truly the Gospel (good news) for Mormons. Absolute perfection is possible, though not by our effort but by God's grace.

Only one Person lived the absolutely perfect life, and He gives us the perfection we cannot attain as a free gift. As quoted above, Jesus said, "He that believeth on me hath everlasting life" (John 6:47). As Paul put it, "For the law of the Spirit of life in Christ Jesus hath made me free from the law of sin and death. For what the law could not do, in that it was weak through the flesh, God sending his own Son in the likeness of sinful flesh, and for sin, condemned sin in the flesh, that the righteousness of the law might be fulfilled in us, who walk not after the flesh but after the Spirit" (Romans 8:2-4).

In response, the Mormon mind moves immediately to James 2:24: "Ye see then how that by works a man is justified, and not by faith only." Of course—but nothing is considered good works in God's eyes apart from faith. The Bible says, "Whatsoever is not of faith is sin" (Romans 14:23). Hebrews 11:6 declares that "without faith it is impossible to please God." James is distinguishing *true* faith from *false* faith. True faith always produces good works. We are saved by faith alone, but the faith that saves us is not alone; it always results in good works. Faith is the root and good works are the fruit. James is not denying this; in fact he uses the word "faith" more times than he uses "works"! He is condemning "dead" faith (2:17). His point is that "I will show thee my faith by my works" (2:18). James believed, as Paul did, that we are not saved *by* good works but *for* good works (see Ephesians 2:8-10; Titus 3:5-8).

The True Gospel

It is true faith in what Christ did for us, not in what we do for Christ, that will get us into the celestial kingdom. Perhaps no passage in the Bible is more emphatic on this point than Hebrews 10:12-14: "But this man, after he had offered *one sacrifice for sins forever,* sat down on the right hand of God, from henceforth expecting till his enemies be made his footstool. For *by one offering he hath perfected forever them that are sanctified.*" Jesus paid it all. On the cross He said, "It is finished" (John 19:30). Looking to His accomplished work, Jesus prayed, "I have finished the work which thou gavest me to do" (John 17:4). The writer of Hebrews declared that "when he had by himself purged our sins, [he] sat down on the right hand of the Majesty on high" (Hebrews 1:3). He sat down because our salvation was accomplished when He "was delivered for our offenses and raised again for our justification" (Romans 4:25). For the "Gospel" (good news) is that "Christ died for our sins according to the scriptures, and that he was buried, and that he rose again the third day according to the scriptures, and that he was seen of Cephas, then of the twelve" (1 Corinthians 15:3-5). All that remains for us to do is to believe. Jesus said, "Verily, verily, I say unto you, He that believeth on me hath everlasting life" (John 6:47).

This is the true Gospel. Any other gospel is a false gospel—even if it comes from an angel! Paul wrote: "I marvel that ye are so soon removed from him that called you into the grace of Christ unto another gospel, which is not another, but there be some that trouble you, and would pervert the gospel of Christ. But *though we or an angel from heaven preach any other gospel unto you than that which we have preached unto you, let him be accursed.* As we said before, so say I now again, If any man preach any other gospel unto you than that ye have received, let him be accursed" (Galatians 1:6-9).

The good news for every Mormon is that absolute perfection is obtainable—not by our own efforts but through Christ's completed work for us, not by our works but by His grace. For as Paul said, "If by grace, then is it no more of works; otherwise grace is no more grace. But if it be of works, then it is no more grace; otherwise work is no more work" (Romans 11:6).

There is a choice to be made by every Mormon: Either continue the endless, frustrating, and often depressing effort to obtain the absolute perfection demanded of God in order to live with our Heavenly Father, or else accept as a free gift, by faith, the absolute perfection of the only One who ever lived an absolutely perfect life and died a perfect death for our sins—Jesus Christ our Savior. For all who are weary of the impossible struggle to live a perfect life, Jesus said: **"Come unto me, all ye that labor and are heavy laden, and I will give you rest"** (Matthew 11:28).

Chapter Notes

1. This discussion is patterned after the excellent book by Mark J. Cares, *Speaking the Truth in Love to Mormons* (Milwaukee: Northwestern Publishing House, 1993).
2. *To Make Thee a Minister and a Witness* (a Mormon priesthood manual, 1990), p. 116.
3. Spencer W. Kimball, *The Miracle of Forgiveness* (Salt Lake City: Bookcraft, 1969), p. 286.

Chapter Nine

Appendix

Terminology Differences

Godhead

Bible: God is a spirit and has always been God. There is only one God: Father, Son, and Holy Ghost.

LDS: Three totally separate gods. Father and Son have resurrected bodies. Holy Ghost is separate spirit being. God was once a man.

Jesus Christ

Bible: God manifest in the flesh. Fully god, not a subordinate deity.

LDS: Our elder brother, born of heavenly parents in preexistence. Brother of Lucifer.

Holy Ghost

Bible: Same as Holy Spirit

LDS: Separate being from God the Father and Jesus the Son. Holy Ghost is a person. Holy Spirit is influence from God and is not a person.

Mother in Heaven

Bible: Nothing to indicate that God has a wife

LDS: Resurrected wife of Heavenly Father. Mother of spirit children before their mortal birth.

Creation

Bible: God alone is eternal. He created matter, time, space, and life and called them into existence.

LDS: Matter is eternal. God did not truly create out of nothing. Organized existing matter to form worlds without number.

Preexistence

Bible: Only the Godhead (Father, Son, and Holy Ghost) has eternal existence. We are all God's creation. No spiritual existence prior to our birth on earth.

LDS: Everyone had a preexistence. Our intelligence (mind) has existed eternally. Born as spirit-children to God and His wife prior to our birth on earth.

Sons of God

Bible: We are God's creation, not procreation. We become a child of God at conversion.

LDS: We are literally the spirit children of God and His wife, born in a prior existence before coming to this earth.

The Fall

Bible: Adam's sin brought both physical and spiritual death to humanity.

LDS: The fall was a blessing. Adam was given conflicting commandments and supposed to fall.

Virgin Birth

Bible: Jesus' conception was a miracle. A virgin was overshadowed by the Holy Spirit.

LDS: God, as a resurrected, physical man, is the literal father of Jesus—same manner as men are conceived on earth.

Salvation by Grace

Bible: Based on each individual's response to God's offer of eternal life through faith in Christ. Salvation is not universal and is not equated with resurrection. If one has salvation, one also has eternal life.

LDS: Christ's death paid for Adam's transgression and secured universal resurrection. Beyond this, we must earn our own place in heaven. Saved by grace after *all* we can do.

Redemption

Bible: Christ redeems us from both physical and spiritual death.

LDS: Christ's atonement redeems us from physical death and assures us of resurrection. Individual redemption is through full obedience.

Gospel

Bible: Good news. Message of Christ's death and resurrection as atonement for our sins.

LDS: All the teachings and ordinances of the LDS Church. True gospel of Jesus Christ restored by Joseph Smith.

True Chruch

Bible: Not an organization. As born-again Christians, we are all part of God's church.

LDS: Only the LDS Church. The true church was taken from the earth after the death of the 12 apostles until Joseph Smith restored it.

Priesthood

Bible: Christ brought end to priesthood of Old Testament and is *only* High Priest after the manner of Melchizedek.

LDS: Only LDS Church has authority to baptize, ordain, and act in the name of God. Two-part system—Aaronic and Melchizedek.

Forgiveness

Bible: Christ offers forgiveness the moment we turn to Him.

LDS: God's forgiveness is granted after repentance and reformed behavior.

Born Again

Bible: We are spiritually dead until our spiritual rebirth.

LDS: Baptism into the LDS Church.

Baptism

Bible: Emphasis is on **believer**—not priesthood authority.

LDS: Must be performed by one having LDS priesthood.

Dealing with Sin (After Conversion)

Bible: God has promised to always forgive when we turn to Him. No need to confess to another person.

LDS: Forgiveness is granted after repentance and reformed behavior. Cannot sin again and again and expect forgiveness. Must confess to priesthood leader.

Temple

Bible: In Old Testament, had high priest and animal sacrifices. Christ ended the need for a temple.

LDS: Claim Joseph Smith restored the original temple ceremony. Temples are used for eternal marriage ceremonies, baptisms, and marriages for the dead, not animal sacrifices.

Eternal Life

Bible: Promised to all Christians. No mention of temple marriage or eternal procreation.

LDS: Exaltation in Celestial Kingdom; godhood and the ability to procreate children through all eternity. Must be married in LDS temple and be a faithful Mormon.

Immortality

Bible: Makes no distinction between immortality and eternal life.

LDS: Universal gift. Ability to live forever but not the same as eternal life. Unable to procreate.

Hell

Bible: No mention of people getting out of hell. Everlasting punishment.

LDS: Place that exists eternally but people stay only a limited time until debt to God has been paid.

Heaven

Bible: One of only two places after death. Eternal life in the presence of God.

LDS: Divided into three kingdoms. Wicked go to Telestial, good people who never joined LDS Church go to Terrestrial, faithful Mormons go to Celestial Kingdom.

Kingdom of God

Bible: All redeemed will be in presence of God. All believers are part of the kingdom.

LDS: Means Celestial Kingdom. Only those in Celestial Kingdom are in God's presence. Those in Terrestrial and Telestial Kingdoms are not in the presence of the Father.

Author Biographies

Francis J. Beckwith

Francis J. Beckwith is Associate Professor of Philosophy, Culture, and Law at Trinity Graduate School, Trinity International University, California campus.

Professor Beckwith has published numerous articles and reviews in the areas of ethics, philosophy of religion, theology, social philosophy, comparative religion, and bioethics, which have appeared in a number of anthologies as well as in scholarly journals and periodicals. He has authored and edited several books, including *See the Gods Fall: Four Rivals to Christianity*, *The Mormon Concept of God: A Philosophical Analysis*, *Baha'i*, *Politically Correct Death: Answering the Arguments for Abortion Rights*, *Affirmative Action: Social Justice or Reverse Discrimination?* and *The Abortion Controversy 25 Years After Roe v. Wade*.

Professor Beckwith earned a Ph.D and M.A. in philosophy from Fordham University, an M.A. in Christian apologetics from Simon Greenleaf University, and a B.A. in philosophy from UNLV. He and his wife, Frankie, make their home in the Anaheim Hills, California.

Norman L. Geisler

Norman L. Geisler is author (or coauthor) of more than 45 books. He has taught apologetics, Bible, and theology for 38 years at some of the top evangelical institutions, including

Dallas Theological Seminary and Trinity Evangelical Divinity School. Presently Dr. Geisler is president of Southern Evangelical Seminary in Charlotte, N.C.

Ron Rhodes

Ron Rhodes is a popular author, conference speaker, seminar leader, and college instructor. He is the founder and president of Reasoning from the Scriptures Ministries, an organization designed to help Christians become biblically literate so they can apply Scripture to modern issues of concern.

Rhodes is the author of *What Your Child Needs to Know About God, The Heart of Christianity, Heaven: The Undiscovered Country, Angels Among Us, The Culting of America,* and two Gold Medallion finalists—*The New Age Movement* and *Reasoning from the Scriptures with the Jehovah's Witnesses.* He has written several Bible study guides and has authored over 200 articles for national publications.

Rhodes received his Th.M. and Th.D. degrees in systematic theology from Dallas Theological Seminary, where he graduated with high honors. He lives in Southern California with his wife, Kerri, and their two children, David and Kylie.

Jerald and Sandra Tanner

Jerald Tanner was born June 1, 1938, in Provo Utah and was baptized into the LDS Church at the age of eight. His great-great-grandfather, John Tanner, joined the Mormon Church in the 1830s and is remembered in historical books for his sizable financial contributions to Joseph Smith and the LDS Church in 1835 when the church was deeply in debt.

Sandra Tanner was born January 14, 1941 in Salt Lake City, Utah. Her parents were married in the Salt Lake Temple. She was baptized into the LDS Church in southern California when she was eight years old. She is a great-great-granddaughter of Brigham Young, the second president of the Mormon Church. Sandra's mother, Georgia Young, is the daughter of Walter Young, son of Brigham Young, Jr., who was the son of President Brigham Young.

As teenagers, before they met each other, they were both challenged by different people and events to examine the origins of Mormonism. Jerald accepted Christ in 1957 and dropped out of the Mormon Church but was still a believer in the *Book of Mormon*. On a visit to Salt Lake City in 1959, Sandra was introduced to Jerald and they soon were jointly involved in research. Jerald and Sandra were married in June of 1959 by a minister of a small church in the San Fernando valley.

They have lived in Utah since 1960 and are the parents of three grown children. They are active members of the Christian and Missionary Alliance Church in Salt Lake City.

The Tanners gave up belief in the *Book of Mormon* in 1962 and since then have authored more than 40 books on Mormonism. They are known for their extensive research into Mormon history and doctrine. The Tanners established Utah Lighthouse Ministry, a non-profit organization, in 1983 as an outreach ministry to the Mormon community.

Besides the many publications issued by their ministry, they also co-authored the book, *The Changing World of Mormonism*, 1980, published by Moody Press. Sandra's personal testimony is related in the book *Why We Left Mormonism* by Latayne Scott, 1990 (Baker). The Tanners have also been interviewed on various TV and radio shows.

Utah Lighthouse Ministry
1358 S. West Temple
Salt Lake City, Utah 84115
(801) 485-8894

Phil Roberts

Phil Roberts is currently director of the Interfaith Witness Division of the North American Mission Board, Southern Baptist Convention in Alpharetta, Georgia.

He taught evangelism and missions for 13 years in the United States and Belgium, and served four years as the Dean of Theology at the Institute of Biblical Studies in Oradea, Romania. An ordained minister, Roberts has pastored churches in England, Germany, Belgium, and the United States. He has published articles on evangelism, international outreach, and historical figures of the faith in a number of scholarly journals and periodicals, as well as assisting in the production of "The Mormon Puzzle" video.

Roberts received a Ph.D. in philosophy from the Free University of Amsterdam, an M.Div. from Southern Baptist Theological Seminary, and a B.A. from Georgetown College, with honors. He lives in Georgia with his wife, Anna, and their two children, Naomi and Mark.